Personal Data Collection Risks in a Post-Vaccine World

ANTHEM ETHICS OF PERSONAL DATA COLLECTION

The **Anthem Ethics of Personal Data Collection** series publishes scholarly works at the intersection of data, ethics and digital technology in the 21st century. This series introduces the personal data movement by highlighting innovative research in public health, violence against women in public spaces, the energy sector, sexual violence in conflict, vocational training, insurance policy underwriting, individual control of enterprise data sharing, and data as labor. The series focuses primarily on the ethical concerns regarding personal data as a natural resource in the era of digital revolution.

Series Editors

Colette Mazzucelli – New York University, USA
James Felton Keith – Keith Institute, USA

Titles in the series

Personal Data Collection Risks in a Post-Vaccine World
Regulating Cross-Border Data Flows
The Ethics of Personal Data Collection in International Relations
Hacking Digital Ethics
The Domains of Identity

Personal Data Collection Risks in a Post-Vaccine World

Colette Mazzucelli, James Felton Keith, and
C. Ann Hollifield, eds.
with Andrea Adams and Anna Grichting

Anthem Press
An imprint of Wimbledon Publishing Company
www.anthempress.com

This edition first published in UK and USA 2023
by ANTHEM PRESS
75–76 Blackfriars Road, London SE1 8HA, UK
or PO Box 9779, London SW19 7ZG, UK
and
244 Madison Ave #116, New York, NY 10016, USA

© 2023 Colette Mazzucelli, James Felton Keith, C. Ann Hollifield editorial matter and selection;

individual chapters © individual contributors

The moral right of the authors has been asserted.

All rights reserved. Without limiting the rights under copyright reserved above, no part of this publication may be reproduced, stored or introduced into a retrieval system, or transmitted, in any form or by any means (electronic, mechanical, photocopying, recording or otherwise), without the prior written permission of both the copyright owner and the above publisher of this book.

British Library Cataloguing-in-Publication Data
A catalogue record for this book is available from the British Library.

Library of Congress Control Number: 2022942865
A catalog record for this book has been requested.

ISBN-13: 978-1-83998-738-0 (Hbk)
ISBN-10: 1-83998-738-3 (Hbk)

Cover Image: Designed by Marc Nelson in Artistic Collaboration with Colette Mazzucelli

This title is also available as an e-book.

CONTENTS

Acknowledgements vii

Foreword by Prof. John Sexton-President Emeritus, New York University
Word Clouds by Leslie Elizabeth Prosy, New York University xi

Introduction by Colette Mazzucelli, James Felton Keith, and Andrea Adams xiii

Part I

Chapter 1 Data to the People? Surveillance Capitalism and the Need for a Legal Reconceptualisation of Personal Data beyond the Notion of Privacy 3
Jakub Wojciech Kibitlewski

Chapter 2 Human Subjects, Digital Protocols: The Future of Institutional Review Boards (IRBs) and Digital Research in Vulnerable Communities 25
Charles Martin-Shields and Ziad Al Achkar

Part II

Chapter 3 Rome vs. Regions: Government in Italy during COVID-19: Implications for the Future of the European Union (EU) 47
Christian Rossi, Colette Mazzucelli, and David C. Unger

Chapter 4 Roma Lives Matter under the COVID-19 Pandemic: But More So for Populist Nationalism 73
Andras L. Pap

Chapter 5 Ethics of Personal Data Collection in Bosnia–Herzegovina (BiH) 101
Mary Kate Schneider

Part III

Chapter 6 Lessons from the Ebola Epidemic in Sierra Leone: The Importance of State, INGO, and Local Network Actors 119
Thynn Thynn Hlaing and Emilie J. Greenhalgh

Chapter 7 The Digital 'Marketplace of Ideas': The Need for a Human Rights-Centred, Multi-stakeholder Approach to Cyber Norms 159
Laura Salter

Conclusion by Colette Mazzucelli, Andrea Adams, and Anna Grichting 181

Afterword by Annette Richardson, Special Advisor, Office of the Executive Director and Under Secretary-General, UN Women 193

List of Contributors 197

Index 203

ACKNOWLEDGEMENTS

This edited volume builds on the research made possible by the cooperation between Nathaniel Raymond, formerly of the Harvard Humanitarian Initiative and presently a lecturer at Yale University, and Colette Mazzucelli, New York University and Pioneer Academics. Colette and Nathaniel brought together a community of researchers and practitioners in Bosch Workshops at NYU in New York and NYU Washington, DC, including Kristin Bergtora Sandvik, Karen Naimer, Christoph Koettl, Stefan Schmitt, Jay Aronson, Ziad Al Achkar and Charles Martin-Shields. Colette thanks Professors Douglas Irvin-Erickson and Yasemin Irvin-Erickson, George Mason University, for the cooperation that led to a cutting-edge Special Issue of *Genocide Studies and Prevention* (GSP), 'Information and Communications Technologies in Mass Atrocities Research and Response', published in 2017. The pedagogically inspired volume, *Genocide Matters: Emerging Issues and On-Going Perspectives* (Routledge, 2013) edited by our colleagues, Professors Joyce Apsel, New York University and Ernesto Verdeja, University of Notre Dame, resonates strongly as we nurture the research in our community.

The cover of this edited volume designed by Marc Nelson and Colette Mazzucelli speaks to the origins of the GSP research, which is grounded in concerns related to structure and agency. Our artistic sensitivity and that of the contributors pertains to the protection of the most vulnerable from the misuses of data, particularly concerning its collection in the most fragile conflict environments. The research support to connect the Special Issue and this edited volume provided by Leslie Prosy, Amber Celedonio, Laura Salter, Annika Squires, Nicole Scartozzi, New York University; Megan Cameron, York University; and Duru Unsal, Pioneer Academics is most sincerely appreciated as are the insights provided by Edward Ablang, Harvard University and Megan Araghi, SOAS University of London and Executive Office, Natural Resource Governance Institute.

The contributors to this volume come from diverse regions in our world. Their analyses shed light on local contexts across continents. Colette expresses appreciation to this volume's peer reviewers, Professors John van Oudenaren, The Woodrow Wilson International Center for Scholars and Douglas Irvin-Erickson, The Jimmy and Rosalynn Carter School for Peace and Conflict Resolution, George Mason University, for their constructive suggestions to Anthem Press. For the inspiring Foreword and Afterword, respectively, Colette thanks President Emeritus and Benjamin F. Butler Professor of Law, New York University, John E. Sexton, and Special Adviser, Office of the Executive Director and Under Secretary-General, UN Women, and Partner, Ambershore Group, Annette Richardson.

Colette is also grateful to fellow Bosch Alumna Professor Emerita C. Ann Hollifield for her outstanding editing, Professor Andrea Adams for her extraordinary dedication to the larger project that animates this research, Anna Grichting, for her lifetime devotion to regenerative urbanism and inspiring project initiatives across continents and Shirley Cloyes DioGuardi for her extraordinary commitment to human rights in our world. In addition, Colette expresses her appreciation to Tina Lam, Nicolette Teta and Dr Michael John Williams for their support related to the Bosch-NYU Workshops. The authors who wrote chapters for a companion volume to this one also shared their insights to enrich our community dialogue. Colette thanks Azza Karam, Celeste Brevard, Sophia Ehmke, Megan Cameron, Jasmine Lee, Mary Davis, Andrea Adams, Suzanne Goodney-Lea and Elsa D'Silva, Lynne Chandler-Garcia and John Riley, as well as Joshua Cooper.

Anthem Press has provided consistent support as the Ethics of Personal Data Collection Series emerged over the past several years starting with Kaliya Young's *The Domains of Identity*, published in 2020, and followed by Andréa Belliger and David J. Krieger's *Hacking Digital Ethics*, published in 2021. We appreciate Bryan Mercurio and Ronald Yu's volume, *Regulating Cross-Border Data Flows: Issues, Challenges and Impact*, to be published in August 2022. Our appreciation as editors is expressed to Tej P. S. Sood, publisher; Megan Greiving, senior acquisitions editor and the Anthem Press Marketing and Sales Teams. Colette dedicates this volume to her late mother, Adelina Maria De Ponte Mazzucelli, who urged her to ask questions from an early age and to her father, Silvio Anthony Mazzucelli, who encourages her writing. Our family orange tabby, Ginevra 'Cuddles' Pario, is a loving feline companion in the midst of fact checking and creative writing.

Ann acknowledges with deep appreciation the Robert Bosch Foundation and the Robert Bosch Foundation Alumni Association's support for the conferences and collaborations that led directly to the creation of this volume. Across its long history, the Bosch Foundation has made fostering international understanding and cooperation a central part of its philanthropic mission. As a grateful alumna of the Bosch Fellowship Program, Ann thanks this volume's community of authors for the pleasure of working together to share the knowledge in the chapters that comprise this important and thought-provoking book.

James needs to thank an old mentor and former US Special Forces soldier, Earl Winters, for giving him a more realistic view of the incentives that threaten our communal and individual agency. He needs to thank his parents, Tawana and Steven Rogers, for giving him enough stability to try anything. Lastly, but most importantly, James needs to thank his husband, Andy Tarradath, for giving him enough encouragement to come out as the person that he is going to be tomorrow. In the middle of a global pandemic, Andy helped James realise that the communal rights we fight for must be built on human rights that allow our communities enough space to identify all of our individual participants.

For Andrea, she recognises God for bringing her into this mission and on this journey. Andrea's work continues to evolve to include publications that address gender-based violence and data privacy. Her work on the board of Red Dot Foundation Global has helped in driving awareness and understanding of the needs and opportunities to support a global community. She seeks to infuse ethics and technology through understanding place-based violence. Through this work, Andrea connected with the lead editor, Colette Mazzucelli. Colette's scholarship and leadership in crafting a narrative that intertwines the messages of the contributing authors around an emerging voice for international relations are groundbreaking. Andrea cherishes Colette's kindness and willingness to embrace her as a full contributor. Andrea also wishes to thank Ann Hollifield for elevating the direction and focus of her work and James Felton Keith for his generous sharing of strategic insights as well as Elsa Marie D'Silva and Suzanne Goodney Lea for their ongoing support and mentorship. Lastly, Andrea thanks her best friend, husband and love of her life, Nigel, for his continued wisdom, encouragement and support.

Anna is very grateful for the invitation to collaborate with Colette Mazzucelli on this important publication. She acknowledges the richness of the interdisciplinary collaborations that Colette has initiated with this book and other publications, through her courses at NYU, and in the recently created LEAD IMPACT Reconciliation Institute technology-mediated education initiative. Anna is equally thankful to Colette for highlighting and nourishing her work on border landscapes and social ecologies, and for introducing her to the spatial concept of 'mesh region'. She would like to acknowledge all her mentors and teachers as well as the colleagues and collaborators who recognise and enrich her interdisciplinary work and research, particularly authors featured in this volume, including John Sexton, Andrea Adams, Christian Rossi, David Unger, James Felton Keith and Annette Richardson. Finally, Anna remembers her late husband, Cheo Jeffery Allen Solder, for his continued support and encouragement, and for sharing his knowledge of African American history.

FOREWORD

John Sexton

We – humankind – are at an inflection point, a critical threshold. We soon must choose between the fear that is the currency of populism and the hope that is harboured by those who, like Teilhard de Chardin, described the possibility of a Second Axial Age.

In his volume, *The Origin and Goal of History*, Karl Jaspers described the period from 800 to 200 BCE as the Axial Age because 'it gave birth to everything which, since then, humankind has been able to be'. It was the era when Lao-tzu and Confucius revolutionised Chinese thought; Buddha, Mahavira and the rishis who wrote the Upanishads transformed philosophy, religion and ethics in India; and the followers of Zoroaster in Persia explored profound questions about the nature of good and evil. In the Levant, Jewish prophets such as Isaiah and Jeremiah sounded calls for higher levels of moral awareness. In Greece, Pythagoras, Socrates, Plato and Aristotle articulated the fundamental ideas of Western philosophy. Before the Axial Age, the dominant form of consciousness was cosmic, collective, tribal, mythic and ritualistic. By contrast, the consciousness born in the Axial Age, which was then extended by successor waves such as Christianity, Islam, the Enlightenment and the scientific revolution, carries a sense of individual identity that permeates the cultures of the world today.

Since the middle of the last century, we have begun to see signs of a Second Axial period. Although first described by theologians, the Second Axial Age also has a progressive, secular dimension that Teilhard predicted – a process of 'planetisation', a shift in the forces of social evolution analogous to biological evolution, proceeding from 'emergence' and 'divergence' to 'convergence'.

The first groupings of humans were familial and tribal, engendering loyalty to a group and separation from other groups. Humanity then diverged, creating different cultures and nations. But the spatial finitude and spherical shape of our planet were intrinsic constraints: so, human beings now occupy all of earth's readily habitable areas, and modern communication and transportation systems mean that groups can no longer detach completely from the world. Today, humankind is pressed into a full planetary community. Even as powerful forces of difference and division incline us against one another, we are being drawn into a global society.

But this global world need not compromise the great gift of experiential diversity. Teilhard saw not a homogenisation but rather 'creative unions', in which diversity is enriched. 'In any domain', he wrote, 'whether it be the cells of a body, the members of a society, or the elements of a spiritual synthesis, union differentiates'. Whether subatomically or globally, elements unite in 'centre-to-centre unions'. Just as physics describes centres of mass in the universe that are drawn together, capitals of the world will be connected even more than they are. They will touch one another at their creative cores, releasing new energy and much deeper understanding. This powerful centre-to-centre contact offers the promise that we, the citizens of these cities and of this integrated world, may discover what is authentic and vital not only about others but also about ourselves.

New York University has embraced this Teilhardian view of the world in reshaping itself over these last two decades in a Global Network University. Founded nearly two hundred years ago in the world's premier 'glocal' city (global and local simultaneously) to be 'in and of the city', NYU found it natural to become 'in and of the world'. Today the university is located in 16 idea capitols on six continents, anchored by full research campuses not only in New York but also in Abu Dhabi and Shanghai. This is not an independent set of 'branches'; rather, it is a fully integrated circulatory system through which faculty, staff and students flow freely – and, along with them, their ideas.

It is in this context that these extraordinary volumes both operate and cooperate, simultaneously touched by this planetisation and shaping it. My NYU colleague, Professor Colette Mazzucelli, both in her work at NYU and as the president of the Global Listening Centre, has practiced a kind of secular ecumenism. At NYU's New York campus she teaches seminars across schools in conflict resolution, religious radicalisation and ethnic conflict – each a story of division. But from these potentially disheartening stories she draws a contrapuntal lesson of hope – through aggressive listening and genuine dialogue. So, it is in this volume that she, James Felton Keith and C. Ann Hollifield offer us a homage to and an example of collective, nuanced conversation that truly advances knowledge and understanding.

This volume, collecting as its content does the thoughts of participants spread throughout our global society, presents genuine centre-to-centre dialogue. And it does in fact release new energy and deeper understanding. It remains for us to emulate this example still more pervasively in all of our conversations.

Congratulations to the editors and the authors. Onward and upward together!

INTRODUCTION

Colette Mazzucelli, James Felton Keith, and Andrea Adams

The literature that references personal data collection risks is growing amidst international scandals, notably the Cambridge Analytica/Facebook interference in the Brexit referendum and 2016 US presidential election as well as other elections in countries throughout our world. Questions of fundamental importance to the study and practice of international relations are being asked as concerns are expressed, including the most pressing that speak to accountability, the ethics of use in local areas and the impact on the vulnerable populations that information and communications technologies (ICTs) promise to serve. Yet, the editors observe that in key texts written to teach international relations, less mention is made of personal data collection risks in countries around the globe. As we address this significant omission in the literature, this introduction notes the observation made by Acharya and Buzan that 'with the possible exception of the emerging ideology of environmental stewardship, no new ideologies of equivalent weight have come along to reshape international relations' (p. 12).

As the call for the protection of personal data increases globally, other uses of data under the colour of state action continue to complicate the issue. The attack by Russia on Ukraine occurred simultaneously with Russia's participation in the UN's Ad Hoc Committee to Elaborate a Comprehensive International Convention on Countering the Use of ICTs for Criminal Purposes. Russia strongly advocated for a new global cybercrime treaty despite the existence of the Budapest Convention on Cybercrime ratified by sixty-six countries, but Russia did not join, stating that the convention violated state sovereignty principles. Yet, alongside its urging that statements to the Secretariat should not include information about the war against Ukraine, Russia pushed the UN to adopt its proposal, which lessened humanitarian rights. All the while Russia has seemingly turned a blind eye to cybercriminals operating within its borders and has openly and actively supported these perpetrators.

These chapters provide a glimpse into the struggles of liberal internationalism and, yet, seem to suggest a way forward. First, there remain concerns about the impacts of the coronavirus pandemic on liberal internationalist principles because the virus severely tested many governments' resolve to support its premise. However, Mearsheimer and Glaser (2019) argue against liberal internationalism's existence suggesting that the order was neither liberal nor international, limited mainly to the West, and included key dimensions steeped in realism. Under a hyper-globalised economy, developing countries can grow more powerful, as indicated by the rise of China, as well as the constancy of Russia as an energy superpower. By adopting policies that clash with national identity, as multinational states increasingly do in a world in which globalisation dominates economy and finance, grievances abound, he argues, which causes liberalism to fall short in addressing conflict inside states. He further notes that the liberal international order (LIO) adopts policies that clash with national identity, which matters greatly, since mixing different peoples through open borders and broadminded refugee policies is usually a prescription for serious trouble. Some states, like China, seem to be able to exist under any order because their growing power and influence suggest they can profit within any system (Weiss and Wallace, 2021). Norrlöf

(2020) warns that emphasising self-sufficiency and protectionist responses to declining competitiveness and job loss puts stress on liberal hegemony. Yet, making liberal economic policies compatible with domestic intervention to promote social goals is compatible with the LIO. Lastly, according to many, the world's entrance into the Anthropocene stage has arrived. Simangan (2020) discusses the resulting climate change, biodiversity loss, forest depletion, droughts, air and water pollution and extreme weather manifestations. She argues that 'the LIO has lost sight of social protection, an integral to the liberal value of human rights, and increasingly favored unlimited economic growth'. The maintenance of liberal internationalism must be reworked to factor in individual- and global-level changes to address these multifaceted problems. The case studies in this volume showcase how countries are working through these multidimensional issues and developing LIO-based solutions within their countries.

As this volume comes to print, the Russian aggression in Ukraine during 2022 poses the most serious challenge to the LIO since World War II, as China watches the evolving situation in Europe and calibrates its own actions regarding Taiwan accordingly. So far, Ukraine may be a story of data privacy. *Security* magazine (23 February 2022) notes that according to the Digital Freedom Index from ProtonVPN, which measures the scope of media and internet access in countries around the world, Russia is ranked as having the 3rd worst level of digital freedom with Ukraine holding the 22nd worst place.

Actions during wartime of blocking communication and targeting communication assets greatly expand the threat of cyber warfare and showcase how state actors wield power; yet, this evolution does not tell the whole story. Networks around the world may be coming to the aid of Ukrainians. Some believe that Ukraine is winning the social media war; yet, the implications of that context are not known. In this environment, the relevance of digital identity and personal data; the robustness, or lack thereof, of agency; a viable mesh region or sound distributed ecosystems shed light on how states fair when state actors fail to respond or respond inadequately to citizen needs.

This introduction addresses three questions, which track the alternative images to Waltz expanded upon in this volume. First, how does the Global Network University (GNU) model, articulated by New York University president emeritus John Sexton in his volume *Standing for Reason: The University in a Dogmatic Age* (2019), facilitate ongoing research in the Keith/Mazzucelli Anthem Press Ethics of Personal Data Collection Series in light of the COVID-19 pandemic?

Second, does the uneven use of technologies between the developed and developing worlds deconstruct the state from the 'black box' of Waltz to the viable mesh region, which nurtures the most fragile nodes without access in a 'post-vaccine' world?

Third, how do nodes utilise personal data and self-sovereignty in ways that disrupt the state, as we revise Waltz's definition of the distribution of influence in GIS 1.2 (the Western tradition of international relations), which is limited in the present context?

The editors and contributors to this volume consider the limitations of existing theories in international relations to address the present context, as personal data collection risks become more significant in a COVID-19 world. The post-pandemic world, as introduced by Zakaria, is likely to be marked by social protests in diverse local settings. In this introduction, the editors explain the necessity to elaborate three alternative images or levels of analysis to those articulated by Waltz in the classic text, *Man, the State, and War* (1959). These images provide aim to provide a much-needed bridge to span the fields of international relations, on the one hand, and conflict resolution, on the other. The alternative images anticipate beyond 2019 rather than remaining fixated on 1959 and prior centuries, thereby allowing us to consider ways to bridge the gap between international relations theory, which is straight-jacketed by realism, and conflict resolution practice (Mazzucelli et al., 2021), which requires an expanded conceptual foundation introduced by the authors as inclusionism in a companion edited volume (Mazzucelli et al., 2022).

In the Western School international relations literature from Thucydides's *The History of the Peloponnesian War* to Waltz's *Man, the State, and War*, realism in its various perspectives focuses on a fixed view of human nature, of the state and of the international system. From ancient times to the present millennium, realism has explained the nature of war and the inherent challenges to nurture the peace in a world dominated by the anarchy of 'no common power' (Lieber, 1988) in an unstable world. In the philosophy of Machiavelli, his counsel to *The Prince* (1532) is that human nature is dark, egotistical and obsessive; power is the pursuit of human nature across the sweep of history. It is the diplomatic history of European states, analysed by Kissinger in *A World Restored* (1957), which allows us to situate our thinking about equilibrium in a specific context, that of the balance of power during the Age of Metternich when the Concert of Europe was responsible to prevent war on the Continent.

In the immediate post–World War II period, Monnet, Schuman, Adenauer and other Founding Fathers of the 'peace project', known as the Communities of Europe, purposefully chose to anchor the economies of the Western countries on the Continent to an embedded liberalism, which privileged the state over the market with the possibility of government intervention to provide a social safety net and mitigate economic as well as social inequalities. As European integration proceeded, a globalisation process, anchored in the neoliberal orthodoxy of the Washington Consensus, exerted an increasing influence in the world, thereby exacerbating fundamental differences between the embedded liberalism model that characterises post-war reconstruction in the countries of Western Europe and the neoliberal model that privileges markets and multinationals at the expense of societies and citizens.

As Heraclitus wrote, 'No man ever steps in the same river twice, for it's not the same river and he's not the same man.' Likewise, observers of European integration recognise that history and politics evolve continuously. In the decades leading to the early part of the twenty-first century, neoliberal ideology has become hegemonic shaping the responses of states. In other words, as embedded liberalism gives way to neoliberalism, the relationship between structure and agency continues to change, thereby widening the gulf between the expectations of disaffected majorities as well as rainbow minorities in European Union member states and those in the top 1 per cent. The grievances of billions in and beyond Europe are rooted in daily experiences whereby their lives are rigidly governed by neoliberal orthodoxy and constricted realism. Realism expects to explain the nature of war for all time. The neorealism of Kenneth Waltz, explained in his 1979 volume, *Theory of International Politics*, framed a static bipolar environment conditioned by the nuclear balance of terror between the United States and the former Soviet Union.

In the early twenty-first century, the international relations literature still posits realism as a dominant paradigm in the Western School. This volume introduces alternative frames of reference that address the deficiencies of liberalism with its lack of sufficient attention to ethnic diversity. By drawing on constructivism with its focus on framing, particularly the influence in instrumentalist terms of narratives shaped by the media, this volume explores that influence by analysing case studies in historical context. In 2020, the world's present, yet unequal, experiences of the triptych, personal data, global pandemic and social protests lead us to introduce personal data (Image I), the mesh region (Image II) and the distributed ecosystem (Image III) to capture the dynamic, transformative nature of the changing relationship between structure and agency.

It is important to organise the contributions of authors in a sequence that builds on itself as the reader progresses forward. The foundation of the work is to provide a general orientation through important terminology and fundamental needs pertaining to college and university institutional review boards (IRBs) to begin the discussion about micro issues that have arisen because of the changing domestic and international relations landscapes. The chapters sequence so as to introduce the concepts (Kibitlewski) and methodology (Martin-Shields and Al Achkar) pertaining to personal data collection in Part I followed by case studies that range from the relatively more liberal in Italy (Rossi, Mazzucelli and Unger) to the illiberal and populist nationalism in Hungary (Pap) to the authoritarian nationalist in Bosnia–Herzegovina (Schneider) in Part II. The case studies in Part III offer the reader a non-Western perspective on the ways in which concepts and methodology elucidate the challenges of personal data collection in localities made all the more fragile in a pandemic environment, notably, Sierra Leone (Hlaing and Greenhalgh) and Myanmar (Salter).

In response to this plea, a community of experts remains in dialogue after two Bosch Workshops at New York University to define the contents of case studies that follow, which build on those in a companion volume. The responsibility of our research community is to grapple with specific issues that define the state of the field in personal data collection risks as the world evolves in a post-vaccine (Zimmerman et al., 2021), rather than a post-pandemic, phase. Case studies, including prominent uses of social media platforms and mobile telephony applications, document human rights' concerns in remote areas. The dilemma of how to use technology effectively, while not harming the vulnerable, constitutes one of the most salient issues. Can technology, a two-edged sword in its applications, promote human empowerment and individual agency? This edited volume highlights the ways in which this question and others identified lead to reflections concerning personal data collection risks as well as their relevance to international relations in research and response.

Our initial question asks us to consider how the GNU model, articulated by New York University president emeritus John Sexton in his volume *Standing for Reason*, facilitates research on personal data collection risks in a post-vaccine world. As students in educational systems around the world make greater use of social media in their learning, research and service initiatives, their interactions with platforms like Facebook and Twitter are steadily increasing. This facet of globalisation is likely to continue as the landscape of higher education evolves in a post-pandemic world (Zakaria, 2009, p. 3). Sexton explains that the origins of the GNU were Eurocentric 'with study-away sites in Madrid in 1959 and Paris in 1969' (p. 87). Not surprisingly, the option of study away was originally for Spanish and French majors and then expanded to include other students. By 2000, sites in Florence and London were added as the NYU student population was encouraged to spend a semester abroad at one of these four academic locations.

It is possibly a matter of synchronicity that as Florence and London broadened NYU's study-away sites, Mazzucelli was initiating a pioneering internet/multimedia seminar at Sciences Po Paris during the fall 2000 semester. Funding provided by the Robert Bosch Foundation in Stuttgart, Germany, allowed the creation of a transatlantic internet/multimedia seminar southeastern Europe (TIMSSE), the first hybrid, in-person and online, graduate offering of its kind in that institution's history (Mazzucelli, 2000-03, http://www.timsse.com/). In a class of twenty-six graduate candidates, more than a dozen countries were represented across the Continent and around the world. One of the goals of such a hybrid learning experience is to experiment with a variety of technology-mediated options available to developing as well as developed countries to increase the plurality of voices in dialogue. In this context, it is possible to spark the intellectual curiosity of students to explore the emerging risks in a changing international environment.

By 2005, the expansion of NYU's study-away sites outside Europe included Accra, Buenos Aires, Sydney and Tel Aviv as well as Shanghai. A consideration of the university's 'relationship to globalisation and its emerging civil society' led to a realisation that without a site in the Arab and Muslim world outreach to 'one-quarter of the world's people' would remain minimal as the university evolved, given that access to 'a repository of a distinguished intellectual and cultural history' was already 'missing from the picture' (Sexton, 2019, pp. 87–88). In the context of this volume, Kibitlewski and Salter refined ideas in their chapters as members of the Conflict Resolution seminar taught as a blended offering in the Program on International Relations within the Graduate School of Arts and Science. New York University is uniquely placed as a GNU to create a community of researchers worldwide to address the concerns raised in this volume. The insights their chapters provide spur the authors in this volume on to further research as we consider why personal data collection risks have received so little attention in the academic world.

Working from the alternative levels of analysis, the contributors in Part I speak to personal data collection risks, whereas those in Part II highlight challenges that speak to the growing relevance of the 'mesh region' in international relations prompting those in Part III to take into consideration the needs of the distributed ecosystem. Like Acharya and Buzan (2019), the authors of this Introduction consider 2008 as an inflection point in the transition from 1.1 to 1.2 GIS. As referenced in the companion volume edited by Mazzucelli et al. (2022), GIS 1.2, in this context, 'means states, networks, and societies analysed from 2008 onwards given the changes taking place in the core and the periphery since the global financial crisis'.

The second question we address in this introduction is how the uneven use of technologies between the developed and developing worlds deconstructs the state from the 'black box' of Waltz to the mesh, which nurtures the most fragile nodes in a 'post-vaccine' world. Waltz (1959, 1979) focuses on human nature, society and system described as a black box, where the primary actors are 'territory-based' nation-states. Waltz's (1979) structured neorealism, like realism, does little to understand the influence of agents other than sovereign nations. The 'black box' suggests that states have but one voice, acting as an integrated unit, even though international organisations actively impact nation-state interests. Realists may see multinational corporations as only a means for creating a monopoly over economic markets, believing that international organisations cannot impact relations between sovereign states (Tariq et al., 2018).

Waltz's focus on structural anarchy as a permissive cause of war has been criticised as not inclusive of some components of order and organisation in the international environment (Sjoberg, 2012). Waltz seemingly admits that beyond being ordered by the presence or lack of government, there may be a substance to the international structure other than anarchy that is invisible (Sjoberg, 2012, p. 7, citing Waltz (1979, p. 89), suggesting a gender-hierarchical theory as a cause of war). Moreover, realism does not consider cooperation as a means for creating mechanisms to deal with conflict and neglects hierarchies' effects between international nation-states on dependent states (Velandia, 2020, p. 4). The short answer is that the proliferation of technology has produced an unpredictable effect between developed and developing countries and within nation-states.

Shifting intra-state dependencies are highlighted in Hlaing and Greenhalgh's chapter about Sierra Leone's Ebola outbreak that outlined state and network cooperation and coordination between multiple non-state actors with critical expertise. In Sierra Leone, the expected response channels based on traditional state alliances, especially ones through the United Kingdom, were ineffective in providing necessary resources to address the outbreak. Hlaing and Greenhalgh's discussion outlined the interactions, goals and outcomes of the state, non-governmental organisations and local networks that supported or hampered the Ebola response. Their chapter details the events supporting critical reconfiguration of traditional non-state organisation's networks that integrated new organisations as partners and relied more heavily on local networks. Their chapter highlights the painstaking method of capacity building to enable and strengthen a mesh network for information dissemination. A lack of trust existed between localities and the nation making it challenging to drive information through the hierarchal 'web of networks' needed to combat Ebola. Local networks connected and strengthened the betweenness centrality by shortening information flow paths through designating local nodes, even in situations where there was a lack of trust. Skype groups were used to disseminate information, even as the country struggled to collect information and perform contact tracing, especially in rural areas. The capability built from their Ebola experiences and the continued existence of these networks resulted in a more successful response to the COVID-19 pandemic. However, this success may have been impacted by the international distribution of resources to fight COVID-19, that is, access to PPE, disregard for contracts, skyrocketing prices, breached contracts and cancellation of orders for medical supplies. As the scramble for pandemic supplies exploded in the international arena, domestic priorities of developed countries may explain the lag distribution but may have threatened the foundations of globalisation for developing countries (Moise et al., 2020). However, the ability to find and secure supplies could only have been accomplished through digital technology (Lee, 2021).

Technology's role is only tangentially addressed by international relations theories. Eriksson and Newlove-Eriksson's (2021) comprehensive review of international relations theory and its treatment of technology notes that under realism suggests that technology's role is understood as a 'force multiplier' while liberalism views technology as a 'liberalising force'. Constructivists view technology as neutral, concentrating on how it helps form identities and social norms, 'along with the reflection that many novel technologies can reshape perceptions of distance' from the effects of one's action (13). Technopolitics see technology as intertwined with or embedded within society and politics rather than outside it and focuses on how technology and politics shape and reshape each other.

By failing to account for technological influences, these theories fail to account for the influence of technology in the international environment. Unlike developed countries, developing countries' policy agendas around technology focus more on developing economic power (Phillips and Phillips, 2019). Moreover, these countries may not feel that international coordination is fruitful because it does not directly address their issues. Further, gaps based on knowledge economies are increasingly significant for individuals in developing countries (Bilon et al., 2018).

Notwithstanding the different policy agendas between developed and developing countries, global technology networks generate power imbalances among nation-states (Farell and Newman, 2019). Developed nation-states and some powerful non-state actors have developed and leveraged positions as focal points or central nodes that give them a strategic advantage. Even though liberal theology includes 'complex interdependence', this interdependence does not produce reciprocal dependencies (50). Instead, these networks can create a weaponised interdependence made up of tangible, enduring power imbalances, where the critical nodes are not randomly distributed; rather, the nodes are territorially concentrated with the ability to produce choke points in the global system (52, 55). They argue against AM Slaughter's (2017) depiction of a liberalistic interdependence network, favouring a structural, Waltz-like perspective of states' influence of technology networks.

Therefore, the effects of the unevenness in the nation-state's use of technology between developed and developing nation-states are still unknown. The answer to Sexton's questions is that technology may promote human empowerment and individual agency through mesh-connected nodes within the global network. However, understanding whether the black box still exists as a single voice is unclear. Anne-Marie Slaughter's (2017) and Slaughter and LaForge's (2021) strategies suggest that the global order can be reformed without state initiatives, suggesting that the messy, contested space can be marshalled by opening it up and liberalising it. They argue that additional spokes and hubs with participation incentives are needed. These additional spokes and hubs should be deliberate and small enough to accomplish a targeted objective. The authors suggest that nation-states acting as hubs should balance the 'shadowy' aspects of the combination of state and mesh influences into an albeit redundant but ever-changing system. The authors suggest that mapping the actors and connections between them would be a starting point. This volume highlights the many faces of the different state and non-state entities, organisations and communities acting alongside states to address personal data exposure and pandemic-related issues.

Three alternative images or levels of analysis have become more relevant to states, networks and societies from 2008 onward given the changes taking place in the core and periphery since the global financial crisis (Acharya and Buzan, 2019, p. 261). In some instances, we propose actions leaders may take relying on the needs expressed by the most vulnerable as disseminated through social media. The first image is that of Personal Data or enlarging the evolving identity footprint of those in the most fragile areas to make the plight of IDPs or refugees visible in ways that can protect the most vulnerable.

The second image deconstructs even the most totalitarian state, to consider the hardest case analyses, that is, Assad's Syria (Mazzucelli et al., 2021) to allow us to view Waltz's state in a modified way, in the form of a 'mesh region', to focus on what anthropologists and architects reference as space and place. The transition from a fragile space to one that exhibits resilience as the transformation from no man's land to community occurs has the potential to facilitate a place for sustainability to take root in the daily lives of the most vulnerable, particularly women and children who are empowered to take action that resists oppression and sustains justice.

A 'mesh describes a type of network that allows any node to link in any direction with any other nodes in the system. Every part is connected to every other part, and they move in tandem' (Gansky, 2010, p. 16). The relevance of the mesh is in its capacity, analysing the present, and its potential, anticipating the future, to expand: a larger and larger mesh in any given region maximises a variety of communications that can, despite incessant possibilities for corruption or oppression, provide a structure of resilience (Slaughter, 2017, p. 108).

The third image in the post-2008 evolution of states, networks and societies is the distributed ecosystem, which relies on initiatives that speak holistically to 'environmental stewardship' during a new era of 'planetary health' (Guinto et al., 2021). In this era, the distributed ecosystem is an alternative focal point to assure the survival of species as extremist violence ticks up, taking advantage of the uncertainty introduced in vulnerable areas around the world by the COVID-19 pandemic. Case studies in this volume are situated in the historical context of conflict in their immediate areas, the plight of IDPs and refugees across regions, and local immersion steps that may be taken to strengthen agency of inhabitants as well as resiliency in a mesh region to counter disinformation as well as extremist narratives.

The third question raised in this introduction concerns how nodes intersect with personal data and self-sovereignty to disrupt the state, as we broaden Waltz's definition of the distribution of influence in GIS 1.2 in the Western tradition of international relations. This question is at the heart of the matter in reflections on ways alternative levels of analysis in 1.2 GIS impact on structure and agency. Waltz's structural or neorealism limits the number of state actors or great powers whose influence determines conflict in the international system. In the early twenty-first century, the interactions between the People's Republic of China and the United States of America, the main protagonists in Waltz's explanation of the distribution of influence in the Western School of international relations, speak to the vertical distribution of power and influence. Although this bipolar world is an evolution away from the Eurocentric focus in the Western School, the universalism inherent in such thinking about international relations and the disjuncture in trying to apply liberal ideas to Myanmar, Sierra Leone or to Hungary in the European Union or Bosnia–Herzegovina (BiH) with its aspirations for EU accession are evident. Agency is constrained in Waltz's analysis, which is problematic in a post-vaccine world given the impact of human behaviour on the exponential nature of COVID-19 transmission. The diversity of responses to the pandemic illuminates the ways in which considerations of culture matter in a post-vaccine world, which is also evolving in a post-Western direction. Yet, as this evolution takes place, we bear witness to the uneven distribution in most of our twenty-first century world of vaccines that new technologies have made possible.

The previously mentioned evolution has significant consequences for social constructivism, which still focuses largely on security analyses in the North Atlantic area and Europe, thereby limiting the focus beyond the West. The chapters in this volume addressing the Myanmar, Sierra Leone, Hungary and

BiH challenge this Western ethnocentrism albeit in quite distinct ways from the case studies analysing China, Iran, Taiwan and India, in the companion volume. This volume counters the notion that such ethnocentrism lends coherence to the field of international relations or that American dominance of the field is acceptable, in Mearsheimer's words, given its 'benign' nature. And yet, realism is still dominant in China and India, given their global aspirations in this century, which leads us to consider the ways in which the alternative levels of analysis may broaden the field of international relations. This evolution is particularly significant as China rises to challenge the United States and as other powers from the Global South advance, relatively speaking, in their development.

The first two decades of the twenty-first century indicate more and more interactions between those countries in the core and those that had been previously relegated to the periphery, the so-called Third World, in the Cold War era. As this revolutionary process intensifies, with technologies and methodologies paving new paths to development, the alternative levels of analysis in 1.2 GIS aim to capture the dynamics of this process. As the nature of the core expands, with some countries in Europe falling back into a semi-core as the barriers separating countries on the periphery erode, the term West speaks to a specific identity that exists as a reference in contradistinction to the rest. The alternative images the authors introduce do not posit the difference between West and rest as +/- given that the verb expand captures the dynamics of the interactions between core and periphery.

This volume underlines an integral aspiration on the part of the editors and publisher alike: to advance the public discourse on personal data collection risks. The dangers to democratic government of illiberal discourses in the network environment analysed by Anne-Marie Slaughter in *The Chessboard and the Web* (2017) are one of the foremost ethical concerns in thinking about community during the early twenty-first century. The manipulation of information as well as data resonates in the research of contributors analysing cases from the Myanmar and the United States to Sierra Leone and Italy. In our experiences, the public square in governments ranging from communist to democratic to oligarchic is increasingly animated by the ubiquitous presence of social media in the lives of billions across the world. The fact that information is increasingly filtered through social media platforms gives states as well as firms more direct influence in personal data manipulation as well as collection risks. As we think about the rights of the community as well as those of the person, this information revolution begs the question on a macro as well as micro level: Why does this state–society transformation matter in international relations?

If we consider the vocabulary of realism, the most dominant theory in the Western School of international relations, the concept of power is central. In her volume *Surveillance Capitalism* (2019), Shoshana Zuboff identifies what she terms 'instrumentarianism' as a new form of power, which asks readers to reconsider how influence may be measured. As Tim Wu asks in the *New York Review*, 'Bigger Brother' (2020):

> How might we measure the influence of Google against that of an outlet like Fox News, which follows a more traditional propaganda formula? Can platform influence really be compared to the power of earlier forms of propaganda, like the broadcasts that united Germany behind Hitler?

Whereas the collection of personal data and corresponding risks by firms dwarfs that collected by states, Zuboff focuses our attention, in terms of the community as well as the individual, on the specific combination of state power and platform surveillance. In an age when more and more states target a particular ethnic community inside their borders, China pushes the envelope in its mix of military-style surveillance technologies with big-data analytics. The Chinese state has the singular capacity to track and control its Muslim Uighur population in Xinjiang. Its surveillance relies on checkpoints, cameras and files, which are constantly updated on virtually every citizen of Uighur descent.

This reality of state control in the early twenty-first century leads us to consider what Tim Wu asserts as critical in thinking about the concerns Zuboff raises:

> The protection of human freedom can no longer be thought of merely as a matter of traditional civil rights, the rights to speech, assembly, and voting that we've usually taken as the bedrocks of a free society. What we most urgently need is something else: protection against widespread behavioral control and advanced propaganda techniques. And that begins with completely rethinking how we control the collection of data. (2020)

Personal data collection risks present a unique dynamism that has not been sufficiently acknowledged in the contemporary literature of international relations. The reality that individuals are at their best when they identify with a community is not at war with the reality that communities are only at their best when they identify with all their individuals. In that regard, we insist on translating the ethic of what Krieger and Belliger in *Hacking Digital Ethics*, the second volume in the Keith/Mazzucelli Anthem Press Series, call the informational self with norms that networks of humanity demand, like flexibility, authenticity, transparency, participation, communication flow and, of course, connectivity.

At the macro level in which Krieger and Belliger reason, the ethical concerns and the risks we face require anti-surveillance protection of a legal nature to prevent indefensible surveillance and incessant accumulation of personal data. Only in this way will the growing power of states to control every facet of the lives of targeted communities be held in check. It is no longer enough to define human rights in terms of limits placed on arbitrary state power in defence of individual freedom, as liberals do. In the second decade of the twenty-first century, billions of people across the planet are interconnected in ways that are a matter of life and death. In a post-vaccine world, the survival of the human species is likely to be dependent on connectivity, which is a core objective of spirituality. This volume asks readers to rethink personal data collection risks in the context of the fragile community, which is comprised of individuals vulnerable to surveillance capitalism as well as what John Sexton identifies in *Standing for Reason* (2019) as 'secular dogmatism', which contributes to the increasing polarisation in societies. In thinking about the relevance of this evolution throughout our world today, the macro and micro levels connect with considerable tensions in play: to counter the dangers of the surveillance capitalism Zuboff defines (2019), as Wu explains, 'a little less knowledge is what will keep us free', whereas to address the pitfalls of secular dogmatism only a great deal more spiritual transcendence may safeguard the peace in community.

Overview of Chapters

This Introduction frames the edited volume in terms of the methodological questions to raise given the range of case studies that follow concerning personal data collection risks in comparative perspective. Part I consists of two framing chapters that speak to the time leading into the COVID-19 pandemic in terms of what this volume defines as an emerging area of study, personal data collection risks in international relations, as the volume introduces empirical cases that reference the 1.2 GIS alternative image of personal data. The opening chapter focuses on the evolution of concerns related to personal data in Western countries and the implementation of regulatory policies in a comparative EU and US context with a focus on the structure that facilitates a type of agency that allows people to reclaim control over their personal data. The second chapter aims to identify and understand new protocol and ethics issues when using digital technology for research in vulnerable communities, as well as to identify new directions for training on human subjects research ethics that account for digital risks. Their forward-looking research is likely to be increasingly relevant to colleges, universities and the service academies.

The chapters in the book speak to this dichotomy, that of the remaining dominance of Waltz's state action, but the impact of state inaction, that shifts the focus to actions of the three alternative images to understand international relations. State inaction might be considered another aspect of realism, but in the twenty-first century, states may be considered not only as 'authors', but also as 'permitters' of actions taken by others. These others are not individuals but networked groups with resources that rival states. Kibitlewski's surveillance capitalism provides an example of the lack of state policy action and its permission, though capitalism, of impacting individual agency surrounding the use and value of personal data. Similarly, Martin-Shields and Achkar's chapter discusses data protection in research by governmental and educational IRBs and the lack of standards to address digital interfaces and the differences in digital data. They also suggest that individual agency is eroding for lack of understanding of what is needed to create protections for vulnerable populations in the digital environment.

Part I looks ahead to concerns related to personal data collection risks in vulnerable communities with a focus on university research as the digital space evolves. In Part II, Pap's chapter does not focus on digital research thereby opening a space for analysis and reflection on the ways in which research may evolve in a new era. In Part III, chapters extend the reach of cases, including two where the General Data Protection Regulation (GDPR) is not applicable, namely, Sierra Leone and Myanmar.

In Chapter 1, the approach of interest to international relations scholars and practitioners is Jakub Kibitlewski's use of the labour theory of value as the analytical lens, which advocates the need for a legal reconceptualisation of data beyond the notion of privacy. The emphasis on an alternative that allows subjects to reclaim control over their personal data speaks to the alternative images to the extent that the consequences are likely to level out the existing power asymmetries in their interaction with platform providers. Kibitlewski analyses debates concerning the implementation of regulatory policies in the context of digital platforms like Facebook, which frequently arise from controversies involving privacy violations. Perceiving the issue of regulation solely from a standpoint of user privacy, however, not only omits some crucial aspects and depth of the problems inherent in the business model of such companies. As revealed by the many empirical examples, this perspective also proves to be inadequate, reactive and ultimate futile in preventing further breeches. Adopting the labour theory of value as its analytical lens, this chapter advocates the need for a legal reconceptualisation of data beyond the notion of privacy. Specifically, a proprietary approach to user-generated data on digital platforms is explored and critically evaluated in terms of a more potent alternative allowing the subjects to reclaim control over their personal information and, thus, level out the existing power asymmetries in their interaction with platform providers.

Kibitlewski references *The Age of Surveillance Capitalism* (2019) to explain that, for Zuboff, the crux of the problem does not lie mainly in the mere selling of audience commodities and their attention to advertisers, but in the 'rendering of our lives as behavioural data for the sake of others' improved control of us' (p. 94). According to Zuboff, the extraction of detailed information about users by platforms is necessarily predatory in character, operating 'through coercion and stealth', enabled by and proceeding through secretive corporate decisions, non-transparent algorithms, abusive contracts, consumer ignorance and lack of real alternatives to the offered products or services (p. 253). The predatory nature of Facebook's approach prevails to the extent that structural aspects of how the platform accumulates capital remain untouched. This is true even if the new changes adhere to the FTC-imposed privacy compliance system to assure greater transparency, oversight and accountability of its commercial activity.

In Chapter 2, Charles Martin-Shields and Ziad Al Achkar assert that, as we move further into the twenty-first century, the digital space is becoming an increasingly ubiquitous area where personal information is stored and managed. The goal of their analysis is to identify and understand new protocol and ethics issues when using digital technology for research in vulnerable communities and to identify new directions for training on human subjects research ethics that account for digital risks. There is a growing literature on the legal and ethical issues around newer digital data management approaches as well as a deep literature on the politics of technology in the lives of vulnerable people. This chapter draws on these literature streams to propose new directions for ethics pedagogy for digital participatory research in vulnerable communities. To do this, Martin-Shields and Al Achkar outline a framework that brings together sociological research on technology in society, particularly Foucault's analysis of the development of hospitals in industrial society, with critical theories of social power structures. This framework is used to analyse how researchers have created tools and guidelines for doing research in vulnerable communities using digital technologies and the role that managing power plays in doing ethical digital research. By identifying the sociopolitical qualities of digital technology and the power dynamics between researchers and vulnerable communities, the chapter proposes new ways of managing research ethics that address the risks that come with doing participatory research using digital platforms.

The three case studies below look specifically at the coronavirus pandemic and the mesh region as it is juxtaposed to environments with either have the foundations of a mesh region demonstrating inadequacy or have mesh networks that don't enjoy the full protection of the state. Inadequacy of state action is a theme related to Rossi, Mazzucelli, and Unger's review of the European Union's failure to fully address the needs of its network, especially as the Italian citizenry was impacted by the COVID-19 pandemic. Failing to use the power of the EU's collective resulted in a lack of policies, tests, vaccines and other needed items resulting in a severely weakened response in Italy. The chapter suggests that inclusionism as an important foundation of the mesh region. They noted that 'the pandemic crisis reveal(ed) the frailties of the decision chain, the communication system, and the perception Italian citizens have of the European Union'. What it also says is that citizens are still relying on 'state-based action', and when those actions are not initiated by the established network, individuals suffer.

Pap's chapter comparing the 'Black Lives Matter' movement in the United States to the plight of Roma 'lives' in Europe shows how state inaction failed to protect different groups during the pandemic. Pap also notes that ethno-racial disparities during the COVID-19 pandemic not only impacted rules for data collection but also fuelled the criminalisation of Roma based on their legal characterisation in countries designating them a 'minority'.

The last case study by Schneider provides another viewpoint about the lack of governmental guidance and action related to data collection and vulnerable populations, especially for researchers in conflict spaces. Schneider suggests that COVID-19 will pose long-lasting challenges to researchers in post-conflict spaces because of the control over international borders and travel restrictions. Without an evolved set of rules set by states to address the new normal, researchers have to fend for themselves and protect their clients as best they can.

Chapter 3, authored by Christian Rossi, Colette Mazzucelli, and David C. Unger, analyses the spread of the novel coronavirus that struck Italy and almost all other European Union member states during spring 2020. Besides the economic consequences, the rules imposed by the Italian authorities tore the country apart, with several institutions, such as the churches and other religious groups, the schools, the universities as well as the cultural sector, unable to function properly. The system approved by the government to track cases of COVID-19, known as *Immuni*, posed clear problems for citizens' privacy. On the international side, Italian authorities found themselves isolated as the European Union seemed politically to disappear with member states responding on their own to the crisis. Italy sought the intervention of the European Commission to enlarge the instruments to fight the economic downturn, which was a direct consequence of the political choices initially taken during March 2020. The European Union provided an uncoordinated response to the crisis. It is undoubtedly true that the EU waived the budget limits and made available new funds to be injected into the economy of member states. Yet, it is also true that not all member states were happy with this solution, particularly the Netherlands and other northern members, including Denmark, Sweden and Finland as well as Austria, the so-called Frugal Five. As Rossi, Mazzucelli, and Unger explain, the COVID-19 crisis highlighted a governance deficit in Italy with a reconsideration needed of the regional model and economic solidarity, a reform of data protection, the necessity to invest more money in a better health service and a different approach towards the European Union.

In Chapter 4, Andras Pap provides an interpretative framework for scapegoating anti-Roma rhetoric and over-policing throughout Europe, which targets a minority group already disproportionately affected by the virus. The case study is situated in the context of the American 'Black Lives Matter' movement as well as current debates on conceptualising and operationalising race and ethnicity, ethno-racial disparities in the effects of the COVID-19 pandemic. Various forms of penal populism and nationalism are analysed in this context to illustrate that COVID-19 exacerbates social inequalities. The chapter begins with an outline of the inquiry's social science context. The points of reference include conceptualising and operationalising race, ethnicity and membership in national groups/communities, in particular in the field of medicine; the discursive and institutional framework of populism, in particular penal populism and penal nationalism; and mapping out four distinct ways as to how the virus may affect certain groups incommensurately and lead to systemic and institutional discrimination. This is followed by an overview of the status of Roma in Europe. The subsequent section provides a case study of Hungary for conceptualising the Roma at the intersection of a racial, cultural or socio-economic minority, as well as an overview of populist policing strategies. The final section shows how Roma have been targeted by populist political rhetoric and securitising law enforcement in lieu of the pandemic.

The evolution of personal data collection risks in international relations is likely to focus increasingly on post-conflict spaces, which is why Mary Kate Schneider's chapter references a field research project at the high school level in BiH. Her research brings to light the challenges of personal data collection in minority as well as majority populations, as these relate to the analysis by Martin-Shields and Al Achkar.

In Chapter 5, Schneider normatively questions how to conduct research in post-conflict spaces. Her chapter addresses the question of ethical data collection of personal information from individuals in BiH. Based on field research conducted as part of a project examining interethnic attitudes among high school students in BiH, the chapter discusses special considerations and best practices regarding sensitive questions and ethical challenges highlighting particularly those challenges associated with conducting research within post-conflict spaces and within spaces claimed by unique populations – namely, public schools attended by minor and minority students. The chapter begins by introducing the project's tripartite methodology, which relies on interviews, focus groups and survey data. Survey questions assess topics including identity, ethnicity, discrimination and social distance. The chapter then explains why the data collected for this project may be considered sensitive, building out implications relating to institutions, access to power and potential for discrimination (both social and professional). Finally, the chapter identifies a host of ethical issues (permission, consent, implicit bias, 'outsider' status, objectivity, neutrality and the question of who benefits from the research) and speaks to how researchers might address each of these. Ultimately, this chapter serves as a case study illustrating the practical challenges associated with personal data collection risks in post-conflict spaces.

The last two chapters are about the evolution of ecosystems and how they support instances where states don't act or act inadequately, but ecosystems are there to provide support for citizens. Hlaing and Greenhalgh commented that the emerging ecosystem developed after the Ebola crisis brought together actors across the three levels of government, acting to strengthen network connections, improve trust, streamline data collection and establish cross-collaboration norms, that improved their response to the COVID-19 pandemic. They were able to keep COVID-19 numbers low despite the lack of state action thanks to this fully developed ecosystem with pandemic experience.

Salter's case study of the issues in Myanmar supports the notion that lack of governmental protection for human rights violations in an 'algorithmically driven, anarchic cyberspace' results in digital hate speech, disinformation, which can lead to violence. The ethnic cleansing of the Rohingya in Myanmar was fuelled by disinformation campaigns, as the distorted 'marketplace of ideas' allowed extremist views to flourish. Moreover, ethical issues of data ownership must extend to digital and corporate spaces to influence the dialogue about democratic values for the 'digital individual'.

These collective case studies are stories of a changing sphere of demand for protection and an indication of where new aspects of protection may come from. Waltz's suggestion that protection comes from the state, even in war times, no longer tells the whole story. Understanding the dimensions and impacts to individual agency, the power of criminal and civil mesh systems, and the robustness of local ecosystems are critical parts of the new relations between and among states.

In Chapter 6, Thynn Thynn Hlaing and Emilie Greenhalgh explain the relevance of understanding challenges during the Ebola outbreak in Africa as the global COVID-19 pandemic intensifies during the 2020–21 period. This analysis underlines why it is important to look at state and networks, as well as institutions and individuals, together in this context. The authors explain why a realist lens is insufficient in this post-colonial, post-conflict context. The exploration of Oxfam's role in Sierra Leone raises questions about community networks as well as key issues from different levels of analysis. This chapter discusses how trust affected the Oxfam response, including a focus on the local population, data flows and information sharing.

Chapter 7 explores human rights in a case study far beyond the reach of the EU's GDPR, namely, Myanmar, given that most of the world's population lives outside the reach of European legislation and remains unaware of the ways in which personal data is misappropriated by firms as well as states. This chapter, authored by Laura Salter, introduces a case study to underline some of the concerns raised earlier by Kibitlewski. Salter's analysis explains that genocidal violence was not solely caused by the presence of Facebook. As a constructivist analysis would indicate, the country's story of ethnic and religious division was already well written. Salter's chapter argues that a digital platform does not, itself, construct violence. Her case study illustrates the heightened role digital platforms now play in manufacturing crises, introducing possible dire ramifications. The manipulation of an unfiltered platform, whose algorithm can intentionally create echo chambers, and which has the capability to target personalised disinformation, can easily act as a catalyst for offline violence and human rights violations. The original question posed in Salter's research speaks directly to one of this volume's main ethical concerns: How may we mitigate the risks of human rights violations and the spread of misinformation in a distorted 'marketplace of ideas'? Her research leads us to reflect on further global actions that could be considered ethical and necessary, taking into consideration an analysis of conflict using the first image of 1.2 GIS, personal data.

This case study exemplifies the role that ICTs now play in structuring the information flow of a society and catalysing the spread of extremism and misinformation. The distortions present in the marketplace of ideas, caused by a profit-centred and data-driven business model, can allow bad actors to manipulate the flow of ideas, aligning new information with pre-existing fears and anxieties in a tailored call to action. The case study clearly demonstrates that this manipulation was uniquely effective and destructive in the post-2011 context in Myanmar, and the effects could easily be extrapolated to other emerging democracies or protracted conflicts. Both corporate ownership of personal data and the challenges of content moderation are relevant in this context. Policymakers must now grapple with whether and how to regulate the 'marketplace of ideas' without treading on the rights of its inhabitants. Salter's chapter employs the conceptual ideal type of a 'marketplace of ideas' to analyse how new distortions present themselves in the global communications landscape and inform individuals' very perception of reality, considering the case study of ethnic violence in Myanmar to illustrate how dangerous online speech in a distorted information infrastructure can lead to offline violence as well as human right violations offline. Her research discusses the benefits of a human rights–centred, multi-stakeholder approach to developing a dynamic cyber norm regime.

The Conclusion by Mazzucelli, Adams, and Grichting assesses the main themes raised by the contributors in their chapters with a focus on the limits of realism to address new challenges raised in the post-vaccine world, which necessitate alternative images to those introduced by Waltz, as the contributors to this volume focus the attention of readers to lines of inquiry taken up in a companion volume, *The Ethics of Personal Data Collection in International Relations: Inclusionism in the Time of COVID-19*, published in the Keith/Mazzucelli Series by Anthem Press (2022).

References

Acharya, A. & Buzan, B. (2019). *The Making of Global International Relations: Origins and Evolution of IR at Its Centenary*. Cambridge: Cambridge University Press.

Eriksson, J., & Newlove-Eriksson, L. M. (2021). Theorizing technology and international relations: prevailing perspectives and new horizons. In *Technology and International Relations* (pp. 3–22). Edward Elgar Publishing.

Farrell, H. & Newman, A. L. (2019). Weaponized interdependence: How global economic networks shape state coercion. *International Security*, *44*(1), 42–79.

Gansky, L., 2010. *The Mesh: Why the Future of Business Is Sharing*. New York: Portfolio Penguin.

Guinto, R. R., Parungao-Balolong, M., Flores, R. J. D., & Bongcac, M. K. (2021). Establishing a community for planetary health in the Philippines. *The Lancet Planetary Health*, *5*(7), e396–e397.

Kissinger, Henry. (1957). *A World Restored*. Boston: Houghton-Mifflin Company.

Krieger, David, and Belliger, Andrea. (2021). *Hacking Digital Ethics*. London and New York: Anthem Press.

Lieber, Robert. (1988). *No Common Power: Understanding International Relations*. Glenville, IL: Scott, Foresman/Little, Brown.

Mazzucelli, C., Rossi, C., & Roggia, V. P. (2021). Revisiting democracy: Intersectionality, youth and the imperative of 'Climate Justice'–Sardinia's 'Europe Day'. In *The demographic dividend and the power of youth: Voices from the global diplomacy lab*, 105. London and New York: Anthem Press.

Mazzucelli, C., Keith, J.F., & Hollifield, C.A. (2022) *The Ethics of Personal Data Collection in International Relations*. London and New York: Anthem Press.

Mearsheimer, J. J. & Glaser, C. L. Whither the liberal international order? 7–50 bound to fail: The rise and fall of the liberal international order. *International Security*, *43*(4), 4.

Norrlöf, C. (2020). Is Covid-19 a liberal democratic curse? Risks for liberal international order. *Cambridge Review of International Affairs*, *33*(5), 799–813.

Phillips, P. P., & Phillips, J. J. (2019). The state of human capital analytics in developing countries: a focus on the Middle East. *Strategic HR Review*.

Sexton, John. (2019). *Standing for Reason the University in a Dogmatic Age*. New Haven: Yale University Press.

Simangan, D. (2020). Where is the Anthropocene? IR in a new geological epoch. *International Affairs*, *96*(1), 211–224.

Sjoberg, L. (2012). Gender, structure, and war: what Waltz couldn't see. *International Theory*, *4*(1), 1–38.

Slaughter, A. M. (2017). *The Chessboard and the Web: Strategies of Connection in a Networked World*. New Haven, CT: Yale University Press.

Slaughter, A. M., & LaForge, G. (2021). Opening up the order: A more inclusive international system. *Foreign Affairs*, *100*, 154.

Tariq, M., Rizwan, M., & Ahmad, M. (2018). Human Nature, Anarchy and Hierarchy as Determining Factors of Realism. *Global Social Sciences Review (GSSR)*, III, 477–487.

Waltz, K. (1959). *Man, the State, and War*. New York: Columbia University Press.

Waltz, K. (1979). *Theory of International Politics*. Reading, MA: Addison-Wesley Publishing Company.

Weiss, J. C., and Wallace, J. L. (2021). Domestic politics, China's rise, and the future of the liberal international order. *International Organization*, *75*(2), 635–664.

Zakaria, F. (2009). *The Post-American World and the Rise of the Rest*. New York: Penguin Books.

Zimmerman, P., Wilson, A., Bosch, J., Grubman, H., Varley, T., McCully, A., ... & Frank, S. (2021, October). Cleveland COVID-19 dashboard: Dynamic summary of disease risk across a diverse inner-city population. In *APHA 2021 Annual Meeting and Expo*. APHA.

Zuboff, S. (2019). *The Age of Surveillance Capitalism: The Fight for a Human Future at the New Frontier of Power*. New York: Public Affairs.

PART I

Chapter 1

DATA TO THE PEOPLE? SURVEILLANCE CAPITALISM AND THE NEED FOR A LEGAL RECONCEPTUALISATION OF PERSONAL DATA BEYOND THE NOTION OF PRIVACY

By Jakub Wojciech Kibitlewski

Introduction

In a keynote speech opening the 2019 F8 Developers Conference in San Jose, California, Facebook's CEO, Mark Zuckerberg, announced his company is about to enter a new chapter in which greater focus will be put on the protection of users' personal information. Having admitted that Facebook '[doesn't] have the strongest reputation on privacy', he then promised 'historically important' changes to the services it offers, including a new, entirely encrypted 'privacy-focused platform' parallel to the already existing traditional social network (Facebook for Developers). The ostensive effort to address user-privacy-related concerns comes at a moment when the platform is mired in multiple investigations, drawing criticism from state actors all around the 'Western' world. For instance, shortly before Zuckerberg's announcement, the Office of the Privacy Commissioner of Canada issued a report in which it accused Facebook of committing 'serious contraventions of Canadian privacy laws and fail[ure] to take responsibility for protecting the personal information of Canadians' (OPC, 2019). More recently, the United States Federal Trade Commission (FTC) approved a record fine of $5 billion after deciding the company violated the FTC's order from 2012 when a settlement was reached following charges of 'deceiving consumers by telling them they could keep their information on Facebook private, and then repeatedly allowing it to be shared and made public' (FTC, 2019). Meanwhile in Europe, Facebook is subject to 11 pending investigations by the Irish Data Protection Commission (DPC) alone, all falling under possible violations of the EU General Data Protection Regulation (GDPR).

These select few examples are merely a fraction of many more instances when the interests of digital platforms appear to stand in direct opposition to the information privacy rights of their users. Moreover, an examination of the structural characteristics of the business model adopted by companies like Facebook, Amazon or Google suggests that further privacy breaches should be anticipated, as they tend to be the rule rather than exception. Since the very logic of capital accumulation that digital platforms rely on is based on personal data collection and its analysis and assembly into information products that are sold to third parties (Fuchs, 2012), it begs a question about the adequacy of applying a privacy-oriented legal framework to effectively protect users' personal information. So far, actions taken to enforce the rule of law in terms of platform users' privacy rights have been retroactive and ineffective, making digital platform providers merely adopt strategies that deflect more radical regulatory policies without significantly changing their business practices (Crain, 2016, p. 93). Thus, as this chapter will advocate, a legal reconceptualisation of data beyond the notion of privacy is necessary if users are to retain a degree of control over their personal data in the digital realm vis-à-vis platform owners.

Chapter outline

The chapter is divided into four sections. It begins with the legal foundation for exercising control over one's personal information within the digital–commercial context. This section briefly outlines and discusses the status quo with regard to currently applicable legal frameworks for the protection of personal data in the United States and European Union. What follows is an examination of the relationship between platform users and operators in order to define and problematise the logic of accumulation utilised by digital platforms. To do so, Marx's labour theory of value is operationalised and applied as the analytical foundation. Most importantly, by identifying the type of activity performed by platform users as unpaid labour (Fuchs, 2012) and situating it within the concept of surveillance capitalism (Zuboff, 2019), this section follows Mark Andrejevic to assert that 'a critique of privacy invasion does not do justice to the economically productive character of consumer surveillance' (Andrejevic, 2010, p. 5) and that 'privacy debates […] come to stand in for discussions that might more directly address the question of who controls the information infrastructure and for what ends' (p. 2). In short, this section argues that if subjects are to retrieve a degree of control over their personal data, a critique of digital platforms needs to be extended beyond the legalistic notion of privacy violations and acknowledge the political-economic underpinnings of their capital accumulation logic.

Drawing on an ownership-oriented legal framework for data developed by Mayer and Ritter (2018), the third section discusses a proprietary approach to personal information as a potentially more effective and proactive alternative in terms of equalising power asymmetries inherent in the political economy of surveillance capitalism. This section argues that reconceptualising data as property opens new avenues for criticism, thus allowing for a more comprehensive debate about regulatory policies aimed at restricting user surveillance performed by corporate actors. By addressing the problematic aspects and possible risks arising from adopting a property law paradigm for personal data, it also asks how far such an approach undermines and, to what extent, reproduces the existing logic of accumulation and its inequalities. Finally, the fourth section serves both as a conclusion of the findings and a brief review of two alternative solutions to the discussed problems. The idea of situating information privacy within the context of human rights and a public service approach to digital platforms is shortly examined and suggested as a point of departure for further research.

Privacy-Oriented Legal Frameworks in Comparative Perspective: EU and the United States

Evaluating the effectiveness and adequacy of a privacy-oriented legal approach to protecting personal information against unsolicited acquisition in the digital sphere necessitates an overview of the main existing regulatory frameworks concerned with data protection. This section focuses on two regulatory regimes in particular: the United States and the European Union. This region-specific focus rests on several important facts. First, both regions are of vital importance for the economic activity of some of the largest digital platforms in the world. Facebook, the poster child for user privacy breaches and the primary concern of this chapter, relies on the European and US markets for the biggest part of its annual revenue (Griswold, 2017). Moreover, both the EU and the United States are currently at the forefront of investigating cases of user privacy rights violations by digital platforms (Privacy International). Above all, however, the region-specific comparative approach serves to emphasise the shortcomings of privacy-based legal frameworks as such, regardless of their respective characteristics.

EU

Europe's personal data protection framework is based on the GDPR, which came into force in 2018. It has been praised as the 'most important change in data privacy regulation in 20 years' (EUGDPR) and 'the toughest privacy and security law in the world' (GDPR.eu, 2019). It is by far the most comprehensive and far-reaching existing legal framework for the protection of individual citizens' personal information, setting regulatory standards for commercial and administrative collection and processing of personal data in 28 countries. The regulation also anticipates extraterritorial application to include EU-based subjects active outside of the union's territory and non-EU actors actively processing data of EU citizens (GDPR, 2016, Art. 3). The framework relies on a specific definition of 'personal data' and its 'processing'. The former is defined as

> any information relating to an identified or identifiable natural person ('data subject'); an identifiable natural person is one who can be identified, directly or indirectly, in particular by reference to an identifier such as a name, an identification number, location data, an online identifier or to one or more factors specific to the physical, physiological, genetic, mental, economic, cultural or social identity of that natural person. (GDPR, 2016, Art. 4)

The latter means 'any operation or set of operations which is performed on personal data or on sets of personal data, whether or not by automated means, such as collection, recording, organisation, structuring, storage, adaptation or alteration, retrieval, consultation, use, disclosure by transmission, dissemination or otherwise making available, alignment or combination, restriction, erasure or destruction' (Art. 4). While the full text of the legal framework is 261 pages long and includes 99 articles grouped into 11 chapters listing numerous principles for lawful data processing and user rights, it is most relevant to invoke the requirement of consent regarding the processing of personal data and the penalties issued in cases of GDPR violations. Recital 32 of the regulation specifies that

> consent should be given by a clear affirmative act establishing a freely given, specific, informed and unambiguous indication of the data subject's agreement to the processing of personal data relating to him or her, such as by a written statement, including by electronic means, or an oral statement [...] if the data subject's consent is to be given following a request by electronic means, the request must be clear, concise and not unnecessarily disruptive to the use of the service for which it is provided. (Rec. 32)

> Depending on the severity of the infringement, non-compliance with the conditions for consent, the principles for data processing or violation of the rights of data subjects can result in administrative fines 'up to 20 000 000 EUR, or in the case of an undertaking, up to 4% of the total worldwide annual turnover of the preceding financial year, whichever is higher' (GDPR, 2016, Art. 83).

It must be acknowledged, however, that the word 'privacy' itself does not appear in the official GDPR document. Consequently, subsuming the protection of personal information under the same notion as privacy might at first glance appear questionable. Nonetheless, considering that the Data Protection Directive of 1995, which was replaced by the GDPR (van der Sloot and De Groot, 2018, p. 103), explicitly links the individual right to privacy with the conditions for personal data processing (e.g. GDPR, 2016, Rec. 2, 7, 10), some room remains to argue that data protection might still be conceived of as being based on, or at the very least related to, the notion of privacy. Furthermore, an independent EU advisory body on data protection and privacy, the Data Protection Working Party, published official guidelines with regard to transparency and processing of personal data under GDPR, referring to a 'privacy-statement/notice' in which the data processing actor is required to clearly elucidate the consequences processing could have for the data subject(s) (European Commission, 2016, p. 7). Thus, as the official legal documents suggest, while the terms 'data protection' and 'privacy' cannot be used interchangeably, it is clear that there is a degree of conceptual association and linkage between the former and the latter.

The United States

Unlike Europe, in the case of the United States, it is difficult to identify a systematic legal regime concerned exclusively with data privacy protection.

The United States does not have a general and federally applicable legal framework regulating the management of personal data and its security. An attempt by the Obama administration to implement one, the Consumer Privacy Bill of Rights Act, which was supposed to provide 'appropriate protection of personal data' (Obama, 2015), never made it past Congress. Rather, the existing laws that address informational privacy, sometimes referred to as a 'patchwork framework' in legal literature (CFR, 2018), are circumstantial and applicable only to specific sectors. For example, the Children's Online Privacy Protection Act (1998) regulates the collection of information about children under 13; the Health Insurance Portability and Accountability Act sets standards for the gathering and management of personally identifiable medical information; and the Family Educational Rights and Privacy Act 'protects the privacy of student education records' (US Department of Education, 2018). However, with regard to the main concern of this chapter, that is data protection and control in the context of commercial practices and user/consumer relations with corporate actors, it is the Federal Trade Commission Act (FTCA) that requires particular attention.

Dating back to the Woodrow Wilson administration, the FTCA was signed into law to prevent 'unfair methods of competition in or affecting commerce, and unfair or deceptive acts or practices in or affecting commerce' (LII §45 (a)). To enforce this, the act established the FTC, which today functions as the de facto main governmental institution providing privacy protection in consumer relations and has the authority to actively intervene in cases of user/consumer privacy breaches and personal data misappropriation (van der Sloot, 2018, p. 88). On its official website, the FTC prides itself on being 'America's top cop on the privacy beat' using the 'FTC Act's general prohibition on unfair and deceptive acts and practices to challenge allegedly illegal conduct involving the privacy and security of all kinds of consumer information' (FTC, 2017). It is important to point out that the FTC has historically relied on the self-regulation of industry in complying with the principles of Fair Information Practices it described in 1998. However, in its May 2000 report to Congress entitled 'Privacy Online: Fair Information Practices In The Electronic Marketplace', the commission presented results of a survey in which it studied the information practices of commercial websites in the United States with regard to their compliance with the Fair Information Practices principles. The results demonstrated that 'industry efforts alone have not been sufficient', and that 'while there will continue to be a major role for industry for self-regulation in the future, the commission recommends that Congress enact legislation that, in conjunction with continuing self-regulatory programmes, will ensure adequate protection of consumer privacy online' (FTC, 2000). Despite FTC's calls for the implementation of a legal framework in order to lay down standards for online privacy protection (like the Consumer Privacy Bill of Rights Act mentioned before), at this writing, the US federal law has not yet experienced any wide-ranging reforms. This leaves the regulation of informational business practices largely to corporate actors, relying on the FTC to hold them accountable only ex post facto.

Both regimes in practice

The procedural dynamic of FTC's interventions in cases of possible data privacy violation is empirically exemplified by its oversight of Facebook's commercial activity. Most recently, concluding a non-public investigation that had opened in March 2018, the commission fined Facebook a record-breaking penalty of $5 billion (FTC, 2019). Apart from financial retribution, FTC has ordered the establishment of a New Facebook Privacy Compliance System. The Compliance System includes an external body of assessors tasked with overseeing the effectiveness of Facebook's privacy protection measures, an independent privacy committee of Facebook's board of directors and designated compliance officers responsible for the company's privacy programme. According to the FTC's chairman, the measures were put in place 'not only to punish future violations but […] to change Facebook's entire privacy culture to decrease the likelihood of continued violations' (FTC, 2019).

Referring to a precedent settlement reached with the company in 2012, when it was charged with allegedly 'deceiving consumers by telling them they could keep their information on Facebook private, and then repeatedly allowing it to be shared and made public' (FTC, 2011), the commission based its penalty on the conclusion that Facebook violated its order which, 'among other things, […] prohibited Facebook from making misrepresentations about the privacy or security of consumers' personal information, and the extent to which it shares personal information, such as names and dates of birth, with third parties' (FTC, 2019). Accordingly, the FTC has come to decide that Facebook failed to comply with the agreement reached in the previous settlement despite the commission's intervention and the issued penalty. Although it will take time to objectively evaluate the effectiveness of these newly adopted measures, the precedent suggests that Facebook is unlikely to fully comply with the privacy restrictions imposed by the FTC. Moreover, as the examination of the structural characteristics of the business model adopted by companies like Facebook in the latter part of this chapter will suggest, further privacy breaches should be anticipated, as they are integral to their logic of capital accumulation.

It is not only the US legal system with its sectoral approach and reliance on self-regulation of the industry, however, that seems incapable of effectively preventing Facebook from committing repeated violations of its users' data privacy. In Europe, the same company is subject to 11 pending investigations by the Irish DPC and is being examined in terms of 'compliance with its obligation under the General Data Protection Regulation' (DPC, 2018). Among a variety of other issues, DPC investigates 'whether Facebook has discharged its GDPR obligations in respect of the lawful basis on which it relies to process personal data in the context of behavioural analysis and targeted advertising on its platform' and whether it has met 'its GDPR obligations in respect of the lawful basis on which it relies to process personal data of individuals using the Facebook platform' (DPC, n.d., p. 50).

Although it is too early to foresee the final verdict of the inquiry, the sole fact that the company is being scrutinised on many different grounds for not complying with Europe's legal standards for the protection of personal data suggests Facebook's commercial activity is at least questionable. Furthermore, the example of the Italian Competition Authority, which fined Facebook a total of 10 million Euros for its aggressive practices in misleading consumers in terms of privacy and personal data processing shortly before GDPR was voted into law (AGCM), shows that an unfavourable conclusion about the legality of Facebook's business practices in the EU would not be a precedent.

In both cases, then, the respective legal regimes allow to undertake only reactive rather than preventive measures. When considered from a standpoint of the economic imperative Facebook relies on to generate revenue, the inability of both the EU and US regulatory regimes to effectively discourage and prevent the platform from abusing its power at the expense of users should hardly come as a surprise. After all, as the following section aims to demonstrate, Facebook and other digital platforms depend on the disclosure of data for their lifeblood, making privacy rights and information sovereignty of their users (thus also the privacy-oriented legal frameworks trying to enforce them) stand in direct opposition to their economic interest. Therefore, debates about more effective regulatory policies targeted at such companies in terms of protecting users' private information require a structural approach that acknowledges the fundamental premises of the logic of capital accumulation on which they depend.

Digital Platforms: Definition

Currently, at least half of the world's six largest companies in terms of market value can be defined as digital platforms (Duffin, 2018). Additionally, leading examples like Amazon, Alphabet (Google's parent company) and Facebook are also among the 200 most profitable businesses globally, with annual revenues reaching $232.9, $136.82 and $55.8 billion, respectively (Fortune). From a technical point of view, what distinguishes them from other companies is their reliance on information and communication technology. In economic terms, digital platforms can be described as assuming the role of mediators on multisided markets, enabling transactions between different sets of actors (Rochet and Tirole, 2013). Put concisely:

> A platform is a digital infrastructure (software-based but sometimes also hardware-based) intended for users to apply either computer code in the conventional sense (i.e., to run applications or fetch data from it), or to apply a set of human uses (delimited, formalised, and patterned by the design of the platform in question) [...] enabling transactions between actors who would otherwise struggle to find each other [...] to reduce transaction costs. (Schwarz, 2017, p. 376)

Crucially, their digital-infrastructural character (utilising software and hardware) and central mediating function allow digital platforms to accumulate and process vast amounts of content and user data which, in turn, can function as a feedback mechanism for self-optimisation purposes while simultaneously 'giving them detailed insights into user behaviour and metrics information' (p. 377). As a result, access to accumulated scores of data about users/consumers and their online activities – a transactional by-product, as it were (Andrejevic, 2013, p. 60) – opens doors to an entirely different market on which the attention of demographically fine-grained and preference-specific audiences can be sold to the highest bidding advertisers (Lyon, 2019, p. 3). Thus, in the case of such companies, one can talk about a multi-sided marketplace business model: on the one hand, there is the offered service/product – Amazon's digital retail platform or its cloud-based services, for instance – on the other, however, platform providers are perfectly positioned infrastructurally and technologically to accumulate, process and then sell data generated by purchases, social interactions and other forms of online activity of their consumers/users to third parties (Djick et al., 2018, p. 9), making them also key stakeholders in the targeted digital advertising business (Perrin, 2018).

While it is true that audiences have played a central role in advertising-based business models adopted by commercial media outlets at least since the dawn of the modern mass circulation newspapers (Schudson, 2011, p. 94), the process by which digital platforms acquire data about their users proceeds in a way unprecedented both in its quality and scale. Given the progressing digitalisation of personal communications and market transactions, a trend likely to be facilitated even further by the coronavirus pandemic and related economic and social restrictions, the central role of platforms as infrastructures enabling such interactions to occur allows them to get hold of data inaccessible to traditional media outlets. Moreover, it is common for relatively few digital platforms to dominate a given service sector of the economy. Nick Srnicek (2017) traces this monopolistic tendency to digital platforms' reliance on network effects: 'the more numerous the users who use a platform, the move valuable that platform becomes for everyone else […] this generates a cycle whereby more users beget more users, which […] lends platforms a dynamic of ever-increasing access to more [user] activities, and therefore more data' (p. 45).

Data accumulation and analysis, then, is a crucial aspect of digital platforms' economic activity, substantially contributing to their financial gains. Arguably, the case of Facebook epitomises this data dependency, for while the social network service it provides had been consistently kept free of charge, advertising profits amount to nearly 90 per cent of its annual revenue (Facebook, 2018). Keeping this in mind, in the context of a critical discussion of data privacy-oriented legislative efforts to regulate the commercial activity of digital platforms, it is of vital importance to remember the very source of the supplied data – the users. Having recognised the central role data plays in how digital platforms make their profit, the active contribution of users/consumers to this process must also be acknowledged and analysed in terms of the power relations between platform users and owners. Christian Fuchs and Shoshana Zuboff's reiteration of the labour theory of value and its application to data-based economies sheds some light on these power dynamics.

The political economy of digital platforms

In his Marxian critique of Facebook's political economy, Fuchs (2012) emphasises the productive role of platform users and identifies their online activity as free labour and thus also the main source of surplus value extracted in the company's process of capital accumulation. Referring to the positive notion of a 'prosumer' (productive consumer) coined by Alvin Toffler to describe the 'progressive blurring of the line that separates producer from consumer' (Toffler, 1980, p. 267), he characterises the capital accumulation strategy employed by Facebook as primarily based on 'outsourcing work to users and consumers, who work without pay' (Fuchs, 2012, p. 143). In this particular business model, it is not the immediately produced commodity in the form of the social networking and communication platform that creates profit. Facebook could not possibly generate enough surplus to preserve the cycle of capital accumulation by merely investing into physical/technological means and purchasing the labour power of its regular employees, while at the same time providing a platform that is entirely cost free for its users. Rather than being sold directly on the market, the platform is made available free of charge and functions as the main avenue for exploitation of labour and the creation of advertising revenue (p. 144).

Whereas Facebook, as any other company driven by capitalist logic, appropriates the surplus labour of its wage workers who create and maintain the platform's infrastructure, it is mainly the platform's users whose unpaid productive consumption contributes to the creation of surplus value and, consequently, the company's profit: 'Facebook sells its prosumers as a commodity to advertising clients; their exchange value is based on permanently produced use values, that is, personal data and interactions' (Fuchs, 2012, p. 146). As each interaction and activity on (but also outside) the platform generates scores of data that are appropriated, accumulated, commodified and sold to third parties interested in reaching particular target groups, Facebook can be conceived of as a repository of audience commodities (Andrejevic, 2009, p. 83) available on demand. Not being remunerated for their labour, the time which Facebook users spent online producing the vast amounts of data is thus exploited to the fullest, making prosumption 'an extreme form of exploitation' (Toffler, 1980, p. 145), with some scholars drawing parallels between the relation of platform owners and users to the power structures inherent in feudal systems. On the other hand, however, considering that Facebook's social networking service is available free of charge, an argument against defining user activity as unpaid labour can be made, provided that one sees the access to the platform as a form of compensation.

Nevertheless, remaining consistent with the Marxian theory on the nature of exploitation in capitalist economies and the central function of compensation in providing labourers with means of subsistence and thus allowing them to reproduce their labour power (Marx and Mandel, 1990, chpt. 23), the qualitative difference between Facebook's wage workers and prosumers becomes evident. Fuchs expressed this difference concisely in his 2014 publication 'Digital Labour and Karl Marx':

> If one decides to see the cost-free access to the service as the exchange (de facto a salary) for user-generated data, one quickly runs into a problem: the prosumer cannot reproduce him/herself with the access to the service. In other words: None of their usage time is remunerated in order to fund subsistence. (p. 104)

Sharing Fuchs's analytical insights about the structural characteristics peculiar to digital platforms, in her latest book *The Age of Surveillance Capitalism*, Shoshana Zuboff (2019) draws attention to still another dimension of the power asymmetries written into their political economy. She describes corporate actors like Google and Facebook as embodying structural changes in the contemporary capitalist market economy, which is based on consumer surveillance and one-sided extraction and commodification of online behaviour (p. 68). While both authors recognise the productive role of users/consumers and their data as fundamental for the processes of production and capital accumulation in surveillance capitalism, Zuboff also emphasises that the act of user exploitation is not exclusively limited to platforms' reliance on unpaid labour. Rather, logically following from the institutionalised extraction of personal data through systematic consumer surveillance, exploitation also extends to the psychological/behavioural sphere. Google, she argues, treats aggregated data as 'raw material' for the manufacturing of 'behavioural prediction products' sold to third parties hoping to minimise risk through exerting influence over the (consumer) choices and decisions of targeted individuals (p. 94). Put differently, for Zuboff, the crux of the problem does not lie mainly in the mere selling of audience commodities and their attention to advertisers, but in the 'rendering of our lives as behavioural data for the sake of others' improved control of us' (p. 94).

The problem, then, lies in massive disproportions in knowledge and the hypothetical ability of platform owners to interfere with people's autonomous decision-making processes. Within the context of privacy concerns and individual agency, the methods with which platforms get hold of user-generated data are also of vital importance. According to Zuboff, the extraction of detailed information about users by platforms is necessarily predatory in character, operating 'through coercion and stealth', enabled by and proceeding through secretive corporate decisions, non-transparent algorithms, abusive contracts, consumer ignorance and lack of real alternatives to the offered products or services (p. 253).

Facebook's repetitive transgressions of user privacy, even after being caught red-handed, appear to only confirm Fuchs and Zuboff's argument. Recognising user data extraction as their primary imperative, it becomes clear that the interests of digital platform owners stand in direct opposition to the information privacy rights and agency of their users. Thus, even if Facebook ends up introducing the privacy-oriented 'digital living room' and a number of additional services announced and promised at the 2019 F8 developers conference, any changes should be regarded as merely cosmetic, calculated to influence the public perception of its actions in the hope to deflect regulatory efforts that would undermine its business model (Crain, 2016, p. 93). This prevails as long as the structural aspects of how the platform accumulates capital remain untouched, even if the new changes adhere to the FTC-imposed privacy compliance system to assure greater transparency, oversight and accountability of its commercial activity.

Data as Property?

Data, thus, appears to be a peculiar asset. It is treated and traded like a commodity, but its spoils are shared exclusively between two parties: digital platforms collecting, analysing and rendering it into data products, and third-party actors like advertisers or data brokers who purchase them for their own means. Meanwhile, the source of raw material used to produce the commodity – the user – holds only very limited rights to them, being entirely left out of the transaction. Zuboff refers to Karl Polanyi's notion of 'fictitious commodities' to highlight this dynamic. Just like labour power, land and money (the three original 'fictitious commodities' listed by Polanyi), data also enters the market as a commodity but is not produced as one (Zuboff, 2019, p. 514).

The difference, however, lies in the fact that unlike the other three examples, data conceived as a commodity does not allow their bearers to dispose of them at will, as they does not fall under a clear property rights regulatory system. This, consequently, makes the exercise of control over data largely arbitrary or dependent on other legal frameworks limited to privacy or (related to the notion of privacy) data protection. Keeping in mind that digital platforms like Facebook have generally been immune to regulations focusing on the control of data premised on the notion of privacy, a proprietary legal approach to user-generated data might be worth exploring. Therefore, following the observations made before, this section introduces a legal paradigm defining data as property and critically discusses it in terms of an effective solution to the inequalities inherent in privacy-oriented frameworks.

Legal efforts aiming to classify data as a marketable good are by no means without precedent. In the United States, the past year has proven especially prolific in legislative initiatives acknowledging the commercial value of user-generated data and the simultaneous lack of user agency in exercising control over them. In June 2019, in a bipartisan initiative to regulate the commercial handling of data in the United States, Senators Warner and Hawley introduced a bill to the US Senate Committee on Banking, Housing, and Urban Affairs entitled 'Designing Accounting Safeguards to Help Broaden Oversight and Regulations on Data'. If passed, the bill would require companies making substantial revenue from selling user data to provide 'each user […] with an assessment of the economic value that the commercial data operator places on the data of that user […] on a routine basis' and to disclose the types and ways in which 'the data of a user […] is used if the use is not directly or exclusively related to the online service that the commercial data operator provides to the user' (GovTrack.us, Sec. 3).

An even more explicit attempt at data proprietisation came in July from a member of the US House Judiciary Committee (HJC), Rep. Doug Collins, who announced the guiding principles for a legislative draft he plans to introduce later this year. Asserting that 'the private sector and the government must recognise consumer data as the property of the consumer', Collins declared his objective to give users more control over their data and protect their privacy rights through a policy that would

> establish a federally-recognised class of online data property that includes data consumers generate on online platforms and devices; recognise in federal law that this data is the property of the consumers who generate it; and enable consumers to oversee the commercial use of their data property and to preclude the use of their data should they choose to do so. (HJC, 2019)

By advocating an alternative approach to user privacy rights protection, policies designed to categorise data as property based on the recognition of their monetary value represent an important shift in legal thought that acknowledges the structural characteristics of digital platforms' political economy. Yet, although marking a crucial change of paradigm, neither of the legislative projects mentioned before, nor any other policy to date, managed to develop a complete 'regulatory framework or model that provides guidance on how transactions using data as an asset are to be constructed' (Mayer and Ritter, 2018, p. 222), leaving critical questions such as the type of data that can be owned or precisely how/when the ownership attaches to data largely unanswered.

In their 2018 article, Ritter and Mayer attempted to fill this gap. Having observed the growing importance of digitalised information for many different sectors of the global industry, in 'Regulating Data as Property: A New Construct for Moving Forward' Jeffrey Ritter and Anna Mayer advocate the need for developing a legal mechanism that would clearly define property rights with regard to data, enabling more effective regulation and facilitating the enforcement of rights and individual control over them. Following the assumption that 'once ownership is well-defined, then the attendant rights can be more precisely expressed – rights to access, license, transfer, modify, combine, edit, and delete data naturally flow from the control that ownership vests' (p. 222), the authors propose an ownership-oriented regulatory framework based on already existing legal constructs. Although it is the automotive industry that lies in the centre of their analysis and is evoked as the potential avenue for empirical application of the measures proposed in the article (p. 240), the premises upon which the framework is based and the fundamental insight that ownership entails improved control can be extended to other economic sectors, including digital platforms. In this context, the semantic basis of the proposed legal construct is especially important. The authors define data as 'any information recorded by electronic or digital means [that] is retrievable, whether perceivable to a human or machine' and identify two types which would be subject to the proposed regulation: (a) industrial data, that is 'any data that is created, processed, stored, or used in commerce, including business-to-business transactions, and excludes any personal information' and (b) personal data, meaning 'any information that may be identified with a data subject or individual person, whether or not formally defined as such by any applicable statute, regulation or other legal requirement' (p. 224).

Such distinction carries a fundamental weight given the fact that while companies such as Facebook often circumvent individual privacy restrictions by anonymising the user-generated data they collect (Bettilyon, 2019), in the end the data still function as an asset, representing an economic value and serving as a source of revenue:

> Once anonymization has served its purpose, the resulting data is truly functioning as industrial data. The distinctions in definitions will enable industrial data to be owned, transferred, and legally protected by distinct legal and commercial rules while also more fully achieving the goals of privacy and data protection laws to truly vest in data subjects meaningful control of their identifiable personal information. (Mayer and Ritter, 2018, p. 226)

Consequently, the type or size of data notwithstanding, if the moment of origin can be identified and sourced back to a specific actor, then the data ownership rights can be clearly defined and codified, hypothetically empowering the proprietors. The fundamental premise on which Ritter and Mayer suggest basing such a legal construct is the reconceptualisation of data in terms of a material asset not different from, for example, real property. Emphasising the physical dimension of (digitalised) information, which is its necessary storage on a solid medium, the authors propose to classify data as a 'physical, tangible matter stored by electronic or similar means' (p. 255), referring to Rolf Landauer's 'Information is Physical', in which he argues: 'information is not a disembodied abstract entity; it is always tied to a physical representation. [...] This ties the handling of information to all the possibilities and restrictions of our real physical world, its laws of physics and its storehouse of available parts' (p. 256).

Building on this assumption about the physical reality of data, they further suggest considering the very act of evidence, that is record, as the moment when digital information comes into existence: '[d]ata creation occurs through one of two methods – either a human user inputs instructions to create a data asset (such as pressure on a keyboard creating the letters of this paper in a digital format) or a machine executes a process that records new data of various classifications' (p. 260). Accordingly, then, once data become stored on a tangible medium, it should be possible to identify and link it to a specific entity, a process whereby ownership rights are established.

Being aware of the many practical and technical difficulties that arise with the application of their proposed framework such as the simultaneous involvement of multiple stakeholders, conflict of interests between the owners of (digital) infrastructures and the data users/producers or the seemingly inconsistent idea of identifying the source of data, while still retaining privacy, the authors evoke blockchain technology and quantum cryptography as possible technological remedies to overcome these issues (p. 264). Given the control that clearly defined ownership rights entail, once the technical hindrances are overcome, a proprietary approach to data such as the one proposed before might present a valid alternative to the retroactive and regularly violated legal frameworks based on the privacy paradigm. Most importantly, however, in the context of digital platforms, reconceptualisation of data based on property law, hypothetically, allows for a more levelled interaction between platform owners and users. This integrates the latter into transactions involving their data and puts them in a bargaining position by giving them increased control over them.

Under such a framework, appropriation of data without consent and remuneration would be a criminal act routinely prosecuted within the boundaries of already existing legal standards. Given the massive scale and scope of data processed by digital platforms every day, consequences for breeches would be dire, possibly forcing actors like Facebook to reform their business model by, for example, introducing a paid, subscription-based service where the access to user-generated information is strictly limited, encrypted and perishable, and thus inaccessible to third parties.

Although restricting the unilateral and unsolicited extraction and appropriation of information by surveillance capitalists clearly necessitates a solution beyond the privacy paradigm, an alternative approach establishing transparent ownership rights with regard to data and its reconceptualisation as a commodity in the full sense of the word also poses a number of potential risks. Some of the major conceivable problems arising from data proprietarisation might be tied to the institutionalisation and normalisation of surveillance capitalism's fundamental imperative. It is reasonable to assume that a shift towards data ownership would asymmetrically target the economically more vulnerable parts of society, incentivising individuals to monetise their most personal information for financial gains. Moreover, the commodification and subjection of human-behaviour-rendered-into-data to the market logic should also be assessed morally, beyond the purely economic dimension worthy of critical evaluation in itself. In the end, reconceptualising data as yet another marketable good might not only reproduce, but perhaps even exacerbate, the inequalities already inherent in the surveillance capitalist model of accumulation by legally sanctioning them. Such a status quo would mark a step away from the digital equivalent of primitive accumulation towards a developed social-economic system with fundamental imbalances in power protected by law.

Conclusion

Debates concerning the implementation of regulatory policies in the context of digital platforms like Facebook frequently arise from controversies involving user privacy violations. As this chapter attempted to show, however, perceiving the issue of regulation solely from a standpoint of privacy omits some crucial aspects and depth of the problems inherent in the business model of such companies. The example of Facebook – the poster child for user privacy breeches – clearly demonstrates that the relative inability to effectively regulate its practices does not depend on regional differences in legal regimes concerned with data privacy protection. Rather, the inefficacy holds true for privacy-oriented legal frameworks and can be traced to the surveillance-based logic of capital accumulation utilised by digital platforms.

An examination of digital platforms' political economy from the labour theory of value perspective reveals that the privacy rights and information sovereignty of platform users (thus also the privacy-oriented legal frameworks trying to enforce them) stand in direct opposition to the primary economic imperative guiding platform owners – data extraction. This, in turn, necessitates a regulatory solution reaching beyond the privacy paradigm. Following this premise, a property rights approach to digitalised personal information based on the work of Mayer and Ritter (2018) was explored as a potentially more effective and proactive legal alternative to ensuring increased control over data on the side of users. Accordingly, a critical evaluation of both frameworks led to two major conclusions: (a) categorising data as property represents an important shift in legal thinking and a more anticipatory turn in regulating the access to and control over user-generated information but (b) its implementation might only cement the existing power imbalance between platform owners and users by providing the process of surveillance-based data extraction with a veneer of legality.

Further research agenda

Considering the shortcomings and limitations of both analysed frameworks, further research concerned with the reconceptualisation of data and the establishment of effective legislative measures addressing disproportions in power, knowledge and means between platform owners and users might benefit from stepping out of the privacy and property paradigms altogether. In fact, several alternative approaches that could serve as potential points of departure already exist. For instance, in an article written in September 2018, Elizabeth Renieris proposes an approach to personal data based on human rights. She argues that while '[...] property rights are alienable in the sense that they can be sold or transferred to another party [...] [h]uman rights [...] attach to each of us individually as humans, cannot be divided into sticks in a bundle, and cannot be surrendered, transferred, or sold [...] [as they] emanate from an internal source and require no evidence of their existence' (Renieris, 2019).

Given the market dominance of American social media platforms specifically, some of the sought-after solutions to problems arising from their monopolistic position might be found in publicly funded or citizen-initiated alternatives. For instance, in a policy proposal for the UK's House of Lords Select Committee on Communications, Clara Sol Krause (2019) suggests that challenging the undesirable data collection practices of companies like Facebook might be achieved by introducing a publicly funded alternative. Pointing out that 'the advertising-based business model and technological architecture of commercial social media platforms facilitate the misuse of personal data and the proliferation of harmful content', Ms Krause proposes the establishment of an independent public service social media platform (PSP) under the auspices of the BBC (p. 3). Emphasising that her proposal should be understood as a long-term initiative and be complementary to the regulation of incumbent social media platforms, she envisions such a service could effectively compete with commercial social media platforms by undermining their profit-driven logic, while at the same time providing a more transparent, accountable and diverse alternative oriented towards the public interest (p. 9). In his article 'Towards the Public Service Internet as Alternative to the Commercial Internet', Christian Fuchs (2017) espouses a similar idea, advocating for an 'alternative internet' based on the 'long and strong tradition of European public service media' (p. 45).

Of course, PSPs come with their own caveats that need to be critically examined before even considering their implementation as valid alternatives to their commercial counterparts. The danger of government surveillance inherent in any public service proposal and possible difficulties arising from incentivising users to switch to a PSP in the face of the network effect logic characteristic of commercial digital platforms are just two of the many potential problems necessary to bear in mind. Any future discussions about more democratic alternatives should also take into account citizen-initiated projects, such as EPOS or Beyond Platforms Initiative, grassroots initiatives aiming to establish decentralised, democratic and sustainable alternatives to purely profit-driven platforms.

Bibliography

AGCM. (n.d.). Autorita' Garante della Concorrenza e del Mercato. https://en.agcm.it/en/media/press-releases/2018/12/Facebook-fined-10-million-Euros-by-the-ICA-for-unfair-commercial-practices-for-using-its-subscribers'-data-for-commercial-purposes [Accessed June 20, 2019].

Andersson Schwarz, J. (2017). Platform Logic: An Interdisciplinary Approach to the Platform-Based Economy. *Policy & Internet* 9(4): 374–394.

Andrejevic, M. (2009). *iSpy: Surveillance and Power in the Interactive Era*. Lawrence, KS: University Press of Kansas.

Andrejevic, M. (2010). Surveillance and Alienation in the Online Economy. *Surveillance & Society* 8(3): 278–287.

Andrejevic, M. (2013). *Infoglut: How the Digital Era Is Changing the Way We Think About Information*. New York: Routledge.

Bettilyon, T. E. (2019). Why 'Anonymized Data' Isn't So Anonymous. *Medium. OneZero*. April 25, 2019. https://onezero.medium.com/why-anonymized-data-isn-t-so-anonymous-535d2db75a2d [Accessed April 25, 2019].

CITP Princeton. (2013). Arvind Narayanan – Digital Feudalism is Upon Us. How Do We Respond? YouTube. www.youtube.com/watch?v=tZR5Oc1F4D4.

COPPA. (n.d.). Children's Online Privacy Protection. https://uscode.house.gov/view.xhtml?req=granuleid%3AUSC-prelim-title15-section6501&edition=prelim [Accessed June 20, 2019].

Council on Foreign Relations (CFR). (2018). Reforming the U.S. Approach to Data Protection and Privacy. http://www.cfr.org/report/reforming-us-approach-data-protection [Accessed June 20, 2019].

Crain, M. (2016). The Limits of Transparency: Data Brokers and Commodification. *New Media& Society* 20(1): 88–104.

Cyphers, B. (2019). A Guided Tour of the Data Facebook Uses to Target Ads. *Electronic Frontier Foundation*. http://www.eff.org/deeplinks/2019/01/guided-tour-data-facebook-uses-target-ads.

Data Protection Commission (DPC). (2018). Facebook Data Breach – Commencement of Investigation. http://www.dataprotection.ie/en/news-media/press-releases/facebook-data-breach-commencement-investigation.

Data Protection Commission (DPC). (n.d.). Annual Report 25 May–31 December 2018. https://www.dataprotection.ie/en/news-media/press-releases/dpc-publishes-annual-report-25-may-31-december-2018 [Accessed June 20, 2019].

Dijck, J., Poell, T., and De Waal, M. (2018). *The Platform Society*. Kettering: Oxford University Press.

Duffin, E. (2018). Biggest Companies in the World 2018. *Statista*. www.statista.com/statistics/263264/top-companies-in-the-world-by-market-value/ [Accessed June 20, 2019].

EUGDPR Home. (n.d.). The EU General Data Protection Regulation (GDPR) Is the Most Important Change in Data Privacy Regulation in 20 Years. eugdpr.org/ [Accessed June 20, 2019].

Facebook. (2018). Facebook Reports Fourth Quarter and Full Year 2017 Results. investor.fb.com/investor-news/press-release-details/2018/Facebook-Reports-Fourth-Quarter-and-Full-Year-2017-Results/default.aspx [Accessed June 20, 2019].

Facebook for Developers. (n.d.). F8 2019 Day 1 Keynote. https://developers.facebook.com/videos/f8-2019/day-1-keynote [Accessed July 30, 2019].

Federal Trade Commission (FTC). (1998). Privacy Online: A Report to Congress. https://www.ftc.gov/sites/default/files/documents/reports/privacy-online-report-congress/priv-23a.pdf.

Federal Trade Commission (FTC). (2000). Privacy Online: Fair Information Practices in the Electronic Marketplace – A Report to Congress. https://www.ftc.gov/sites/default/files/documents/reports/privacy-online-fair-information-practices-electronic-marketplace-federal-trade-commission-report/privacy2000.pdf.

Federal Trade Commission (FTC). (2011). Facebook Settles FTC Charges That It Deceived Consumers by Failing to Keep Privacy Promises. ftc.gov/news-events/press-releases/2011/11/facebook-settles-ftc-charges-it-deceived-consumers-failing-keep.

Federal Trade Commission (FTC). (2017). Your Cop on the Privacy Beat. https://www.ftc.gov/news-events/blogs/business-blog/2017/04/your-cop-privacy-beat.

Federal Trade Commission (FTC). (2019). FTC Imposes $5 Billion Penalty and Sweeping New Privacy Restrictions on Facebook. http://www.ftc.gov/news-events/press-releases/2019/07/ftc-imposes-5-billion-penalty-sweeping-new-privacy-restrictions.

Fortune. (n.d.). Global 500. fortune.com/global500/2019/search/?hqcountry=U.S.&profits=desc [Accessed June 20, 2019].

Fuchs, C. (2012). The Political Economy of Privacy on Facebook. *Television & New Media* 13(2): 139–159.

Fuchs, C. (2014). *Digital Labour and Karl Marx*. New York: Routledge. 24.

Fuchs, C. (2017). Towards the Public Service Internet as Alternative to the Commercial Internet. *ORF Texte* 20: 43–50.

GDPR.eu. (2019). What is GDPR, the EU's New Data Protection Law? https://gdpr.eu/what-is-gdpr/.

General Data Protection Regulation (GDPR). (2016). Official Legal Text. https://gdpr-info.eu/.

GovTrack.us. (n.d.). Designing Accounting Safeguards to Help Broaden Oversight and Regulations on Data (S.1951). https://www.govtrack.us/congress/bills/116/s1951 [Accessed October 4, 2019].

Griswold, A. (2017). Facebook's Overall Revenue by Region. Atlas. www.theatlas.com/charts/SJF080k_l.

Helmore, E. (2020). Tech Giants' Shares Soar as Companies Benefit from Covid-19 Pandemic. *The Guardian*, Guardian News and Media. www.theguardian.com/business/2020/jul/30/amazon-apple-facebook-google-profits-earnings.

HIPAA. (n.d.). Health Insurance Portability and Accountability Act of 1996. https://www.govinfo.gov/content/pkg/PLAW-104publ191/pdf/PLAW-104publ191.pdf [Accessed June 20, 2019].

House Judiciary Committee (HJC). (2019). Collins Releases Principles to Protect Online Data Property and Privacy. https://republicans-judiciary.house.gov/press-release/collins-releases-principles-to-protect-online-data-property-and-privacy/ [Accessed December 20, 2018].

Justice and Consumers and European Commission. (2016). Guidelines on Transparency Under Regulation 2016/679 (wp260rev.01) – European Commission. http://ec.europa.eu/newsroom/article29/item-detail.cfm?item_id=622227.

Krause, C. (2019). *Policy Proposal for the House of Lords Select Committee on Communications.* London: London School of Economics and Political Science, Coursework Submission.

LII/Legal Information Institute. (n.d.). 15 U.S. Code § 45 – Unfair Methods of Competition Unlawful; Prevention by Commission. www.law.cornell.edu/uscode/text/15/45 [Accessed June 20, 2019].

Lyon, D. (2019). Surveillance Capitalism, Surveillance Culture and Data Politics. In: Bigo, D., Isin, E., and Ruppert, E. (Eds.), *Data Politics: Worlds, Subjects, Rights.* Abingdon, Oxon: Routledge.

Marx, K., and Fernbach, D. (1992). *Capital: A Critique of Political Economy.* Vol. 2. London: Penguin Books in Association With New Left Review.

Marx, K., and Mandel, E. (1990). *Capital: A Critique of Political Economy.* Vol. 2. London: Penguin Books in Association With New Left Review.

Mayer, A., and Ritter, J. (2018). Regulating Data as Property: A New Construct for Moving Forward. *Duke Law & Technology Review* 16: 220–277.

Obama, B. (2015). Administration Discussion Draft: Consumer Privacy Bill of Rights Act of 2015. Obama White House. https://obamawhitehouse.archives.gov/sites/default/files/omb/legislative/letters/cpbr-act-of-2015-discussion-draft.pdf [Accessed June 20, 2019].

Office of the Privacy Commissioner of Canada (OPC). (2019). News Release: Facebook Refuses to Address Serious Privacy Deficiencies Despite Public Apologies for 'Breach of Trust'. https://www.priv.gc.ca/en/opc-news/news-and-announcements/2019/nr-c_190425/.

Perrin, N. (2018). Amazon Is Now the No. 3 Digital Ad Platform in the US. EMarketer. www.emarketer.com/content/amazon-is-now-the-no-3-digital-ad-platform-in-the-us [Accessed June 20, 2019].

Privacy International. (n.d.). Cambridge Analytica, GDPR – 1 Year on – A Lot of Words and Some Action. https://www.privacyinternational.org/news-analysis/2857/cambridge-analytica-gdpr-1-year-lot-words-and-some-action [Accessed April 30, 2019].

Renieris, E. (2019). Do We Really Want to 'Sell' Ourselves? The Risks of a Property Law Paradigm for Personal Data Ownership. *Medium.* https://medium.com/@hackylawyER/do-we-really-want-to-sell-ourselves-the-risks-of-a-property-law-paradigm-for-data-ownership-b217e42edffa.

Rochet, J. C., and Tirole, J. (2013). Platform Competition in Two-Sided Markets. *Journal of the European Economic Association* 1(4): 990–1029.

Schudson, M. (2011). *Discovering the News: A Social History of American Newspapers.* New York: Basic Books.

Soto-Acosta, P. (2020). COVID-19 Pandemic: Shifting Digital Transformation to a High-Speed Gear. *Information Systems Management* 37(4): 260–266.

Srnicek, Nick. (2017). *Platform Capitalism.* Cambridge: Polity.

Toffler, A. (1980). *The Third Wave.* New York: Bantam Books.

US Department of Education. (2018). Family Educational Rights and Privacy Act (FERPA). www2.ed.gov/policy/gen/guid/fpco/ferpa/index.html.

van der Sloot, B., and De Groot, A. (Eds.). (2018). *The Handbook of Privacy Studies: An Interdisciplinary Introduction.* Amsterdam: Amsterdam University Press.

Zuboff, S. (2019). *The Age of Surveillance Capitalism: The Fight for a Human Future at the New Frontier of Power.* London: Profile Books.

Chapter 2

HUMAN SUBJECTS, DIGITAL PROTOCOLS: THE FUTURE OF INSTITUTIONAL REVIEW BOARDS (IRBS) AND DIGITAL RESEARCH IN VULNERABLE COMMUNITIES

Charles Martin-Shields and Ziad Al Achkar

Introduction: New Pedagogy for Digital Human Subjects Research

Ethics in human subjects research, whether in medical or social sciences, has been a key topic in researchers' training for decades in the United States and United Kingdom (UK). In the United States, the history of IRBs in evaluating and overseeing the conduct of ethical human subjects research has its roots in legislation. The 1974 National Research Act was signed into law after a series of congressional hearings on human subjects research and gained greater momentum in response to the Tuskegee syphilis study (Chadwick, 1997). In the UK the processes have been more decentralised with research ethics committees distributed across research sectors and universities, but since the early 2000s there have been greater efforts to develop national standards for both biomedical and social science human subjects research in the UK. While these standards are world leading, world-leading, and many developing countries are adopting their own human subjects research frameworks based on them, the advent of widespread digital data collection presents new challenges for researchers and educators to address in ethics and research protocol pedagogy. This is especially true when research is being done in and with vulnerable subjects in developing countries.

How we address this question has implications for general society as well as academic research. Complex power relations emerge in this space between a university's IRB's conception of ethical human subjects research and a technology's terms of use, including those between the researcher and participant, and the researcher and software company. As the nature of research adapts and incorporates technological changes, the IRB will increasingly be the facility that mediates the power of different actors in a digital human subjects research process to make sure research participants are protected.

Increasingly, the interface between digital research and peoples' daily online behaviour is blurring. When we, for example, use Twitter, it is possible that this mundane activity is producing data that can be used by a researcher. This type of relationship would be governed by a platform's terms of use, to which a researcher who uses Twitter or social media data must conform. But there is a great distance between a technology platform's terms of use, which fundamentally protects the business interests of the software firm, and the standards for doing human subjects research that the researcher is expected to uphold. Within this space are elements of power. There is the software firm where data is provided and housed, and for which data is a profit-making medium; the researcher, who is seeking to undertake research using digital data and has a wider scope of knowledge than the research participants about what this work entails; and the university itself, for which ethical human subjects research is tightly interwoven with managing the risk of culpability in the case that harm comes to a research subject. Between these actors and the research subject is the IRB, which must assess and mediate the power of the different actors to protect both the research subject and the firm, researcher and university from each other. So how does an IRB, traditionally an analogue construct, moderate different aspects of power in the digital era?

The first issue to address is understanding the unique risks that digital systems bring to human subjects research. Digital survey tools like KoBo Toolbox have been used for a number of years to do traditional survey research, but these are different than digital platforms that involve third-party software and cloud data storage. Doing a survey is ethically different than using social media platforms for experiments or remote sensing/passive data collection in vulnerable communities. The passive/remote sensing tools bring up a basic issue in research protocols, the main area where the research subject has power: informed consent. Because social media and remote sensing systems derive their utility by being autonomous and may remain in a fixed location gathering data many times over, the process of defining an informed consent process is made more complex. The second issue, the 'permanence' of digital data, is less tangible and demands a wider range of risk analysis on the part of the researcher. Unlike paper, a digital record can be replicated and shared widely in a way that defies deletion. What does this mean for research protocols and ethics in vulnerable communities, especially those who may be at risk for years after the research takes place? The first section of this chapter will address these issues in relation to standard approaches to human subjects research protocol training and lead into the second section that grapples with the current gaps in ethics and protocol training when using digital tools.

The second section of the chapter goes into greater detail on what is covered in traditional ethics and protocol training, with a specific focus on social sciences. It will unpack the issues that arise with informed consent, managing power relations and other sociological components that are critical to ethical human subjects research. After doing this, the section will explore how this training falls short in preparing researchers to use digital tools in their research, exploring the skills and training gaps that would need to be filled to fully prepare researchers to work digitally with vulnerable communities.

In many ways what makes digitally-based research unique is that the relationships and power dynamics between the researcher and subject are interjected by the digital medium. Inherent to this medium are user agreements, issues with data ownership and the role that third-party software providers play in supporting or undermining best practices in ethics and research protocols. Thus, the purpose is not to develop a tool-to-match process by which we identify specific rights, requirements or risks with each specific technology that would apply to each scenario, but rather develop a holistic approach that guarantees rights of individuals and groups whose data is collected that would transcend a specific technological innovation. The role of digitally literate and equipped IRB would be to therefore evaluate how the proposed project or technological tool used guarantees the rights of individuals, reduces risks and safeguards against harm.

The chapter closes with final conclusions on the future of digital research, including both the opportunities and risks that come with using new digital tools to do human subjects research and what these mean for society more broadly.

What Makes Digital Research Unique(ly Risky)?

The current state of research protocol and ethics training covers a wide range of ethical and risk management issues. Topics like informed consent, data protection, and privacy and anonymity are well-covered ground in most human subjects research and ethics courses. The problem is that digitally intermediated research, using social media platforms and proprietary data collection systems, introduces a whole suite of risks that go beyond legal processes like informed consent or procedural issues like securing respondent data on a host computer. This section will cover three ways in which digital systems can lead to breakdowns in different aspects of human subjects research protocols: the first is the automatic nature of digital systems, the second is the 'permanence' of digital data and the third is the speed of technological change outpacing regulatory or oversight capacity. When we overlay these three aspects of digital data collection across the standard rules and regulations that go into ethics protocols, we can begin to see how digital platforms for data collection present new, unique risks for doing human subjects research in an ethical way.

The first issue, passive and automatic data collection, brings up specific problems of informed consent. For example, if a researcher is using drones to collect imaging data of a village or populated area how do they make sure that each round of data collection meets consent rules? WeRobotics, a social impact firm that focuses on the effective and inclusive use of drones and robotics in humanitarianism and development, provides a framework that could be applied in an IRB framework. They recommend limiting flight time and data collection to only that which is necessary, coordinating with communities and sharing information on flight activities, and knowing/respecting local regulations and political sensitivities when flying drones. This may be easier to manage if we are the pilots and are flying the drones at a specific time on specific days for a set number of flights; in such a case we would write the entire flight schedule into the informed consent form, have meetings with residents and show them footage after the first flight, and generally make sure that the research subjects are aware of the entire process. But what if we are doing an experiment that relies on the drones to fly autonomously in response to certain environmental conditions? We may not know how many times they will fly, the image quality, who will be out of their house during flights and the impact that flights during sleeping hours may have. Again, this can be written into an informed consent document and routine meetings with communities can help identify tensions, but the randomness of the flights can add complexity to consent. Following the WeRobotics approach, we have to go beyond just flight management – a researcher needs to get training on flying drones and risk management that is specific to drone operations, create contingency plans for accidents and make their data collection strategy as publicly known. If an IRB is making power central to an ethics process, training and planning are precisely the kind things that a researcher would need to do to manage and direct their power vis-à-vis the communities with which they are doing research.

At the sharpest end of consent issues are remote sensing tools. For example, a researcher may want to do an experiment that tracks locals' mobility. This kind of data collection is done by cities all the time, and urban planning researchers have used passive systems to track urban mobility for years (e.g. Bhatta et al., 2010). In these cases, though, these were not overtly vulnerable populations, and the research subjects were using public infrastructure – a sign explaining what data are being collected and where to find more information could be sufficient, depending on local ordinances. But what if one is working in a vulnerable community, for example, one affected by violent conflict? The use of drones and sensing systems has led to ethical problems in practice settings such as peacekeeping operations (Andrews, 2017; Lidén and Sandvik, 2016).

Using passive sensors to register movement and sounds for research purposes creates serious informed consent problems. From a methodological perspective, we may want to know how people move in the natural rhythm of their day, explaining that there are unseen sensors in the environment could adversely affect their normal behaviour. There is another problem, too: What counts as a single round of data collection? Normally any time someone gathers data, they have to ask permission. This is impossible if sensors are picking up new data hundreds or thousands of times a day. Finally, what happens when someone refuses to consent? The sensor is operating in an open space, and the researcher may not know if the anonymised data the sensor picks up is from the person who did not consent. One could just shrug and run the research, but this runs directly contrary to standard ethical practice. This creates a large problem for researchers and raises important questions of what the protocol ought to be in those cases. Should the dataset be completely deleted? Are there mechanisms to remove the data from parties who did not consent without jeopardising the validity of the data for research purposes?

When someone deletes a Tweet or digital record, did it really 'go away'? We can extend this point using Twitter as the case. There are many times someone tweets something embarrassing, then deletes it only for it to live on in cached or screen-grabbed form on the internet. At a basic level, when we or any other researcher who does survey research captures data in a digital format or transfers responses from paper to digital format, the data cease to be something that can be destroyed in a physical sense. Compounding this, scientific publishing increasingly requires replication data to be publicly available, so once the dataset is online, there is no longer the option of 'deleting' it. In this example though, we as the researchers had full control over the collection of the data, anonymising it and controlling its public release. For vulnerable people who participated in the research, I can have a high degree of certainty that their safety and privacy will be protected even if the data are online.

This certainty decreases when there are third-party or automated systems involved in the data collection. If data goes to a third-party server after being collected, how does a researcher know that the data protection and privacy protocols were followed? Especially for researchers working in politically sensitive environments, if your computer is connected to an unsecure Wi-Fi port, a hostile actor can target your laptop and may be able to steal the information from the hard drive (http://werobotics.org). This is critical because metadata behind the front-end data can be an effective tool in identifying who participated in the research, and a motivated actor can easily take advantage of this. Image and sound files, in particular, come with a great deal of information embedded in them. We only need to imagine the problem of compounding effects, if the data, with identifying information intact, is released onto unsecured internet platforms or websites. In effect, there would be no way to delete data that posed direct risks to research subjects, who require anonymity and privacy for their safety.

The OCHA guidelines for responsible data use offer here a helpful mechanism to classify information and to manage its release based on sensitivity of the data and the risk assessment that is made. A similar approach could be developed for IRB purposes. One of the key challenges that arise from digital research is the pace by which new technologies and innovations are developed, and the inability of existing regulatory systems or ethical boards to keep up. This is a problem that IRB faces as well. Second, the pace of innovation also means that the large majority of the population is unable to fully grasp the changes that are happening and the risks or harms that can result from them. For example, many people still fail to consider how uploading large amounts of personal information onto platforms could be used to try to influence their voting behaviours, or that their information is repackaged and sold to third-party data companies.

These are not the only three risks that arise when doing human subjects research with vulnerable communities using digital tools. But they represent three risks that will be ubiquitous to digital, often online, research done at any level of scale. Using these as key examples for further analysis, the following section will explore how and if digital risks and gaps are addressed in ethics and human research subjects training.

How Does the Concept of Power Help Improve IRBs and Digital Research Protocols Training?

Having addressed three main risk areas, this section asks what gaps exist in human subjects research pedagogy with regard to digital research mediums, and how managing power – as opposed to creating specific technical guidelines – can help IRBs navigate digital human subjects research. Particularly in the social sciences, much of the curricula focuses on interpersonal processes – the importance and process of gaining informed consent, privacy and anonymity, and risk management when working with vulnerable or traumatised respondents. Power is very directly addressed in this traditional research mode – the researcher, by virtue of knowing more about the project and empirical strategy, has power over the research subject. Recognising these interpersonal dynamics is critical to doing ethical human subjects research, but what is lacking for a research space that is increasingly digital is training on how multi-directional power manifests across different tech actors. This does not mean that training on the interpersonal components of ethical research is unnecessary; indeed, the issues around power differences and ethics between researcher and subject demand their own reassessment in a digital research space.

One of the challenges facing IRBs when it comes to new innovations and technologies is linked to William Oburn's cultural lag theory. Ogburn posits that when changes happen to a system or society, there is a period of time between the diffusion of the new technologies and when the people in the system adapt their behaviour to using these technologies. This lag or 'period of maladjustment' means that for a period of time, there is a gap in how one (a society, system, institutions) adapts to technological changes.

This 'period of maladjustment' is one that is often rife with possibility for social conflict as the people who lead the change are faced with resistance by those lagging behind.

Langdon Winner (1986) reflects on a couple of points that are helpful to ponder as we evaluate the relationship between digital communication technologies and a modern-day IRB and research ecosystem. Winner (1986, 25) writes that 'In our accustomed of way thinking, technologies are seen as neutral tools that can be used well or poorly, for good, evil or in between.' Winner argues that technologies do not escape from our social interactions and indeed 'enhance the power, authority, and privilege of some over others'. Deploying digital technologies for data collection purposes inevitably adds a new layer to the power dynamics between the researcher and the research participant(s). Kimball Marshall (1999, 83) extends this point further and notes that 'technology is purposive. It is applied to achieve a goal'. He makes a point to distinguish between technology and science in that 'science seeks knowledge while technology applies knowledge to the manipulation of the natural world to achieve a goal'. Daniel McCarthy (2013) argues that we need to look at how technologies influence social systems through time, arguing that different technologies have different impacts on communities depending on their status and power. This is an inherent dilemma that researchers normally face but which will continue to grow as a problem with further deployment of remote sensing techniques for data collections.

Read, Taithe, and MacGinty (2016, 1324) highlight similar concerns when it comes to data collection, noting that 'data technologies serve themselves first and foremost, but they also empower their supporters. [...] The most significant empowerment that data technology risks bringing is that of those who believe in the potential of technology'. In other words, data collection empowers those who lead the projects or initiatives to the detriment of those whose data are harvested. The promise of technological improvement may, therefore, not be all that it seems.

Problems of power distribution and impact of these technologies are articulated by David Chandler (2015) as he notes the limits of the promise of technological innovation. Chandler writes that 'Big Data does not seem to be very empowering for those who most need social change'. Rather it allows you to be aware of your realities, of the circumstances you are in and reveal the limitations of your current position. Chandler seems to articulate that change is limited to those already powerful and in positions to be able to maximise the utility of these functions. These are important questions for researchers engaged in remote sensing work to address, and for IRBs to evaluate.

IRBs also will have to reckon with what Couldry and Mejias (2018) describe as 'data-colonialism', that is the practices and behaviours of organisations that resemble the 'predatory extractive practices of historical colonialism with the abstract quantification methods of computing'. Algorithms and computing techniques are increasingly used to turn social and human relations into data points that are of value for private firms (marketing, advertising, etc.) and governments, which can use them for security purposes (tracking and monitoring, social credit, etc.). These models are extractive and predatory in nature because the individuals whose data are being collected are unaware of the extent and scale to which it is being done (to them), and the scale to which their everyday life has been commodified.

Madianou (2019) introduces 'technocolonialism' as a manifestation of this phenomenon in the relationship between humanitarian organisations and the populations that they look to serve, highlighting a digital inequality that exists between the two of them. Madianou notes that technocolonialism reinforces extractive behaviours in the humanitarian sector and furthers inequalities, as refugees and aid recipients continue to generate new data, which in turn generates new value for organisations and private firms who benefit from them. Data or technocolonialism concerns call for an approach that is critical of this power and the extractive behaviour and processes and allows us to begin to deconstruct and resist data colonialism. Ricaurte (2019) points to the critical role that the state and, for the purposes of this chapter, universities play in systematically reinforcing this model. Ricaurte highlights the need to consider new data governance and data regimes that would ensure rights for individuals and reduce digital inequality. Increasingly there are calls for a new Belmont Report that would articulate new rules and regulations that incorporate the pressing need to tackle the risks and new challenges IRBs face from the use of digital data for research (Raymond, 2019).

What is important, though, is to understand how using digital media in the research process reshapes the basics of ethical research practice. These changes take place in both technical and legal spaces, which are often not covered in traditional ethics training but are central to understanding the ethical and duty-of-care risks that arise when using digital tools. The following sections will map the traditional components of research ethics and human subjects protocols onto the aligned digital technical and legal issues researchers need to be aware of when developing a protocol.

We can start with the traditional issue of informed consent. The legal implications represent the most direct issue. From a legal standpoint, the researcher is laying out to the research participants to what they are agreeing to participate. Under normal circumstances, for example, when doing a survey study, the researcher can easily state that the data will be collected and used in a certain way. They can explain how it will be transferred from paper questionnaire to a .csv file, then used to write an academic article. This is easy because the researcher has multiple tangible ways to show the participants what they are consenting to; this could include showing them the survey instrument, where the .csv file will be stored and secured on a computer, and an example of a journal article, and so on.

A large-scale research project, such as the Heinsberg study in Germany, which created a randomised representative sample of respondents from the 'ground zero' of Germany's COVID-19 outbreak, serves as an analogue example around which we can evaluate the challenges of going digital. The research team essentially turned a district in Germany into a laboratory, observing infection rates among the representative sample of respondents to create an estimate of the total number of infections in Germany (Streeck et al., 2020). This was all done face to face, with biological samples taken from residents of Heinsberg. In this situation it is relatively straightforward to obtain consent. But what if a researcher wanted to use passively collected digital information, such as mobile phone location data, or cameras that could track the body temperature of a subject?

It gets harder when a piece of digital software is used that requires accepting a 'terms of use' agreement that the researcher did not write. In this case, it is important to provide some basic training on the legal principles behind terms of use and how to make them understandable to research subjects.

Consent has technical implications too. As mentioned in the previous section, autonomous and sensing tools create particular risks to informed consent. This can be managed with basic training on how sensing systems work, what happens between the sensor and the server to which it sends data and how the chain of data custody from sensor to researcher is managed. Following the example of training in the basics of understanding terms of use, basic training in how data are transferred from remote location to server to researcher can go a long way in helping researchers clarify what happens to the data that vulnerable communities are providing them. This could include introductory training on server software and the operation of wireless data transfer systems. The idea is not to turn a researcher into a software engineer, but to give them the technical knowledge to understand what is happening at the data collection point so they can clarify it to the research subjects.

This kind of technical training extends into the privacy and identity protection spaces, too. As digital technologies become increasingly accessible to non-technical users – for example, out-of-the-box solutions for remote sensing or software packages that provide users with easy front-end systems for gathering 'big data' – the risks to identity and privacy protection increase significantly. One example of privacy risks that can arise from bulk collection of remote sensing data was revealed in a *New York Times* expose on privacy and cell phone data collection. Though cell phone data collected by some carriers are anonymised, through access of public data, individuals can be easily identified and their movements can end up being tracked when the two datasets are combined (Thompson and Warzel, 2019). Basic training that covers tools like VPNs and TOR, and explains what a file's metadata is and how it can be abused, is important. Also important is instruction on the basics of managing data and hardware so that a researcher can guide an IT consultant or colleague through setting up a digital solution that is part of a research protocol.

Another facet of the technical limitation issue involves a third-party software provider that may not have full access or comprehension of the algorithm or technologies that they are developing. Complex algorithm or software that is built over many iterations and years leads to 'blackboxing'. Blackboxing is where the process that leads to the output of the software or algorithm isn't understood and developers are unclear how they've reached that point. A recent example of this was seen with Apple's launch of its credit card business. Individuals with identical information were given wildly different credit limits, and the company's officials were unclear as to why that happened (Vincent, 2019). This is important to digital research because it adds another layer of complication into how we develop frameworks and guidance for researchers regarding how to best ensure that the rights of individuals are preserved, while minimising risk and safeguarding against harm.

Developing deeper knowledge across these technical and legal areas is only a starting point. Traditionally, the sociological side of research ethics has focused on power, and the balance of power in the relationship between researcher and research subject. Digital platforms bring new and complex power issues into play, at times bisecting the chain of data custody and terms of use that exist between the researcher and subject. Software firms themselves bring their own power to a project, since their business models increasingly rely on using data submitted or shared by communities to tailor their advertising and data services offerings. The following section will explore this level of ethics in digital human subjects research, and highlight both the new power dynamics that arise, how technical knowledge can empower researchers to be good stewards of their research subjects' trust, and innovative ways to manage risks when doing digital research with vulnerable communities.

Balancing the Power among Researchers, Their Subjects and Third Parties

> The Signal Code developed by researchers at the Harvard Humanitarian Initiative articulates a 'rights-based approach' for collecting data from vulnerable populations. The code creators argue that the focus on rights of individuals is critical to be able to then pursue a needs-based approach, arguing that without establishing rights for individuals, pursuing a needs-based approach may prove to be insufficient, at best, or cause harm, at worst. As such, the Signal Code stipulates that individuals have a basic set of five rights when it comes to data: 'The Right to Information, The Right to Protection, The Right to Data Privacy and Security, The Right to Data Agency, The Right to Redress and Rectification'. The code is developed as a result of increasing reliance on technological tools to capture large data from population in the onset of humanitarian crises. These tools include remote sensing technologies, geospatial information, technologies to capture biometric data and information communication technologies that can collect telephone data. The Signal Code argues that the rights-based approach applies to all users who engage in activities to 'collect, analyze, process, transmit and communicate, share and publish, and support access to information as part of meeting the humanitarian needs of crisis-affected populations before, during, and/or after crises occur', as such, the Signal Code looks to apply a holistic approach for data collection from start to end. The Centre for Innovation offers a holistic approach to development of a data responsibility framework, which established core elements that help build and develop principles, and places ethics around the project. Therefore, all processes and applications build towards an ethical use for data. Another manifestation of responsible data use rights and principles is advocated by the *Feminist Data Manifest-No*, in which there is an emphasis on the importance of contextualisation of risks and harms. The *Manifest* argues that there is a need to understand that developing generalisable rules without accounting for the context of specific individuals, communities or groups would ultimately reinforce inequalities. The *Feminist Data Manifest-No* recognises the need to centre any work on humanity and an appreciation of the individuality of each person.

Identifying technical fixes and training is only part of the solution. These questions and issues do not arise in a vacuum, and the known issues about power balances between researchers and subjects are magnified in a digital space. One major difference between traditional data collection and the use of online digital platforms for collecting data is how data ownership and use are delineated. When a researcher gathers data for a survey on a tablet and transfers it to their computer, they remain the 'owners' of that data. They control how it is stored, replicated and distributed. When a researcher gathers data using a cloud service, social media or third-party instruments for passive data collection, those data often become the property of the technology or software provider. What happens with that data, how it is replicated or released to other parties, is often outside the researcher's ability to influence. Thus, power dynamics and the associated expectations between researcher and subject are magnified: not only might a subject feel compelled to share data, but they would be doing so in a space where their data could be used by a third party in a way that the researcher has little or no power to influence. What digital platforms add to human subjects research are new intermediating layers of power, defined in legal terms by software providers and economic and social terms between researchers and their subjects.

Some of the biggest questions in this space already are being raised in the humanitarian response sector, as NGOs and international organisations increasingly are exploring and entering into cooperative agreements with multinational technology firms. One recent example that has garnered a great deal of interest is Facebook's new cryptocurrency Libra, which is being adopted by global NGOs like Mercy Corps (Cheney, 2019). Deploying such a tool into high-risk environments with vulnerable populations is fraught with ethical and privacy considerations. At a basic level, the data that are inherent to using a platform like Libra is owned by Facebook, which makes its money selling targeted data to third parties. Can an NGO or humanitarian response agency meet its duty of care and its privacy commitments to the communities they serve while also working with firms like Facebook? This is a question that has evolved for over a decade as crowdsourcing, machine learning and digital volunteer groups have become increasingly involved in humanitarian response (Collins, 2013). The academic side of humanitarian research has picked this up as a theme to be studied with application to practice (Sandvik et al., 2014; Read et al., 2016; Hunt et al., 2016), with legal scholars bringing the conversation into closer alignment with the ethical and protection issues researchers face when doing human subjects research with vulnerable communities (Sandvik et al., 2017; Maitland, 2019).

Since researchers have an ethical commitment to protecting respondents' data, which in many cases can run contrary to software providers' goal of selling those data, what are the emerging tools that can be used to balance power between end users and technology firms? One approach is the establishment of data trusts, which are comanaged between citizens, governments and firms. Data trusts can take the form of a fiduciary trust between citizens, government and data firms (Wylie and McDonald, 2018). These kinds of fiduciary agreements give all parties input into how data are used; they are enforceable in different jurisdictions, and they are flexible, while also preventing capture of data by private actors. This can create an ethical, transparent mechanism for storing and using sensitive data, like medical information, that are often collected during human subjects research in vulnerable communities. Indeed, these trusts currently are being explored by the National Health Service in the UK (Mahonic, 2018) as a tool for protecting and managing sensitive data, while training machine learning software. Data trusts are still a concept that is being developed, and different governance entities have different definitions and approaches for understanding them. For this reason, academic researchers and faculty tasked with doing human subjects research training should be aware of what constitutes a trust from a legal standpoint and understand when the scope of a project requires one. Not all research requires a trust or fiduciary arrangement; yet, understanding the model can help researchers develop informed consent protocols and data management processes that are responsive to the risks that come with using third-party software for data collection.

Fundamentally, ethical human subjects research protocols are grounded in an understanding of, and engagement with, power dynamics between researcher and subject. The previous sections dealt with the individual-level factors that arise when using computing mediums to gather data; cases in which the researcher maintained control of the data through the entire process, and the 'terms of use' for the data were directly governed by an informed consent agreement between the researcher and respondent community. In many ways, the current methods of teaching research ethics provide the tools to navigate this kind of digital space and require only some supplementary technical training on managing data across different private platforms. The real power dynamics and complexity take place when integrating third parties into the research process and managing the power dynamics that they bring to the table. This is where formal training in understanding 'terms of use' and digital data management becomes crucial. The researcher in such cases should bring to the informed consent process both an understanding of how they themselves relate to the research subject and their ability to ensure that research subjects understand how their data will be used by third parties. With better knowledge of the overall digital ecosystem, researchers can make better decisions about which software solutions to use and when to stay off digital platforms all together, thus meeting their duty of care and ethical commitments to the potentially vulnerable communities with which they are doing research. There is a critical need to evaluate whether digital products are truly the appropriate solution. Often, the pursuit of digital solutions leads to further complications and risks that are unnecessary and do not provide an added value to the research process. We must be wary of falling into the trap of digital utopianism and pursue a critical lens in how we design research processes and data collection.

What Does the Digitally Engaged IRB Look Like?

Human subjects research, especially cooperative research that includes participation by international organisations and private sector actors, is increasingly going to reach into peoples' lives as we move further into the digital era. This means that when we think of IRBs, we have to step beyond the notion that they are an entity that deals only with the interests of university-based scientists and the subjects they study in either labs or managed field conditions. While this notion of researcher and researched always came with a power dynamic, it was one governed by a set of legal and ethical principles that were managed technically. Researchers collected their data and had a relationship with the research participant; there was a space for the researcher to explain the risks, and the job of the IRB was to make sure the ethical protocols the researcher developed for managing the relationship with the research subject did this sufficiently. Even in cases of higher-risk research, such as clinical trials or experiments that involved deception, there was space for the researcher and participant to interact face to face during a debriefing. In the digital world, there is so much scope for using digital information provided by people based on the acceptance of a software firm's 'terms of use', that the human relationships where power could be moderated are impossible to maintain.

For a modern IRB, ethics processes that focus on the specific relationship between a researcher and subject are no longer sufficient. Traditional means of ensuring privacy and anonymity in human subjects research are not fit for purpose when working with social media data, for example. Unlike a household survey, where we as the researchers are in control of what gets entered into the database, scraping the data from a platform like Twitter means that potentially identifying information is being used in research involving real people. There may be a digital veneer between the researcher and the subject, but in the end, data provided by a real person is being used in research. Are these data actually the subject's data? Probably not. The data people provide on social media platforms are likely to be the property of the social media firm, once it has been posted. Before even getting to the stage of using data though, there are a number of legal hurdles that have to be negotiated between researchers and software firms.

A good example is the experience Gary King and Nathaniel Persily (2020) shared about getting access to Facebook data on the sharing of weblinks (URLs). They organised this through Social Science One, a global committee of academics working on social science, social media and computing. Even with the combined talent of the best social scientists, law scholars and computer scientists, organising a large Facebook data release that met the needs of Facebook and the needs of researchers was an extraordinarily complex undertaking. Complex statistical techniques favoured by Facebook for anonymising data made the data unreliable for research, so statisticians and legal experts from Social Science One had to then find a technical and legal solution for keeping data anonymous, while keeping it useable. Once there was agreement on statistical, storage and legal issues, Social Science One continued acting as the gatekeeper for the data.

The mix of expertise in the Social Science One community in many ways makes it what a modern digital human subjects review board should be. They have the multifaceted knowledge required to deal with social media firms and assure researchers have the skills to use the data ethically and effectively. This allows them to act on behalf of the Facebook (or other social media) users, who may not be able to directly consent to their online behaviour being used as data for research.

But if Social Science One is the platonic ideal of what effective review and management of large-scale digital data looks like, this also presents a problem. Not every university of research institution has a mix of faculty with the variety of skills Gary King and Nathaniel Persily have brought together. Indeed, many institutions would struggle to make sure all these skillsets were present on their IRBs. So how do researchers with such resource limitations do digital work ethically? A starting place is using tools like the Signal Code as a guide to the questions they and their IRBs should be asking. If researchers start by asking the right questions, and know what those questions are, then they can seek out the experts necessary to evaluate a project. IRBs can do the same thing. Social Science One is not an IRB and, indeed, as part of any request to get access to the data they host, a researcher needs an IRB ethics approval from their home university. Thus, IRBs themselves need to either be upskilling or developing a better institutional understanding of the questions that come into play when evaluating digital human subjects research.

Conclusions: Shaping a New Approach to Human Subjects Protocol and Ethics Pedagogy

As technology changes the way we do research and makes data from invisible or vulnerable populations potentially easier to gather, the way that ethics and human subjects protocols are taught has to evolve. Researchers and the technology community are increasingly seeing how found data creates risks that traditionally were only seen in face-to-face research, including risks to privacy and safety (Zhang, 2016; Gibney, 2017). Scholars, including Matthew

Salganik (2017), are taking on the challenge of evaluating and finding new ways to teach social science research protocols in an increasingly digital research environment.

As digitalisation blurs the lines around what kinds of human subjects protocols are required to protect the identity of research participants, it is increasingly apparent that the social sciences need to prepare researchers with a broader range of technical and legal knowledge. This is especially the case when researchers work with third-party software providers, particularly if those providers use data collected on their platforms for commercial purposes. This is exactly the kind of tension that arises when a study like Heinsberg's COVID-19 experiment moves from face to face to tracking digital footprints. The reality, though, is that a focus on eliminating or managing risks hinges on *knowing* all the risks. With the speed that new technologies and digital research techniques are evolving, this approach to digital research ethics is impractical at best. Every researcher will not have the collection of expertise, such as is represented by Social Science One, available to them. Thus, having references like the Signal Code as ethical guides for understanding the different ways power manifests in digital human subjects research, and understanding how to make sure that power is managed in a way that protects vulnerable participants, will be critical to future research ethics.

Broadly speaking, research ethics is one of many areas of society that is reaching what is referred to in German as an *Umbrück*, which loosely translates as a 'bridging over'. We are on one bank, and the territory behind us contains all the lessons of a pre-digital world. We have to cross over to a world where digital systems are both actively and passively part of our lives. This Umbrück crosses over the space between pre- and post-digital worlds, thereby representing the changes and re-imagining of how we train ourselves to do ethical digital research in vulnerable communities. If we manage it well, ethics and research protocol pedagogy can help us get the most out of using digital tools for research, while lowering the risk of carelessly or accidentally putting at risk the people whose lives could be made better through effective scientific research.

Bibliography

Andrews, S. M. (2017) 'Drones in the DRC: A Case Study for Future Deployment in UN Peacekeeping'. *Intersect: The Stanford Journal of Science, Technology, and Society*, 10(2), 1–10.

Bhatta, B., Saraswati, S., and Bandyopadhyay, D. (2010) 'Urban Sprawl Measurement From Remote Sensing Data'. *Applied Geography*, 30(4), 731–740.

Chadwick, G. L. (1997) 'Historical Perspective: Nuremburg, Tuskegee, and the radiation experiments'. *Journal of the International Association of Providers of AIDS Care*, 3(1), 27–8.

Chandler, D. (2015) 'A World Without Causation: Big Data and the Coming of Age of Posthumanism'. *Millennium: Journal of International Studies*, 43(3), 833–851.

Cheney, C. (2019) 'Facebook's Digital Currency Libra: Why Nonprofits Are Joining'. *Devex*. https://www.devex.com/news/facebook-s-digital-currency-libra-why-nonprofits-are-joining-95142. Accessed 25 June 2019.

Collins, Katie. (2013) 'How AI, Twitter and Digital Volunteers Are Transforming Humanitarian Disaster Response'. *Wired*. https://www.wired.co.uk/article/digital-humanitarianism. Accessed 25 June 2019.

Couldry, N., and Mejias, U. A. (2018) 'Data Colonialism: Rethinking Big Data's Relation to the Contemporary Subject'. *Television & New Media*, 2. DOI: 10.1177/1527476418796632.

Gibney, E. (2017) 'Ethics of Internet Research Trigger Scrutiny'. *Science*, 550(7674), 16–17.

Hunt, M., Pringle, J., Christen, M., Eckenwiler, L., Schwartz, L., and Davé, A. (2016) 'Ethics of Emergent Information and Communications Technology Applications in Humanitarian Medical Assistance'. *International Health*, 8(4), 239–245.

King, G., and Persily, N. (2020) 'Unprecedented Facebook URLs Dataset Now Available for Academic Research Through Social Science One'. *Social Science One Blog*. https://socialscience.one/blog/unprecedented-facebook-urls-dataset-now-available-research-through-social-science-one. Accessed 1 July 2020.

Lidèn, K., and Sandvik, K. B. (2016) *Poison Pill or Cure-All: Drones and the Protection of Civilians*. London: Routledge.

Madianou, M. (2019) 'Technocoloniamism: Digital Innovation and Data Practices in the Humanitarian Response to Refugee Crises'. *Social Media + Society*. DOI: 10.1177/2056305119863146.

Mahonic, A. (2018) 'Can Data Trusts Be the Backbone of Our Future AI Ecosystem?' https://www.turing.ac.uk/research/research-programmes/artificial-intelligence-ai/programme-articles/can-data-trusts-be-backbone-our-future-ai-ecosystem. Accessed 26 June 2019.

Maitland, C. (2019) 'Digital Developments: Harbingers of Humanitarian Change?' WRC Research Paper No. 15. https://www.cigionline.org/publications/digital-developments-harbingers-humanitarian-change. Accessed 25 June 2019.

Marshall, K. P. (1999) 'Has Technology Introduced New Ethical Problems?' *Journal of Business Ethics*, 19(1), 81–90.

McCarthy, D. R. (2013) 'Technology and 'the International' Or: How I Learned to Stop Worrying and Love Determinism'. *Millennium: Journal of International Studies*, 41(3), 470–90.

Raymond, N. (2019) 'Safeguards for Human Studies Can't Cope With Big Data'. *Nature*, 568(7752), 277.

Read, R., Taithe, B., and Mac Ginty, R. (2016) 'Data Hubris? Humanitarian Information Systems and the Mirage of Technology'. *Third World Quarterly*, 37(8), 1314–1331.

Ricaurte, P. (2019) 'Data Epistemologies, The Coloniality of Power, and Resistance'. *Television & New Media*. DOI: 10.1177/1527476419831640.

Salganik, M. J. (2017) *Bit by Bit: Social Research in the Digital Age*. Princeton, NJ: Princeton University Press.

Sandvik, K. B., Jacobsen, K. L., and McDonald, S. M. (2017) 'Do No Harm: A Taxonomy of the Challenges of Humanitarian Experimentation'. *International Review of the Red Cross*, 99(904), 319–344

Sandvik, Kristin Bergtora, Jumbert, Maria Gabrielsen, Karlsrud, John, and Kaufmann, Mareile. (2014) 'Humanitarian Technology: A Critical Research Agenda'. *International Review of the Red Cross*, 96(893), 216–242.

Streeck, H., Schulte, B., Keummerer, B., Richter, E., Höller, T., Fuhrmann, C., Bartok, E., Dolscheid, R., Berger, M., Wessendorf, L., Eschbach-Bludau, M., and Hartmann, G. (2020) 'Infection Fatality Rate of SARS-CoV-2 Infection in a German Community With a Super-Spreading Event'. *medRxiv*. DOI: 10.1101/2020.05.04.20090076.

Thompson, S., and Warzel, C. (2019) 'Twelve Million Phones, One Dataset, Zero Privacy'. *The New York Times*. https://www.nytimes.com/interactive/2019/12/19/opinion/location-tracking-cell-phone.html?fbclid=IwAR0o6mLT-uKNWdWtnQuww-NeWvse9DsrdYubiV_AT1jqLu_0lxd1eJoQJEw. Accessed 1 July 2020.

Vincent, J. (2019) 'Apple's Credit Card Is Being Investigated for Discriminating Against Women'. *The Verge*. https://www.theverge.com/2019/11/11/20958953/apple-credit-card-gender-discrimination-algorithms-black-box-investigation. Accessed 1 July 2020.

Winner, L. (1986) 'Do Artifacts Have Politics?' In: Winner, L. (Ed.), *The Whale and the Reactor: A Search for Limits in an Age of High Technology*. Chicago: University of Chicago Press, 19–39.

Wylie, B., and McDonald, S. M. (2018) 'What Is a Data Trust?' https://www.cigionline.org/articles/what-data-trust. Accessed 26 June 2019.

Zhang, S. (2016) 'Scientists Are Just as Confused About the Ethics of Big-Data Research as You'. *Wired*. https://www.wired.com/2016/05/scientists-just-confused-ethics-big-data-research/. Accessed 26 June 2019.

PART II

Chapter 3

ROME VS. REGIONS: GOVERNMENT IN ITALY DURING COVID-19: IMPLICATIONS FOR THE FUTURE OF THE EUROPEAN UNION (EU)

Christian Rossi, Colette Mazzucelli, and David C. Unger

Introduction

The experience of European integration provides a challenge to classical realism. The newly partnered states of Western Europe constructed a community narrative of 'no more war' embodied by the creation of a security community embodied in economic integration of Original Six of the Treaty of Rome – with its original six members – France, West Germany, Italy, Belgium, the Netherlands and Luxembourg, and West European military integration within NATO (Kupchan, 2010). With these steps, Western Europe turned its back on the fratricide that led to three Franco-German conflicts in less than 70 years, which resulted in two world wars (Stern, 2007).

The twentieth-century international system had Europe as its reference point: first, as the subject of empires in decline; and, subsequently, after World War II, as the object of superpower competition with a divided Germany at the front line (DePorte, 1979). During the Cold War, the debate was dominated by Waltz's focus in the international relations literature on bipolarity, namely, the ideological and material competition between the United States and the former Soviet Union. Structural realism, also called neorealism, placed the emphasis squarely on the international system, the so-called third image (Waltz, 1959). In hindsight, the waning years of the last century may be perceived as a bridge decade between the fall of the Berlin Wall on 9 November 1989 and the destruction of the Twin Towers on 11 September 2001 (Chollet and Goldgeier, 2008). That period from 11/9 to 9/11 bore witness to the rise of the internet as the driver of the latest phase in the history of globalisation, namely, the information and communications technology revolution. This latest turning point in world history featured a frequently disorienting experience of contrasts between old-world hierarchies and new social networks (Ferguson, 2019).

The early twenty-first century has experienced a series of three inflexion points. The first came right at the end of the bridge decade with the attacks on the United States in 2001. Less than a decade later, the world experienced the financial crisis of 2007–8, which left many Western countries in a state of future shock (Aliber and Kindleberger, 2015). The global financial crisis reignited a long-standing debate about neoliberalism (Slobodian, 2018) as the linchpin of the Washington Consensus. The orthodoxy of the neoliberal model retains a focus on Waltz's systemic analysis even though the world is rapidly changing as we begin a third decade in the new millennium. The onset of the novel coronavirus pandemic is the singular event to define a society that is more and more interconnected around the world, in other words, what is termed 'global international society' by leading international relations scholars (Acharya and Buzan, 2019) in 2020. Taken in conjunction with climate change, the pandemic reorients our systemic focus from the ego of realism to the eco of inclusionism.

On the one hand, this reorientation is the search for a twenty-first-century narrative of European integration. Europe's latest existential crisis before the COVID-19 pandemic struck is one in which Italy remains on the front line:

transnational migration. The narrative of 'Never again' (Hayes and Roth, 2012), which references the aim to make genocide impossible, remains an elusive one in the post-1945 era, as Italy's recent angry political debates over refugees in Europe indicate (IRC, 2020). On the other hand, the quest for a new community design is necessary given the rapid transformation of the EU in successive enlargements since the Maastricht Treaty ratification. Italy is the founding member state whose domestic specificity most resembles the EU27's North–South as well as East–West diversity. In the time of COVID-19, present challenges of migration and enlargement make Italy a pivotal case study to question neorealism and neoliberalism (Baldwin, 1993).

In 1959, Waltz presented a philosophical inquiry into the nature of war that contributed to international relations by introducing three images of analysis. Wars are caused by individuals (or human nature, more generally speaking), the domestic configuration of states and/or the anarchic structure of the international system. Scholars have discussed these 'levels of analysis' with a prescience that speaks to our present situation: 'and if it is not closed soon, the repercussions may be ominous not only for the study of man, but for man himself' (Singer, 1960). Just when leaders aimed to make publics believe in the onset of a new phase in the Cold War, the publication of Waltz's *Theory of International Politics*, in 1979, anchored neorealism as the dominant international relations lens in 'an American social science' (Hoffmann, 1977) much to the chagrin of those seeking pluralism in theory as well as practice (Acharya and Buzan, 2019).

Neorealism underlines the inherent stability of a bipolar system in which the balance of terror highlights the central place of the United States and the Soviet Union as the dominant nuclear powers in the structure of the international system (Waltz, 1979). A bipolar system is more stable, in Waltz's reasoning, than a multipolar one. The structure is one of hierarchy with a vertical orientation: power dictates from the top down. The soldier and the diplomat are its most important assets thinking in terms of the chessboard (Aron, 2003). The rise of the Web (Slaughter, 2017) in the twenty-first century leads to a consideration of different players, other than states, in the system. The structure is one of disparity with a horizontal orientation: power is shared. Firms and data have an increasing relevance in a world of 7.8 billion people whose individual and collective experiences are more and more interconnected for better and for worse.

The lack of global leadership by the United States and China during the COVID-19 pandemic exemplifies in certain ways the power vacuum of the G-Zero World (Bremmer, 2012). In other ways, the pandemic is a harbinger of the increasingly multipolar world that has emerged since the end of the Cold War (Cohen-Tanugi, 2008). Environmental stewardship takes on ever increasing significance as the nexus between climate change and global pandemic creates an urgent need: to cooperate for the survival of our planet. In this situation, the EU's value-added ticks up; yet only if its construction is redesigned to function much closer to the peoples whose distinct voices aspire to replace directives from Brussels. By working from this premise, our chapter integrates alternative levels of analysis more relevant to 1.2 global international society (GIS) in 2019 than international relations in 1959 (Mazzucelli and Keith, 2020).

Evolving research points to a direct linkage between the destruction of nature and disease outbreaks (Conservation International, 2020). Such a link suggests the distributed ecosystem, or the third image in 1.2 GIS (Mazzucelli and Keith, 2020), is this chapter's point of departure. During spring 2020, Italy experienced the brunt of the pandemic's first wave. Europeans mistakenly believed what happened in China was an 'Asian problem' relying on information provided by the World Health Organization, whose officials underestimated the gravity of the situation (Harari and Vitacca, 2020). A treacherous pathology that spreads through the air, as millions of people travel across the world, knows no sovereign borders. The first diagnosis of a positive COVID-19 patient in Lombardy on 22 February led to a complete lockdown in March disrupting free movement of persons, one of four freedoms in the Single European Market (SEM).

The COVID-19 pandemic is changing the way billions experience their immediate environments, which constitute a distributed ecosystem that has yet to be designed with nodes (Slaughter, 2017) for planetary survival. In Italy, borders are being implicitly redrawn as lockdowns occur and travel restrictions evolve. 'Borders are the scars of history', as Robert Schuman, an architect of European construction, explained (Borrell, 2020). A challenge for Italy in the EU is to draw the lessons from history being made by COVID-19. An initial lesson is that the scars of pandemic history are primarily within the member states rather than among the EU27. In Italy, this reality necessitates reference to the regions, particularly those hardest struck, notably Lombardy followed by Piedmont and Veneto (Statista, 2020), as well as the nation-state. In this context, the mesh region, or the second image in 1.2 GIS, introduced with the family as a unit of analysis, is this chapter's next focal point.

In this context, a 'mesh describes a type of network that allows any node to link in any direction with any other nodes in the system. Every part is connected to every other part, and they move in tandem' (Gansky, 2010). The relevance of the mesh is in its capacity, analysing the present, and its potential, anticipating the future, to expand: a larger and larger mesh in any given region maximises a variety of communications that can, despite incessant possibilities for corruption or oppression, provide a structure of resilience

(Slaughter, 2017). A focus in this chapter is on the agency that makes bottom-up policy-making to address the pandemic in Italy more plausible. The mesh provides a region with the structure of an underlying network that is reciprocal in the interactions nurtured through a return on investment in exponential social network expansion, which can engender trust over time (Fukuyama, 1996).

The distinct and devastating nature of the pandemic's second wave striking Italy during fall 2020 (Paterlini, 2020) raises the most fundamental change to consider given its COVID-19 response in an EU context. Clearly, there is a need to organise new health paths; this is a process in which data collection as well as observation, measurement, description, analysis and evaluation figure prominently (Harari and Vitacca, 2020). The challenge to improve healthcare in local areas within the most vulnerable regions is a call to the scientific community and local populations to share their experiences. Diverse healthcare systems across the EU member states make the earlier functionalist idea of international government, asserted by Woolf in the literature at the turn of the twentieth century, less relevant.

The challenges the COVID-19 pandemic pose to integration in Europe point to a relaunch for the twenty-first century rather than disintegration (Leigh, 2020). The 2020's relaunch (Michael, 2020) distinguishes itself from the functionalist model of technocratic integration, which dates to The Schuman Plan of 9 May 1950 (Gillingham, 1991). The idea that expresses the purpose of the EU 2020 relaunch is *build it back better*. At its core is the democratic principle that finds expression in the experience of integration realised from the bottom up starting with the voices of peoples in diverse societies across the Continent. These voices speak to unity in diversity contradicting regulations from Brussels starting with the General Data Protection Regulation (GDPR). The GDPR sets the stage for conflict that is inherent in the first image of 1.2 GIS, or personal data, as explained in context of the evolving nature of identity (Mazzucelli and Keith, 2020).

As the challenges Italy faces in Europe indicate, identity is experienced in the plural not the singular. In his commentary on *Identity and Violence*, when speaking of 'The Illusion of Destiny' (Sen, 2007), one of India's most famous development economists discusses ways in which it is possible, in his experiences, to negotiate among various identities at once – '[…] an Asian, an Indian citizen, a Bengali with Bangladeshi ancestry, an American or British resident, an economist, a dabbler in philosophy, an author […]' Italy's frontline encounters with trans-regional migration beg the question 'Who is My Other?' (Kapuściński, 2009). This inquiry is complicated by the ways in which identity is defined increasingly with reference to personal data, explained relationally in terms of community rather than individual

(Mazzucelli and Keith, 2020). At the heart of conflict, more so in the time of COVID-19, is abuses of personal data by firms and governments.

The impact of COVID-19 in Italy gives the country's specificity in Europe new meaning. The implications of measures taken by the government in Rome call Italy to come to terms with its specificity (Unger, 2020). The exponential rate of transmission region by region, particularly during the second wave of COVID-19, allows the authors to refocus our lens on what there is to observe in this case. As our colleague Pat Caruso reminds us, 'When you change the way you look at things, the things you look at change' (WE Prison Fellowship, 2016). A regional comparison matters in tracking daily progress of COVID-19, as the consideration of family contacts informs the evolving story. The Italian context reveals tensions among different levels from the national in Rome to the regional in the hardest struck areas to the local, as the involvement in political decisions of local mayors indicates (Garavaglia et al., 2020).

Social media communications by Italian mayors are a new form of outreach to the Italian people as the pandemic evolves in different areas of the country (Horowitz, 2020). The state cannot always be relied on to address the pandemic in effective and efficient ways: subunits and society must step up to address urgent tasks for democratic governance. As this analysis explains, each of Waltz's levels of analysis is too constrained to accommodate the security risks posed for Italians in the EU (Krastev, 2020) or for the billions of humans and non-humans whose lives are in question during a new era of 'planetary health' (Guinto, 2020). In this era, personal data is more integral to individual and collective health concerns; the mesh region, including key cities, is a modified feature of the state to access given evolving global public health challenges, and the distributed ecosystem is an alternative focal point to assure the survival of species.

The tensions that endure between the technocratic nature of the functionalist model and the democratic orientation of federalist ambitions limit the degree to which citizens animate integration in Europe during the early years of the twenty-first century. There is a marked difference between the EU's constructive response to climate change, which speaks more to its unity, and the lack of European response to the COVID-19 pandemic, which points to the logic of diversity (Hoffmann, 1966). Italy is the founding member state of the European Community in which tensions and contradictions abound. The more the Italian government relies on technocrats to advance integration in Europe, the less its citizens accept Italy's participation in a SEM that no longer promotes freedom of movement within either domestic or European borders. As much as the original six tried to replace centuries of war on the Continent, exclusionary nationalism persists to make conflict within Italy, rather than between member states, a dominant feature of European construction in the early twenty-first century. This fact is evidenced by the rise of the Far-Right from France to Poland. In this context, it is impossible to transition from a twentieth-century narrative of 'no more war' to a twenty-first-century narrative of 'never again'.

In this chapter, inclusionism is referenced as a new 'ism' through which to see Italy and Europe in 1.2 GIS, a lens that recognises what realism, in all its variants, denies: the lack of capacity in current structures to respond proactively to present-day challenges. Moreover, the inherent deficiencies of solutions that build on such inadequate structures can only lead to greater inequalities. In contradistinction, there is the kinetic, constitutive and interactive relationships between human beings and personal data, which define a more integral type of agency to complement the innate relevance and responsibility of people, not only states, in the perpetuation of climate change as well as the spread, and, likewise, the mitigation of the COVID-19 pandemic worldwide. Likewise, billions in our world increasingly confront the transnational nature of social protest, triggered, although less driven, by isolated experiences, that is, the murder of George Floyd, and animated more by the structural inequalities, the missed opportunities and the systematic discrimination against the majority of the world's peoples by the market-driven 'instrumentarian power' (Zuboff, 2019) of a technologically determined minority elite. These developments are by no means new having evolved with globalisation from the last century to the present era.

And yet states that have a history of respecting human rights have already endeavoured to start 'hacking digital ethics' by distributing human rights beyond their own borders. The EU's GDPR is many things, notably a deliberate effort to distribute rights via each one of its citizens' travel. In this capacity, European citizens' personal data is a part of the make-up of many systems across the globe. This granular level of analysis is an opportunity to understand how an expanding global society exists rather than clinging to what older hierarchies aim to maintain as the legacy of a previously static Cold War system. The challenge is in the conflict that regulations from Brussels engender inside member states, notably Italy, which has one of the least successful records of compliance with European legislation. As historians question the causes of war (MacMillan, 2020), whether conflict is rooted in human nature, as realists posit, or the product of leadership that aims to manipulate narratives to set groups against each other in a particular cultural setting, as instrumentalism explains, Italy is marked by a struggle among the central government, its regions and localities hardest struck by the pandemic. The poor Italian response to the second wave of COVID-19 leads to a call for more agency rather than simply a structural change in the direction of a federalist EU.

Italy's well-known North–South divide has inhibited the country to act as France does under the Fifth Republic. The present approach to integration on the Continent is a convenient proxy to use the EU as a substitute for the Italian state. Italy's problem of 20 years of no economic growth was brought on by measures adopted to meet the first wave of Economic and Monetary Union agreed to in Maastricht. The urgency to fix this problem of economic stagnation, especially given the impact of the pandemic lockdowns, is the relaunch this chapter discusses. Italy's participation from the base in society needs to be rebuilt by bridging divides across the country.

The COVID-19 pandemic brought forward a series of contradictions within the EU and Italy. These contradictions threaten the very existence of the Union as well as the cohesion of Italy. Indeed, the outbreak of the novel coronavirus led the EU and Italy to seal off their borders. On the one hand, the member states began to curtail freedom of movement within the EU. On the other, Italy started to prevent Italian citizens from moving within the country. These recent developments have influenced the European Treaties as well as the Italian Constitution. In Italy, the legal hierarchy has been considerably impacted. The need for rapid decision-making did not allow time to avoid the influence exerted on freedoms enjoyed by citizens and protected by the supreme law of the country, the Constitution.

The Specificity of Italy's Democracy: Domestic Institutional Complexities and Personal Data Concerns

The early months of the COVID-19 pandemic hit Italy particularly hard. By the time the first wave of cases began receding in April, nearly twenty-five thousand Italians had died, at that time the highest recorded death toll in Europe. In several north Italian provinces where COVID-19 infections were initially concentrated, hospitals and intensive care units were stretched to and beyond their capacity.

What put Italy at the centre of the pandemic storm? And why was the hospital crisis most acute in some of its richest, most economically vibrant regions, home to some of Italy's best, most modern hospitals? Virologists and epidemiologists will be debating these questions for years, but some likely economic, demographic and structural causes already seem evident. Airports, like Milan's Malpensa, and urban centres like Bergamo are at the heart of today's globalised Italian economy. Business travellers frequently shuttle back and forth between Italy's Po Valley and Asian production hubs like China, where the first outbreak of the COVID-19 virus was detected. Italy's population is among Europe's oldest, with almost one in four residents over the age of 65, an age group significantly more vulnerable to serious complications from COVID-19, including death. Italians also tend to congregate in high population density clusters, live in multigenerational households and gather for extended family celebrations. The northern Po Valley region where the epidemic hit hardest is Italy's most industrialised, and there appears to be a correlation between industrial pollution, with its fine dust particles, and susceptibility to severe COVID-19 respiratory symptoms. Finally, Italy's decentralised and underfunded national healthcare system, administered at the regional level, is notoriously prone to waste, inefficiency, bureaucracy and outright corruption, with funds that could go to hiring more doctors and nurses diverted instead to overpriced medical construction projects. On top of this, the short-sighted fiscal austerity drives of recent decades led to significant underinvestment in public health, resulting in fewer doctors, nurses, hospitals and hospital beds by the time the pandemic hit.

Perhaps the biggest single factor explaining Italy's high early death toll was that it was the first major Western democracy forced to cope with the pandemic. The Italian government was dealing with a new threat in real time without much precedent elsewhere to guide and with its own standby plans for dealing with pandemics ill-suited and badly out of date. Treatments later found to be effective were not yet known. Procedures that may have spread contagion and worsened patient's recovery prospects had not yet been identified and eliminated. Stockpiles of personal protective equipment (PPE) for medical staff had not yet been built up.

Nor was this the EU's finest hour. Italy, despite being a charter member, found itself in those early months largely on its own, with little Continent-wide administrative coordination, no significant sharing of PPE and no meaningful infusions of emergency fiscal resources to pay for acquiring PPE and other needed equipment from outside the EU, or for recruitment of desperately needed additional doctors and nurses. Quite the contrary. Brussels remained mired in the ludicrously inappropriate role of fiscal austerity enforcer it had taken on during the euro debt crisis of the preceding decade. Instead of mobilising a continental fire brigade to help douse Italy's raging pandemic flames, Brussels' 'frugal four' austerity coalition called for tightening the fiscal faucets to guard against hypothetical threats of future inflation.

Seen retrospectively, Italy made many costly mistakes during the first phase of the pandemic. But seen in the context described before, we might reach a very different conclusion – that Italy confounded the many foreign and domestic critics who had long held it up as a poster child of ineffective governance and, by the summer of 2020, found its way to a remarkably effective first wave response. The number of active cases of COVID-19 in Italy fell from 108,257 on 19 April (the first wave peak) to 12,422 on 31 July, a decline of 88 per cent. The remainder of this section will look at how Italy got to this better place, looking especially at the respective roles of the national government in Rome and regional administrations throughout the peninsula. We will then look at how and why that first wave success gave way to catastrophic failure in the pandemic's second wave, which saw cases explode from 12,422 on 31 July to 805,947 on 22 November (the second wave peak). We will try to see whether it is possible to draw any constructive lessons for the future from this unhappy turnaround.

The first wave – January–April 2020

In the absence of a well-coordinated, adequately funded, EU institutional response to the COVID-19 emergency from Brussels, the Italian government was left to cope on its own with a complex of politically difficult and sometimes financially costly challenges: for example whether and how strictly to override constitutional norms and EU agreements in order to restrict the spread of the virus by sealing internal and external borders, how to quickly ramp up hospital and intensive care capacity, rapidly expand the pool of professionally trained doctors and nurses and acquire huge supplies of good quality PPE – like masks, gowns and face shields – and how to go about developing the large-scale programmes of testing, contact tracing and quarantine that epidemiologists soon began recommending. These challenges might have been met more efficiently, implemented more smoothly and resourced more adequately at the EU level. But for the first six months of the pandemic, they weren't.

Based on widely held stereotypes about Italian misgovernment, stereotypes prevalent not just among non-Italians but among Italians themselves, and considering Italy's very real problems of bureaucracy, corruption, organised crime and incurably fractious party politics, passing the ball to Rome looked like a sure invitation to pervasive dysfunction. And yet […]

Despite many costly misjudgements and operational breakdowns, and at a terrible cost in lives and livelihoods, Italy's political institutions rose to meet most of these challenges. In contrast to supposedly better-governed countries like the United States, the United Kingdom and Sweden, Italian caseloads fell sharply after their mid-April peak, Italian hospitals and emergency rooms ceased to be overwhelmed and a phased reopening of the economy proceeded without major setbacks.

The first eight months of 2020 can be seen as a severe stress test of Italy's society and democracy, a test from which Italy emerged with surprisingly good grades.

Following the first reports of a new coronavirus spreading from China, Italy's government reacted relatively quickly. By the end of January, it had banned flights from China and initiated airport health checks and controls on other international flights. A few weeks later, on 23 February, when the first Italian clusters of cases were diagnosed, the Italian government designated a 'red zone' strictly limiting movement in or out of the most affected northern provinces. As the pandemic spread, the red zone was expanded, on 8 March, to include most of northern Italy.

Even though COVID-19 cases remained largely confined to northern regions, sealing off the most economically productive and politically vocal portions of the country posed such enormous challenges that just one day later the government locked down all of Italy. All residents except emergency workers were ordered to stay at or near their homes. Schools were closed, athletic events and other large gatherings were cancelled and signed forms were required for travel even to the food stores and pharmacies that remained open. These measures were rightly seen at the time as unprecedentedly swift and drastic steps by a Western democratic government to curtail basic freedoms (http://www.governo.it/it/coronavirus-misure-del-governo).

Hindsight tells us that Rome's initial steps were neither swift nor drastic enough. Areas that should have been included in the initial red zone were not. Had the government acted more quickly, and more drastically, and included more areas in the initial red zone, thousands of lives might have been saved and the most affected hospitals might never have been overwhelmed.

Italy's European neighbours might have learned from Italy's initial mistakes. But in the subsequent weeks and months, as the virus struck hard at many of these neighbours, Italy's lessons were applied unevenly, and in some cases too hesitatingly, also likely costing thousands of lives.

Few imagined in early March that Italy would need or choose to keep many of those early restrictions in place for months. But for weeks the number of Italians newly infected with COVID-19 kept rising. Even after the curve of new infections turned downward in late March, current caseloads kept growing for several more weeks, reaching the first wave peak of 108,257 on 19 April. A week later, Rome decreed a programme of phased reopenings, to start in mid-May. Observing the costs that other countries, particularly the

United States, were paying for premature reopenings, Rome at first moved cautiously, despite pressures from businesses facing the prospect of mounting losses. Government aid packages and tax relief helped keep those political pressures more manageable, giving the government somewhat greater scope to keep remaining restrictions in place.

Prime Minister Giuseppe Conte did not, and, given Italy's constitution and political culture, could not, have made all the needed decisions by himself. But he made ample use of the decree powers available to him under Italy's legislation, thereby assuring himself the last word on the timing and extent of the country's lockdown and, later, on the phased lifting of emergency restrictions. Like most heads of government, especially in democratic countries, Conte consulted with scientific advisers, official and unofficial, whose advice he followed somewhat selectively. But he could not simply ignore these advisers, who broadcast their views through the media whenever they felt Rome wasn't listening to them.

The Conte government in Rome, supported in Parliament since September 2019 by an unnatural and uneasy coalition joining the establishment centre-left Democratic Party and the insurgent populist 5-Star Movement, and smaller groupings like former prime minister Matteo Renzi's breakaway Italia Viva party, had to find ways to keep its diverse constituent parties on board. Some of these thought reopening the schools should take priority. Others stressed reopening factories or small shops. Some called for strict and uniform national policies, directed from the top. Others wanted to give more say to Parliament or the regional governments. If any of the coalition parties broke ranks, Conte could not be sure that his decrees would be ratified by Parliament. In the early weeks, Conte cultivated the image of a wartime leader and found unexpectedly wide popular support. As the pandemic, and the restrictions, dragged on, he appeared more like a political manager, and that initial popular consensus began to give way to a more politicised fragmentation.

Rome also had to negotiate with regions. Given the decentralised features of Italy's governing structure, particularly the fact that the national health service SSN (Servizio Sanitario Nazionale, created in 1978) operates through the country's nineteen regions and two autonomous provinces, Italy's responses to the COVID-19 challenge had to be constantly negotiated and renegotiated between Conte and the elected regional presidents. In many of the northern regions where the first wave of the pandemic struck hardest, these regional governments were dominated by centre-right opposition parties intent on minimising the impact of Rome's restrictions on the local business communities from which they drew much of their political support. Informal negotiations also took place between the regional governments and their most economically and politically influential constituents, including business associations, labour unions and the elected mayors of cities and towns within their regions. Whatever party they came from, all the regional presidents were also advised by local health officials and academics.

Competing pulls came not just from the political parties but from civil society, especially from its key economic actors. Rome had to balance the interests of richer industrialised northern regions like Lombardia, Emilia-Romagna, Veneto and Piemonte with those of poorer southern regions like Campania, Puglia, Calabria and the islands of Sardegna and Sicilia. It also had to balance pressures from Po Valley regions whose economies depended on an early reopening of industrial facilities against coastal, scenic and historic areas whose largest single source of income has long been tourism, domestic and foreign. The richer northern regions had much stronger healthcare systems than the poorer south. But in the northern regions hit hardest by the pandemic, even those stronger systems were for a time overwhelmed by the sudden surges of infected patients.

In early phases of the reopening, the north–south dichotomy presented Rome with another special set of political challenges as some southern regions sought to protect themselves against contagion from travelling northerners, many of whose families had migrated north from the job-poor south decades earlier and still had relatives living there. Summer, as we shall see, brought a different set of regional variations and challenges.

In July, the EU re-entered the picture. Spurred by the overwhelming magnitude of the intertwined health and economic crisis, European heads of government approved a multi-year, €750 billion coronavirus recovery package, of which Italy's projected share will be €210. As part of the price for approval of this package by the fiscally frugal north European bloc, the share made up of outright grants was lowered and the share made up of soft loans was increased. Still, the package was notable for breaking through former taboos against pooling EU credit to reduce borrowing costs. But with much of Italy's centre-right opposition, and some within its government coalition, wary that any EU funds will come tied up with EU fiscal supervision, the modalities of spending Italy's share of the recovery funds have become, predictably, caught up in Italian party politics.

This was not textbook democracy – far from it. The input from above was more technocratic than democratic in spirit. Experts proposed mitigation strategies mainly based on successes and failures elsewhere, national politicians then decreed a politically brokered selection of these from above without seeking much local community input from below. Expertise matters, but ideally expert advice should help guide democratic decisions. Uniform policies were applied nationally without taking adequate account of important local differences. Key decisions were made by executive decree, effectively bypassing Parliament and opposition parties. Italy's established political parties, like the Partito Democratico, and newer movements like the Lega and 5-Star, served more as platforms and vehicles for their national and regional political leaders than as conduits for their grassroots constituents.

This simplified the political challenges for Rome, but at the expense of democracy and popular buy-in to policies that ultimately depend on voluntary public compliance. Local mayors and communes were given little discretion until the later stages of the reopening process. The input from below was more corporatist than democratic in form, with industry lobbies wielding far more influence than the rest of civil society. What is best for the tourist industry or agriculture is not necessarily what is best for public health.

All of this sometimes clamorous input from parties, scientific advisers, large and small business, regional governments and large and small businesses was necessary in a democratic society, but it complicated decision-making, delayed timely responses, produced inconsistent policies and eroded public confidence. Some of the price for that was paid in the second wave, when people, feeling increasingly disconnected from national policymakers in Rome and hearing mixed and contradictory messages at the regional and local level, let down their guard for summer vacations, school reopenings, and so on. That second wave began in August and has not yet played itself out.

In our view, most of this political and civil society back and forth constructively influenced the policies Italy adopted during the first wave. Despite the staggering and unnecessarily high death toll, the policies ultimately arrived at eventually helped Italy bend the infection curve downward to the point where, by the end of July, the weekly average of new cases was down by roughly 95 per cent from its March peak and the number of active cases, which peaked a month later, had descended by 88 per cent.

Subsequent waves – August 2020 and beyond

By the end of June, Italy's infection rate per capita had been driven down well below that of many other European countries. But within weeks, with governmental restrictions rolled back and public messaging from many regional governments encouraging a return to normal life, many Italians, especially younger people, returned to traditional summer forms of socialising and travel. People began congregating in bars and on beaches, sharing the popular belief that young people did not become seriously sick from COVID-19 (most did not. But even those with milder cases were capable of spreading them to more vulnerable seniors). Tourists from northern European countries with higher infection rates began flocking across recently reopened Schengen zone borders, actively encouraged by regional governors from tourist dependent areas, like the Italian Riviera region of Liguria. Italians took their own traditional August vacation trips abroad to countries with higher infection rates like Croatia, Greece, Malta and Spain, sometimes bringing new infection clusters back with them on their return. Recent and not-so-recent immigrants made their annual summer visits to their countries of origin to reunite with extended families left behind. Summer also brought the usual seasonal surge of migrant agricultural workers and clandestinely arriving would-be immigrants to southern and other agricultural regions. Often, these migrants were packed into crowded living and working quarters, seeding new infection clusters.

Throughout August and early September, the number of new infections kept rising, while the average age of people hospitalised or instructed to isolate at home went down. Older, more vulnerable people were taking more care to protect themselves, but that was not easy to do in Italy's many multigenerational households, especially as cooler weather began to drive family life back indoors.

By the end of August, current COVID-19 cases had more than doubled to 26,078. By the end of September, they nearly doubled again to 51,263. Despite the rising numbers, Rome pressed ahead to reopen schools on 14 September, a date first set months earlier at a time when the incidence of COVID-19-infected people was forecast to be significantly lower. National, regional and local governments worked hard to make school buildings and classrooms as safe as possible. But sending children back to school, especially older children, meant a lot more human circulation, and a lot more opportunities for contagion outside school premises. For example, public transit became more crowded, as commuters, teachers and students travelled on the same buses and trains during the same morning hours, so much so that capacity limits meant to limit contagion on buses and trains had to be relaxed. When contradictory goals came up against practical limits, it was the practical limits, rather than the contradictory goals, that were made to give way.

Cases continued to rise exponentially. By mid-October they had surpassed the highest level (108,257) reached in the first wave. Before the end of October, they had more than tripled again to 351,386. On 22 November, the second wave finally peaked at 805,947 current cases. That was a staggering 65-fold increase in a little more than three and a half months. One in seventy-five Italians was now ill was COVID-19. By the end of December, more than thirty-five thousand Italians had died in the second wave alone, far more than had died in the springtime first wave.

Almost as shocking was the Conte government's slow, weak and badly belated response to this second wave surge. Rome had long ago acknowledged, with the benefit of hindsight, that many more lives might have been saved in the spring had it moved it more quickly to impose regional blockades, lockdowns and quarantines in the earliest days of the first wave. Those costly spring delays consisted of days, or at most weeks, and they came at a time when not much was understood about the virus's pattern of contagion and the nature of community spread.

Yet in the fall, Rome let weeks and months of exponential growth go by without mounting a suitably energetic response. With regional governments, business lobbies and ordinary citizens pressing hard to avoid a second lockdown no matter how quickly cases, hospitalisations and deaths were rising, Rome waited until mid-October to act, only to find its politically brokered half measures repeatedly overrun by the rampant virus. More drastic restrictions were needed than limiting bar and restaurant service hours and curbing indoor dining. But until late November, efforts to please voters and business lobbies by preserving a semblance of normal Christmas shopping and travel seemed to take precedence over urgently stopping a runaway public health emergency that was once again straining hospitals and intensive care facilities to the breaking point, this time not just in northern regions but throughout Italy.

Compared to Rome's ultimately successful first-wave record, its second-wave performance suffered from a costly negative feedback loop of longer policy delays, more fractious party politics inside and outside the governing coalition, lessened government credibility and increasingly strained public patience with observing restrictive rules. Colder weather made things worse, but even given the added complications of indoor living, Italy's policy responses to the second wave fell grievously short of its first wave performance.

Throughout the first and second waves, one crucial type of democratic input was and remains sorely missing – the kind of public buy-in that could have added needed local nuances to restriction and reopening policies, sustained public confidence over the longer term and assured wider compliance with masking, distancing, reporting, contact tracing, quarantining and obeying travel restrictions over time. Big city mayors were generally consulted, but the mayors of smaller- and medium-sized cities were not even kept consistently informed. Traditional town meetings and council hearings would likely have been difficult, and sparsely attended, under pandemic conditions. But much more could have been done with Zoom and other technologies that kept cabinet members, scientific advisers and regional presidents in near daily touch. If we can conduct schools online we should be able to practice democracy online.

Maps of Italy's Regions. Source: Wikipedia.com

Italy's Pleas, the Early Absence of EU Solidarity, and the Special European Council Response, 17–21 July 2020, Response

EU governance has changed since the 1950 Schuman Plan created the European Coal and Steel Community (ECSC). The European project was born as a compromise between two theories: functionalism (Mitrany, 1966) and federalism (Milward, 1984). Both were viewed as alternatives to the nationalism the project's founders rejected, seeing it as a consequence of the refusal of nationalism, seen as the root of the recent wars in Europe. To achieve a period of enduring peace, the two main theories proposed different methods. Functionalism proposed the creation of separated international functional agencies to preside over one specific area. Federalism, as suggested by Altiero Spinelli in his Manifesto of Ventotene (Per un Europa libera e unita. Il Manifesto di Ventotene, 2017), proposed instead the creation of a European Federation. The underlying idea of both approaches was that post-war Europe should be rebuilt avoiding the creation of 'nation-states' as before the war to avoid rekindling rivalries between European states, and perhaps another war in the future. Spinelli's Manifesto was adopted by the Union of European Federalists, founded in 1946, and became the core of the ideas of a federal Europe (Bache et al., 2015: 8). The concept eventually brought forward by the French and German governments in drafting the Schuman Plan, under the auspices of Jean Monnet, was a mixture of both approaches and can be identified as functional-federalist. Monnet was aware of the economic inadequacy of the European nation-states and he thought that the best way to reconstruct a dynamic post-war Europe was to create a large common market (Monnet, 1962: 205). According to Monnet, the free-market system was not the best idea for Europe. It needed to be guided by supranational institutions able to adopt common economic policies and reasonable planning procedures. The creation of the ECSC, and later of the European Economic Community, and lately of the EU generated a full-scale debate among academics over several positions in which the evolution of the European project could be situated: neofunctionalism (Haas, 1958; Keohane and Nye, 1989), intergovernmentalism (Hoffmann, 1964, 1966), liberal intergovernmentalism (Moravcsik, 1993) and supranational governance (Stone Sweet and Sandholtz, 1997) to cite the most famous. Over the past 70 years, the European project evolved from 6 member states to 27. The international scenario changed from the bipolarity of the Cold War to multipolarity of the post–Cold War era. The governance of the EU has evolved, and the hierarchy within the Union has dramatically changed over the years. The main subjects of the European functions at the project's origin and treaties beneath the Union have adjusted accordingly.

Looking at today's EU governance a critical point is the decision gap, which still exists in the EU despite the new institutional architecture designed by the Lisbon Treaty of 2007. As stated previously, the pandemic displayed, in its entirety, the lack of political cooperation in the EU (Fasanaro, 2020: 72–74) and underlined the necessity of a revival of political coordination over a set of closely interconnected subjects such as health, environment and climate change. Environmental policies were among the last to be created and moved under the European umbrella only in 1973. This belated consideration was the poor appeal of those policies to people, governments, and industries. Still, the significant impact of climate change has increased these policies' importance over the years, and they are now considered paramount. It is important to note that even in such vital areas, the EU's response has sometimes been ineffective and, due to the internal legislative hierarchy, quite challenging to implement and less credible in the international scenario. Since 1990 the European Environment Agency has supervised, informed and monitored environmental policies but the agency's proposals still must pass through the hands of the commission, of the member states and partially of the European Parliament (https://www.eea.europa.eu/). Besides environment and climate change, another important point is the fragility of European borders, which can be a physical barrier for people but not for pollution.

The outbreak of the novel coronavirus pandemic posed several problems for the future relevance of the EU and its endurance. The federal-functionalist model created by Jean Monnet has been overwhelmed by the challenges now facing the EU. Another deep and more audacious reform is now clearly required, perhaps with the federalisation of some functions that cannot be effectively carried out through today's excessively divided and differentiated national health systems. The Italian National Health Service (SSN), administered at regional level and too differentiated, is a vivid example of the necessity of viable reforms perhaps built at the European level. Besides the pandemic, the departure of the United Kingdom from the EU poses a serious challenge for the future of the European project. The coronavirus and the Brexit are raw nerves of EU cohesion and are the two sides of the same coin. The EU's lack of response to the pandemic generated a wave of doubt and disaffection towards the European institutions, while the exit of such an important member state may prove, should it succeed, that life is possible beyond the EU.

Of course, the Union is not in immediate danger, but it is vital that its members inject new vitality, new programmes, new tasks, a new raison d'être into the project in order to rekindle the European dream for the most disenchanted Europeans – the young people who are the necessary pillar for the future. Young people can be the foundation for building bottom-up projects of renewal of the European institutions. These must be renewed, since if we deeply look into one of the major consequences of the pandemic, besides the failure of the health services, we find the jeopardising of democratic processes. Parliaments, including the European Parliament, partly due to physical distances and lack of communication, played a minor and sometimes non-existent role in deciding a strategy for fighting the virus, with all the decision-making left to unsupervised governments and extra-governmental bodies. Citizens felt undefended by Parliaments' checks and balances. A lesson must be drawn for the future in order to regain sufficient space for the Europe's people in the decision-making process. Year 2020 can be remembered as the year of pan-European disillusionment, or alternatively a low point from which the young people can reshape their spaces and rebuild their European future together (Rossi and Zuddas, 2020). During European history there have always been points of fracture, which sometimes provided the occasion for a new constructive impulse. Will the COVID-19 crisis be one of those turnaround moments?

Since the outbreak of the novel coronavirus the EU moved in two directions: one practical, the other political. The EU commissioner for Health and Food Safety since January 2020 alerted the member states to report immediately to the EU the information and share analyses about the virus. The first meeting at the EU level occurred in mid-January at the Health Directorate-General where the

Health and Security Committee evaluated a low risk of virus spreading in the EU. The European Centre for Disease Prevention and Control stated that there was not enough information to declare an emergency in the whole EU, noting that the Chinese city of Wuhan, centre of the infection, had direct flights with France, Italy and the United Kingdom, confirming that there were no instructions for the member states to take action.

After the outbreak of the first case in Europe, on 24 January, the EU activated the EU Civil Protection Mechanism for the repatriation of EU citizens from China and an appeal was made in order to find scientific solutions through the funding of a special Horizon 2020 programme dedicated to Sars-Cov2. Despite this first alarm, the EU authorities did not seem to understand that coordination was needed. For an entire month, the EU Commission and member states continued to underestimate the virus circulation in Europe, concentrating their efforts on repatriating citizens and helping China with medical devices. Only at the end of February, after a massive virus outbreak in Italy, the European Commission started a procedure, according to a Resolution dated 2010, for a joint procurement of medical devices on behalf of the European member states. The 2010 Resolution was agreed after the H1N1 pandemic when the council adopted a draft directive concerning the application of patients' rights in cross-border healthcare and set out a series of countermeasures to be ready in case of a future pandemic, particularly with the development of a vaccine.

The worsening crisis in Europe prompted EU member states to stop flights with China and other countries affected. The consequence was a severe threat to the Schengen Treaty when member states started to close borders to other European countries, notably Italy, thereby de facto suspending the Schengen Treaty. At that point, the Commission decided to issue guidelines to avoid significant disruptions to the internal borders, with the idea of sealing off the external borders, therefore protecting the Schengen principle and saving the right to have controls among member states in case of exceptional circumstances. This last point was of paramount concern to the commission since the Founding Fathers of the European project imagined Europe without internal borders. Europe is a very old land that only recently is appearing united on the international scene, where once there were rival empires, now there are the states, but there is also a new entity, the EU whose internal borders can be the worst danger and nightmare (Truzzi, 2017). The EU Commission also noted intense disorientation among European citizens about the EU response after the crisis, particularly in Italy, whose citizens felt abandoned by the EU authorities. Consequently, President Ursula von der Leyen explained the European Commission's actions, and with a message primarily directed towards the Italian people, reassured citizens that the EU was giving its solidarity support to surmount the pandemic together.

The deterioration of the economic situation in spring 2020 convinced the EU to drop existing budget constraints to intervene effectively with economic measures. Despite all these efforts, the EU is undergoing a deep crisis in the perception of its citizens. The popular national perception was that member states, each of which was in lockdown with the notable exception of Sweden, were left alone fighting the pandemic. There is now a perception that the EU is moving forward, although slowly, with the agreement of the states. The European Commission decided on extensive assistance proposing to activate the EU's Emergency Support Instrument to help the healthcare systems of EU member states in their fight against the coronavirus pandemic with an injection of 2,364.3 billion Euros (540 billion of funds already in place for the three safety nets, for workers, for businesses and for member states, 1074.3 billion for the budget 2021–27 and 750 billion of recovery effort) even with the fierce opposition of the 'frugal four'.

Looking at events, the EU acted as a mere support for the member states without any real coordinating role or proposing impetus. For instance, only in mid-April 2020 did the EU launch a scientific platform to collect data about the novel coronavirus to rally the efforts of the scientific community and to speed up the research for a vaccine or a cure. A major side effect of the pandemic was the crisis caused to families, mostly affected in their income, due to the severe lockdowns, subsequent job market failure and drop of spending levels. Therefore, the commission decided to adopt a package to help facilitate bank lending to households and businesses throughout the EU. The aim of this package was to ensure that banks could continue to lend money to support the economy and help mitigate the significant economic impact of the coronavirus pandemic. Another significant EU intervention has been to ease regulations on state aid, which were partly waived by the commission on 30 April, with a detailed list of permissions given to the member states. Italy, particularly, applied for a list of measures to help enterprises in crisis using this temporary framework. The assistance scheme is for companies registered in Italy whose activities have been particularly affected by the coronavirus outbreak. The aid will take the form of direct grants, aimed at supporting companies facing liquidity shortages and ensuring the continuation of their activities. This assistance is directed towards several fields of operation.

Clearly, the EU was more comfortable trying to have a coordinating role among the member states than providing an impetus to transform the larger context of EU governance as the pandemic intensified. What the EU authorities tried to do was to save the idea of a common border by giving expert advice to member states, gradually to reopen their borders after their closure as the pandemic worsened, in order to save the Schengen spirit. The commission gave recommendations and advice to resume travels within the EU and outside, thereby allowing people to join again with friends and family.

The first aim of this policy was to help the tourism sector, which was highly affected by the pandemic, while also protecting the health of citizens as well as providing advice regarding general security.

Another field where the EU decided to intervene has been that of combating fake news and disinformation. The pandemic has been followed by a massive impact of fake news or misleading information with attempts by foreign countries to influence EU citizens and public debates in the EU. The EU High Representative, on behalf of the commission, introduced a response and actions to tackle misinformation about the pandemic, most particularly about the EU response.

The coronavirus pandemic seems to be a stress test for the EU, member states, and citizens. The crisis undermined the idea of an EU as a common family of people and nations. The EU did not succeed even in having a unique position in setting basic rights for people who felt their democratic liberties were under threat. The EU member states had to fight alone against the COVID-19 pandemic. European citizens felt like they were no longer part of a peace and stability project. The EU response to the pandemic seems to be another fracture point in Europe's history and with lessons to learn for the future development of the European common project. Member states and citizens should open a further debate over the future, especially after the departure of the United Kingdom from the Union, deciding whether it is worthwhile to reintroduce Altiero Spinelli's historic project of a federal Europe (Glencross and Trechsel, 2010).

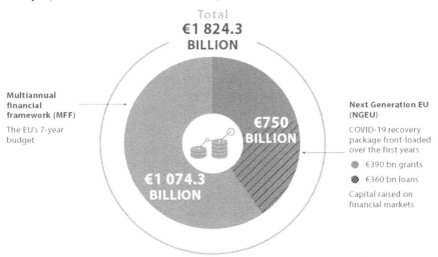

EU budget 2021-2027 and recovery plan. Source: https://www.consilium.europa.eu/en/infographics/recovery-plan-mff-2021-2027/

Conclusion

A lesson can be drawn from this extraordinary period of the novel coronavirus pandemic during which the normal course of life for people and states has been shaken to its foundations. The EU must rethink its internal governance as well as the relationships with and among member states. The pandemic crisis reveals the frailties of the decision chain, the communication system and the perception Italian citizens have of the EU. This last aspect must be looked at with careful attention as Italians and Europeans no longer feel part of a common project. It is imperative to set forth a new series of common rules and fields of intervention. As stated previously, the federal-functionalist model created at the beginning of the European project no longer works. The larger size and diversity of interests in the Union overwhelm European institutions created for an earlier time. The different challenges that a globalised world introduces call for a new approach to European integration. Public health and climate change have something in common. These policies must be tackled at the European level by creating an agile federal system, which is able to govern for and by the people through decision-making processes that connect directly to society. The EU's future is younger generations presently living through a period of turmoil caused by the uncertainties of climate change and global pandemic. Future generations need to be placed at the centre of the European relaunch. The Green Deal and European Action for Young People should be a priority for member states in the Next Generation EU program. In the early twenty-first century, the EU27 have the occasion to demonstrate that the European dream is still not accomplished. There are many pages to write and more adventures to live in a community that aspires to its own experience of unity in diversity. The pandemic, a disease fed by globalisation with its border crossings, has led to a loss of freedom of movement with decisions taken by technocrats who believe in their right to impose restrictions in the service of democracy. As we explain, such decisions taken in the name of the people must be negotiated, including citizens with their buy-in, rather than implemented as thunderbolts from Zeus at the apex of the Italian and European political systems.

References

Acharya, A. and Buzan, B. (2019). *The Making of Global International Relations: Origins and Evolution of IR at Its Centenary.* Cambridge: Cambridge University Press.

Aliber, R. Z. and Kindleberger, C. P. (2015). *Manias, Panics and Crashes: A History of Financial Crises.* Houndmills, Basingstoke, Hampshire; New York: Palgrave Macmillan.

Aron, R. (2003). *Peace and War: A Theory of International Relations.* New Brunswick, NJ; London: Transaction.

Bache, I., Bulmer, S., George, S. and Parker, O. (2015). *Politics in the European Union.* Oxford: Oxford University Press.

Baldwin, D. A. (1993). *Neorealism and Neoliberalism: The Contemporary Debate.* New York: Columbia University Press.

Borrell, J. (2020). Schuman Day in 2020 – My Personal Take on the European Idea [Online]. *European American Chamber of Commerce.* Available at: https://eaccny.com/news/chapternews/schuman-day-in-2020-my-personal-take-on-the-european-idea/.

Bremmer, I. (2012). *Every Nation for Itself: Winners and Losers in a G-Zero World.* New York: Penguin Books Ltd.

Chollet, D. H. and Goldgeier, J. M. (2008). *America Between the Wars: From 11/9 to 9/11: The Misunderstood Years Between the Fall of the Berlin Wall and the Start of the War on Terror.* New York: BBS Publicaffairs.

Cohen-Tanugi, L (2008). *The Shape of the World to Come: Charting the Geopolitics of a New Century.* New York; Chichester: Columbia University Press.

Conservation International. (2020). 2020 Impact Report [Online]. Available at: https://www.conservation.org/about/2020-impact-report.

DePorte, A. W. (1979). *Europe Between the Superpowers: The Enduring Balance.* New Haven: Yale University Press.

Fasanaro, Laura. (2020). Complessità e cambiamento nell'Unione Europea degli anni Duemila. La visione di Romano Prodi e il ruolo della Commissione. In: Laschi Giuliana, Calandri Elena and Paoli Simone (Eds.), *L'Europa adulta. Attori, ragioni e sfide all'Atto Unico alla Brexit.* Bologna: Il Mulino.

Ferguson, N (2019). *The Square and the Tower: Networks and Power, From the Freemasons to Facebook.* New York: Penguin Press, An Imprint of Penguin Random House LLC.

Fukuyama, F. (1996). *Trust: The Social Virtues and the Creation of Prosperity.* New York: Free Press Paperbacks.

Gansky, L. (2010). *The Mesh: Why the Future of Business is Sharing.* New York, NY: Penguin Group.

Garavaglia, C., Sancino, A. and Trivellato, B. (2020). Italian Mayors and the Management of COVID-19: Adaptive Leadership for Organizing Local Governance. *Eurasian Geography and Economics* 62(1): 76–92.

Gillingham, J. (1991). Jean Monnet and the European Coal and Steel Community: A Preliminary Appraisal. *Jean Monnet*: 129–162.

Glencross, A. and Trechsel, A. H. (2010). *EU Federalism and Constitutionalism: The Legacy of Altiero Spinelli.* Lanham, MD: Lexington Books.

Governo Italiano Presidenza del Consiglio dei Ministri. (2020). Coronavirus, le misure adottate dal Governo [Online] Available at: http://www.governo.it/it/coronavirus-misure-del-governo.

Guinto, R. (2020). COVID-19: Reimagining the Political Economy of Planetary Health [Online]. Coronavirus (COVID-19) Blog Posts Collection – BMJ Journals. Available at: https://blogs.bmj.com/covid-19/2020/04/27/covid-19-reimagining-the-political-economy-of-planetary-health/.

Haas, E. B. (1958). *The Uniting of Europe: Political, Social, and Economic Forces 1950–1957.* Stanford: Stanford University Press.

Harari, S. and Vitacca, M. (2020). COVID-19 Spread: The Italian Case. *Respiratory Medicine and Research* 78: 100771.

Hayes, P. and Roth, J. K. (2012). *The Oxford Handbook of Holocaust Studies.* Oxford: Oxford University Press.

Hoffmann, S. (1966). *Obstinate or Obsolete? The Fate of the Nation-State and the Case of Western Europe.* S.L.: S.N.

Hoffmann, S. (1977). An American Social Science: International Relations. *Daedulus* Vol. 106 No. 3: 41–60.

Horowitz, J. (2020). Comic Insults Aside, Mayors Act as Sentinels in Italy's Coronavirus Tragedy. *The New York Times*, 26 April. Available at: https://www.nytimes.com/2020/04/26/world/europe/italy-mayors-coronavirus.html.

International Rescue Committee (IRC). Italy [Online]. Available at: https://www.rescue.org/country/italy.

Kapuściński, R. (2009). *The Other.* New York: Verso.

Keohane, R. O. and Nye, J. S. (1989). *Power and Interdependence.* London: HarperCollins, Cop.

Krastev, I. (2020). Europe's Pandemic Politics: How the Virus Has Changed the Public's Worldview [Online]. *European Council on Foreign Relations.* Available at: https://ecfr.eu/publication/europes_pandemic_politics_how_the_virus_has_changed_the_publics_worldview/.

Kupchan, C. A. (2010). *How Enemies Become Friends: The Sources of Stable Peace.* Princeton: Princeton University Press.

Leigh, J. (2020). *The Emergence of Global Power Politics: Imperialism, Modernity, and American Expansion 1870–1914.* PhD Thesis, The London School of Economics and Political Science (LSE).

Macmillan, M. (2020). *War: How Conflict Shaped Us.* New York: Random House.

Mazzucelli and Keith. (2020). *New York University, International Relations in the Post-Cold War Era, Module Session.*

Micheal, L. (2020). Relaunch or Disintegration? What Covid-19 Means for the Future of Europe [Online]. The London School of Economics and Political Science. Available at: https://blogs.lse.ac.uk/europpblog/2020/12/14/relaunch-or-disintegration-what-covid-19-means-for-the-future-of-europe/.

Milward, A. (1984). *The Reconstruction of Western Europe 1945–51.* London: Methuen.

Mitrany, D. (1966). *A Working Peace System.* London: Oxford University Press.

Monnet, J. (1962). 'A Ferment of Change'. *JCMS: Journal of Common Market Studies* 1(3): 203–211.

Moravcsik, A. (1993). Preferences and Power in the European Community: A Liberal Intergovernmentalist Approach. *JCMS: Journal of Common Market Studies* 31(4): 473–524.

Paterlini, M. (2020). On the Front Lines of Coronavirus: The Italian Response to Covid-19. *BMJ*: m1065.

Rossi, C. and Zuddas, A. (2020). Le politiche dell'Unione europea per una maggiore partecipazione giovanile ai processi democratici. In: Barberis Giorgio (Ed.), *Libertà, uguaglianza, sicurezza. Un dibattito fra storia del pensiero e teoria politica.* Monticello: Ronzani Edizioni Scientifiche.

Sen, A. (2007). *Identity and Violence: The Illusion of Destiny.* London: Penguin.

Singer, J. D. (1960). International Conflict: Three Levels of Analysis. *World Politics* 12(3): 453–461. Available at: https://www.jstor.org/stable/2009401.

Slaughter, A. (2017). *The Chessboard and the Web: Strategies of Connection in a Networked World.* New Haven: Yale University Press.

Slobodian, Q. (2018). *Globalists: The End of Empire and the Birth of Neoliberalism.* Cambridge, MA: Harvard University Press.

Spinelli, Altiero and Ernesto, Rossi. (2017). *Per un'Europa Libera e Unita.* Il Manifesto di Ventotene, Tipografia Print, Monterotondo.

Statista. (2020). Italy: Coronavirus (COVID-19) Deaths 2020 [Online]. Available at: https://www.statista.com/statistics/1104964/coronavirus-deaths-since-february-italy/.v

Stern, F. (2007). *Five Germanys I Have Known*. New York: Farrar, Straus and Giroux.

Sweet, A. S. and Sandholtz, W. (1997). European Integration and Supranational Governance. *Journal of European Public Policy* 4(3): 297–317.

Truzzi, M. (2017). *Sui Confini. Europa, un viaggio sulle frontiere*. Roma: Exorma.

Unger, D. (2020). Op-Ed: I'm an American in Italy. We're on Coronavirus Lockdown. It's Horrific [Online]. *Los Angeles Times*. Available at: https://www.latimes.com/opinion/story/2020-03-11/coronavirus-italy-quarantine-infection.

Waltz, K. N. (1959). *Man, the State, and War*. New York: Columbia University Press.

Waltz, K. N. (1979). *Theory of International Politics*. Long Grove, IL: Waveland Press.

WE Prison Fellowship. (2016). *Warden Exchange, Third Residency and Graduation*. Minneapolis, MN.

Youtube. (2008). Laurent Cohen-Tanugi: It's a Multi-Polar World [Online]. Available at: https://www.youtube.com/watch?v=EghlN8yV_OE.

Zuboff, S. (2019). *The Age of Surveillance Capitalism: The Fight for a Human Future at the New Frontier of Power*. New York: PublicAffairs.

Chapter 4

ROMA LIVES MATTER UNDER THE COVID-19 PANDEMIC: BUT MORE SO FOR POPULIST NATIONALISM

Andras L. Pap[1]

The aim of this chapter[2] is to provide an interpretative framework for scapegoating anti-Roma rhetoric and over-policing throughout Europe, targeting

---

1 Research Professor, Centre for Social Sciences, Institute for Legal Studies; Professor, Eötvös University (ELTE), Faculty of Business Economics; Budapest, Hungary; Adjunct (Recurrent Visiting) Professor, Central European University, Vienna, Austria.
2 The research was supported by the DEMOS – Democratic efficacy and the varieties of populism in Europe' H2020 RIA project, as well as the 129018, 129245 and 134962 Hungarian National Research and Innovation Grants.

a minority group which is already disproportionally affected by virus. The case study is situated in the context of the American 'Black Lives Matter' movement, as well as current debates on conceptualising and operationalising race and ethnicity, ethno-racial disparities in the effects of the COVID-19 pandemic as well as various forms of penal populism and nationalism, and shows that the virus exacerbates social inequalities. The chapter begins with outlining the social science context of the inquiry. The points of reference include conceptualising and operationalising race, ethnicity and membership in national groups/communities, in particular in the field of medicine; the discursive and institutional framework of populism, in particular penal populism and penal nationalism; and mapping out four distinct ways in how the virus may affect certain groups incommensurately and lead to systemic and institutional discrimination. This is followed by an overview of the status of Roma in Europe. The subsequent section provides a case study of Hungary for conceptualising the Roma at the intersection of a racial, cultural or socio-economic minority, as well as an overview of populist policing strategies. The final section shows how Roma have been targeted by populist political rhetoric and securitising law enforcement in lieu of the pandemic.

The Social Science Context

The social science context of anti-Roma rhetoric and over-policing members of the Roma community throughout Europe (and Central-Eastern Europe in particular) is manifold. The first section is aimed at dissecting and providing an overview.

Black Lives Matter vs. Roma Lives Matter

There is a significant interest in analysing the recent uprise of the Black Lives Matter movement in lieu of the COVID-19 crisis (McCrudden, 2020), highlighting how institutional discrimination within and beyond law enforcement disproportionately burdens African Americans and augments the impact of the pandemic. Patterns of social marginalisation and institutional discrimination in the criminal justice system and in particular within the operation of the law enforcement machinery are parallel in lieu of the African American and the European Roma community. However, unlike in the case of African Americans, as the fifth section will show, the spread of the COVID-19 virus brought a surge in targeted anti-Roma rhetoric and scapegoating, often coupled with disproportionate law enforcement action enforcing social distancing and lockdown measures. This rhetoric includes an open ethno-racial and culturalist essentialism securitising Roma 'culture' and lifestyle as a threat for spreading the virus.

Conceptualising and operationalising race and ethnicity

A second point of reference for the case study is the broader project (the author is engaged in) deciphering legal approaches to conceptualising and operationalising race, ethnicity and membership in national groups/communities. Here the field of medicine opens a thrilling angle of scrutiny. In social sciences the (socially) constructed nature of these categories is a given, uncontested dogma, and partly due to privacy regimes, there is also a reluctance in law and policy-making to provide strict definitions for ethno-racial concepts. However, it poses a significant challenge that an ambiguity in terms of the targeted communities and membership boundaries for minority protection mechanisms and social inclusion measures may hinder the achievement of policy goals, and the potential for abuse can open avenues for further discrimination and marginalisation. The past years did bring changes in how the meaning of the terms of national and ethno-racial identity is assigned and conceptualised in social sciences and humanities and to a certain degree in politics and law. The shift centres on the destabilisation of categorical frameworks, where race and ethnicity (and gender) as social classifications apparently seem to have lost stability, self-evidence and clarity, thus transracial (like transgender) people seem to legitimately move between ethno-racial (and gender) categories.

This trend is epiphanised by the multiracial movement, the growing body of literature on 'racial passing' (see, for example, Hobbs, 2014; Chanbonpin, 2015; Hunter, 2011; Ignatiev and Garvey, 1996; Ignatiev, 1995; Kelly and Nagel, 2002; Kennedy, 2003; Overall and John, 2004) and Brubaker's (2016b) recent works on 'racial migration', which explores how race and gender are conceptualised as more similar than different in the sense that the juxtaposition of the fluidity and artificiality of gender with the immutability and givenness of race is being questioned (also see Sharfstein, 2007). Reflecting on the Rachel Dolezal case (see, for example, Brubaker, 2016a, 414–48),[3] Brubaker

---

3 The highly publicized 2015 case concerned the 37-year-old Rachel Dolezal, American civil rights activist and former African studies instructor, and president of the National Association for the Advancement of Colored People chapter in Spokane, Washington, when she resigned following allegations of having committed cultural appropriation and fraud, after her white parents stating publicly that Dolezal is a white woman passing as black. Dolezal claimed that her racial identity is genuine, albeit not based on biology or ancestry, as she was born white. See, for example, Brubaker (2016a, 414–48).

uses trans narratives as a 'master story', arguing that race and ethnicity may actually be additional forms of identity and social practice that are fluid in the ways that chosen identities are (like work, marriage, bearing children, religion, or the management or transformation of bodies). 'Transracial people' can legitimately move between ethno-racial categories (Brubaker, 2016a, 414–48). The colour line may be sharp and rigidly policed in theory, but is often blurred and porous in practice. Even multiple forms of betweenness or new categories outside existing frameworks can be conceptualised, blending and blurring putative objectivity with affiliative self-fashioning; race, like gender, is 'something we do rather something we have' (Brubaker, 2016b). As Brubaker points out, even the core questions are multilayered: Do race and ethnicity have a fixed meaning susceptible to verification or are these categories expressive and affiliative through self-discovery and public disclosure? Voluntarists, constructivists and liminals argue over whether one can change 'genuine' racial identity (or even reject the existence or legitimacy of such categorisation) or if it is only the social validation of particular public expressions that can be altered. Brubaker (2016a, 414–48) also emphasises that illuminative as the race–gender parallel is, racial identity undoubtedly has supra-individual elements such as biogenetic and trans-generational history; genealogical facts of ancestry; social facts of classification systems and categorisation practices; and historical facts of enslavement, oppression and discrimination. Social scientists emphasise the lack of linguistic and conceptual resources, cultural tools and proper vocabulary for thinking about racial identity in subjectivist-individualist terms, as an inner essence independent of the body and knowable only to the individual. Even the conceptual multiplication of sex and gender is absent from discussions on race or ethnicity (Brubaker, 2016a, 414–48; for more also Pap, 2017).

In sum, the starting dilemma is that social sciences in an increasing fashion deconstruct the notions of 'nationality' (in the minority context) race, ethnicity and identity, removing the false image of 'objective' criteria defining belonging to these groups. At the same time law intensively operates with them, ignoring that the concepts used in the legal, normative texts no longer have (if they ever had) a fixed meaning, therefore the target group of any policy measure defined by the law becomes blurred and subject to abuse (both by the implementing agency and by the potential beneficiaries).

Membership in racial and ethno-national communities also raises a number of questions related to data protection and privacy. In Europe, challenges raise in regard to the new data protection regime of the European Union. (Regulation (EU) 2016/679 of the European Parliament and of the Council of 27 April 2016 on the protection of natural persons with regard to the processing of personal data and on the free movement of such data, and repealing

Directive 95/46/EC (General Data Protection Regulation)). Race, ethnicity and national origins are sensitive data, and revealing is subject to either explicit legal authorisation or the consent of the data subject.

The lack of solid and up-to-date vocabulary is particularly stark in the field of law. It should be taken into account that law, especially human rights law, habitually operates with the concepts of race, ethnicity and nationality when setting forth standards for the recognition of collective rights, protection from discrimination, establishing criteria for asylum, or labelling actions as genocide, or requiring a 'genuine link' in citizenship law, without actually providing definitions for these groups or of membership criteria within these legal constructs.

Ethno-racial disparities in the effects of the COVID-19 pandemic not only elevated the relevance of data collection in lieu of the virus, but also rebooted debates on algorithmic discrimination in pharmacology or transplantation (see, for example, Vyas et al., 2020 or Kolata, 2020), as well as the question of whether vaccine trial contractors enrol enough minorities (Reuters, 2020), or whether policies in distributing vaccines should involve ethno-racial measures to counterbalance the above disparities. The issue of how approaches to race and ethnicity in the medical field relate to social science, and legal and policy conceptualisation, is, hence, a fascinating one, where analysis and scholarship (see, for example, Kazuko and Vacano, 2018), be it general or area specific, are still scarce (Twohey, 2020).

'Classic' and benevolent penal populism

The third contextual dimension of the case study is the discursive and institutional framework of populism, in particular penal populism and penal nationalism. These can operationalise in three distinct forms. The traditional, 'classic' form of penal law enforcement and criminal policy-related populism (in rhetoric and/or in policy-making) involves singling out and othering racially or ethno-culturally defined internal or external groups as enemies. In my recent works (Pap, 2020), I identified a second and third, more intricate type of penal populism. The second pertains to the proliferation of protected groups, which is arguably a form of identity politics-led populism. The third, elaborated in the fourth section, pertains to policies and legislation that are not, and not even intended to be enforced, and mostly serve the purpose of paying 'legislative lip service' to the international community, or international organisations (or the European Union, in particular), or to be used as a bargaining chip in international relations (as a point of reference in negotiating with neighbouring states where large ethnic kin populations reside). Let us elaborate on these shortly.

In regard to the former case, the inquiry rests on six premises. The starting point is the claim that hate crimes are and should be conceptualised as minority and not identity protection mechanisms. Second, it is further contended that legislators should enumerate all potential (mostly visible, immutable, fundamental) protected characteristics that are habitually connected to the aforementioned vulnerability, as criminal law is very different from anti-discrimination law. In anti-discrimination legislation, the more protected characteristics included, the better, the more inclusive and potent the law will be, in fact even open-ended lists are progressive, allowing to outlaw discrimination for previously undefined 'other' characteristics. In criminal law, less is more: legal certainty requires narrowly tailored, thoroughly circumscribed definitions, otherwise the 'nullum crimen sine lege', 'no crime without law (legislation)' principle would be violated. Thus, criminal legislation should resist the identity politics-driven race and lobby for recognising more and more identities and should not give in to accusations of unethical or politically insensitive creation of a hierarchy of valued identities, as, for example, violence and vandalism is a criminal offence, and victims are not unprotected or abandoned even if no special hate crime provisions are applied in their case. If we expand the list of protected characteristics, we actually marginalise the vulnerable ones by relativising their vulnerability. As a third claim, it is also argued that the proliferation of protected characteristics is where identity politics turn into a form of penal populism. Fourth, it is furthermore argued that hate crime legislation catering to identity protection can open the gate for what Lynne Haney (2016) calls penal nationalism, a special form of penal populism, which can equate punitiveness with a national sovereignty and protection along a variety of forms for reimagining community and the lines of social exclusion. Fifth, it is also contended that the systematic failure to apply criminal legislation, in line with jurisprudence and international case law, actually amounts to a form of institutional discrimination, a phenomenon widely documented by domestic and international organisations. Here, desuetude inflates normativity of the legal system, and hence raises rule of law concerns. Thus, finally the research introduces the concept of 'benevolent populism', for the broadening of the concept of populism by including legislation that may have the international community or international organisations as reference points, when introducing legislation that is not intended to be enforced. In a similar vein, Godzisz (2019, 291–306) used the theory of Europeanisation as an explanatory frame (and 'fundamentals first' as an operational guideline), explaining how hate crime laws are enacted as part of the democratisation process in the Balkans. This expands the reference point of populism beyond the national electorate (and within that, the 'silent majority') to international organisations or even regional/local pressure groups.

The other inquiry, to be elaborated below in the third section, using the example of Hungary, points out that conceptualising the multifaceted Roma community as an ethno-cultural one, and a commitment to connect ethno-cultural features with law enforcement tasks, is another form of an operationally empty legislative declaration, as in the specific context, ascribing to the principles to police 'multicultural communities' has few, if any operative consequences. This project, too, relies on the concept of 'benevolent populism', which here is applied for legislation that does not necessarily involve more severe social control, and which arguably has the international community or international organisations as reference points, when introducing legislation that is not, and not even intended to be enforced, partly because it is inapplicable and unsuitable per se. Legislation thus appears to be no more than a politically and public policy-wise low-cost, and mostly symbolic 'virtue-signalling' (albeit ideologically diffuse and incoherent). These cases show that the reference group of penal populism can also go beyond the 'silent majority', and populist legislation may include lobby groups as well; furthermore, populism in penal legislation can materialise in other forms than more stringent laws.

Systemic and institutional discrimination and the disproportionate effects of the COVID-19 virus

The fourth contextual dimension of the case study is the intersection of institutional discrimination (in particular in the field of law enforcement) and group-specific effects of the COVID-19 pandemic. A large body of scholarly literature and public discussion targets the disproportionate effect of the COVID-19 virus on minorities and vulnerable social groups. For analytic purposes, there are four distinct ways in how the virus may effect certain groups incommensurately.

The first scenario is when due to biological or cultural reasons, the virus will have a stronger effect on certain groups independently from social or state actions. For example, the elderly (see, for example, United Nations, 2020) or people with asthma (see, for example, Raterman, 2020) are more exposed and more vulnerable to COVID-19. Likewise, Catholics may be prone to more exposure, as attendance at the Sunday mass (which involves communal singing) is mandatory. Also people incarcerated or living in refugee camps or incarcerated in prisons, where social distancing is impossible, will be exposed to contamination more severely.

The second type involves emergency or healthcare measures that will automatically affect certain groups negatively. For example, for the hearing impaired, mandatory masks reduce communication channels (Taylor, 2020).

Social distancing or lockdown measures can interfere with religious practices and rituals, for example mourning and burial within a short time after death (see, for example, Stack, 2020). Also, with lockdowns, people with disabilities and homeless people will be affected more severely (Barnes and McDonnel, 2020; also see, for example, Bernstein et al., 2020; Sturm et al., 2020).

The third cluster refers to cases when the virus enlarges systemic marginalisation and vulnerability of certain social groups. For example, in the United States, the African American and Latino population is three times more prone to coronavirus contamination (not independently from weaker socio-economic position, greater exposure due to job market shares, more crowded housing and commuting facilities) and is twice as likely to die (also not independently from a generally worse health status, obesity and diabetes in particular) than whites (Oppel et al., 2020; also see, for example, Faleiro, 2020, or United Nations Human Rights Office of the High Commissioner, 2020b, or Cultural Survival, 2020). As the *Economist* reports, in England a black man is nearly four times more likely to die from the disease than a white man of a similar age; in the state of New York, in the first months of the pandemic, black and Hispanic children were more than twice as likely to lose a parent or caregiver to COVID-19 than those who were white or Asian. In Britain, all non-white groups (except Chinese women) have been more likely to contract and to die from COVID-19 than whites. In America, a 40-year-old Hispanic person is twelve times as likely to die as a forty-year-old white person. In São Paulo, Brazil's richest state, black people under the age of twenty are twice as likely to die from COVID-19 than their white counterparts. Sweden tallied deaths early in its epidemic and found that those born abroad were several times more likely to die than those born in Sweden. Bangladeshi men are three-and-a-half times more at risk of dying of COVID-19 than white men of the same age. (A lack of data on race hampers efforts to tackle inequalities, The Economist, 2020.) Women (and especially minority women) are also more severely affected by a heightened risk of unemployment (in the tourism and the garment sector, where they are overrepresented and more severely affected) (World Trade Organization News, 2020), extra burdens of domestic care and labour, face a drastic rise in intimate partner or gender-based violence (the UN estimates an increase of 15 million cases for every three months of lockdown) (CARE International and International Rescue Committee, 2020; see also Interpol, 2020), are more exposed to forced marriages and to more severe obstacles to social services (such as well prenatal care or access to crisis prevention centres). Unsafe abortions are in a surge and are often lethal (see, for example, Women Enabled International, 2020; Barnes and McDonnel, 2020). The virus is expected to cut off 13–44 million women from contraceptives and lead to an additional 1 million pregnancies

(CARE International, 2020). The virus brings a setback in various facets of development, for example, 2 million more cases of female genital mutilation (Save the Children's Resource Centre, 2020) and 4 million more child marriages (for more, see Orchid Project. Working Together to End Female Genital Cutting, 2020).

And finally, the fourth scenario concerns state action, either through over- or underperformance that disproportionally effects or targets certain groups. This could mean inappropriate access to healthcare services or overpolicing. An example for over-policing is how BAME people were fined more than white population under coronavirus laws Police in England (Busby and Gidda, 2020).

A Note on Methodology

Spatial limits of the chapter do not allow a further development or assessment of the issues raised in the contextualising framework. What follows is a brief overview of the status of Roma in Europe. Next comes the case study of Hungary for conceptualising the Roma at the intersection of a racial, cultural or socio-economic minority, as well as an overview of a controversial, arguably benevolent populist, policing strategy (applying a multicultural framework for the Roma). The subsequent section shows how Roma have been targeted by populist political rhetoric and securitising law enforcement policies in the COVID-19 era. Here examples will be brought from outside Hungary, as there no such relevant cases were reported. Yet, the models for conceptualisation and policies are pooled in the European space, hence theorising can be relevant. Also, the available date is yet scarce, and at the time of the submission of the chapter the COVID-19 crisis and pandemic is far from being over, and further developments need to be incorporated in the analysis in time.

Roma in Europe

The term 'Roma' is used as an umbrella term, encompassing a wide range of different people of Romani origin such as Roma, Sinti/Manush, Kale(Calé, Kaale), Romanichels and Boyash/Rudari. It also encompasses groups such as Ashkali, Egyptians, Yenish, Dom, Lom, Rom and Abdal, as well as traveller populations, including ethnic Yenish, travellers or those designated under the administrative term 'Gens du voyage', and people who identify as Gypsies, Tsiganes or Tziganes, without denying their specificities (EU Roma Strategic, 2020, 1). The term 'Roma' thus refers to heterogeneous groups, living in various countries under different social, economic, cultural and other conditions, and it denotes multifaceted subgroups that overlap, but are connected by historical roots, linguistic communalities and a shared experience of discrimination in relation to majority groups. 'Roma' is therefore a multidimensional term that corresponds to the multiple and fluid nature of Roma identity (Izsák, 2015, 2–3).

Originating from India a millennium ago, Roma have dispersed worldwide and there are no official or reliable statistics on the global population (Izsák, 2015, 3–4).[4] Roma are the largest ethnic minority in the region and 6 million reside within the European Union (Izsák, 2015, 2–3; Jovanovic, 2020).[5] Most Roma, approximately 11 million, live in Europe, where their presence dates back to the fourteenth century. In many regions, Roma were forced into slavery, a practice which continued into the nineteenth century in Romania. In the 1930s, the Nazis in Germany saw Roma as 'racially inferior' and murdered hundreds of thousands during World War II. Roma continued to be discriminated against and oppressed. For example, between the 1970s and 1990s, the Czech Republic and Slovakia sterilised around ninety thousand Romani women against their will (Motoc, 2015).

According to a 2016 survey by the European Union Agency for Fundamental Rights (FRA), 80 per cent of Roma are at risk of poverty compared with an EU average of 17 per cent. Thirty per cent live in households with no tap water and 46 per cent have no indoor toilet, shower or bathroom; 30 per cent of Roma children live in households where someone went to bed hungry at least once in the previous month; 53 per cent of young Roma children attend

---

4 In Turkey, data indicates that the Roma population ranges from 500,000 to 5 million. In Latin America, Roma have been arriving from Europe since the beginning of European colonization, and a 1991 study by the United Nations Educational, Scientific and Cultural Organization estimated the population to be approximately 1,500,000. Recent government data indicates a population of over half a million Roma in Brazil. It is generally accepted that approximately 1 million Roma live in North America today; however, that data is incomplete, as the census in the United States does not include Roma as a category. Roma groups are also present in Central Asian countries, where they are known collectively as Lyuli. Unofficial estimates indicate there may be significant populations in Egypt, the Islamic Republic of Iran, Iraq, Israel, Jordan, Lebanon, the Occupied Palestinian Territory and the Syrian Arab Republic (Izsák, 2015, 3–4).
5 (Izsák, 2015, 2–3). As the director of the Open Society Foundation Roma Initiatives Office explains, if the Roma were to live in one country in the EU, without counting the Roma in the candidate countries, it would have a population of 6 million – bigger than Denmark or Finland or another ten member states. Apart from its size, the youthfulness of the Roma population makes it even more relevant. As for demographics, for example, in Hungary, the number of Roma below 15 years old is three to four times higher than the number of non-Roma in that group. In Romania, children under 15 – the new generation of labour market entrants – make up almost 40 per cent of the total Roma population, compared to 15 per cent among the general population (Jovanovic, 2020).

early childhood education, often less than half the proportion of children their age from the general population in the same country; only 30 per cent of the Roma surveyed are in paid work, compared with the average EU employment rate for 2015 of 70 per cent; 41 per cent of Roma feel they have been discriminated against over the past five years in everyday situations such as looking for work, at work, housing, health and education; and 82 per cent of Roma are unaware of organisations offering support to victims of discrimination (FRA, 2018a). The European Commission's Eurobarometer survey on discrimination in Europe, conducted in 2015, confirms the persistence of anti-Roma prejudice. On average (in the EU-28), 20 per cent of the respondents would feel uncomfortable if one of their colleagues at work were Roma. Less than half (45 per cent) would be comfortable or indifferent if their son or daughter had a relationship with a Roma person, and only 18 per cent have friends or acquaintances who are Roma (FRA, 2018b).

Conceptual and Policy Inconsistencies: The Hungarian Case

Conceptualisation and policy dilemmas

Given the multifaceted nature of Roma communities, the conceptualisation of 'what the Roma are' and how Roma policies should be designed is a core question in Europe. Targeting will need to be completely different when referencing rights holders for minority (cultural) rights, beneficiaries of social inclusion policies or victims of discrimination. The Hungarian case will show how both domestic and EU policymakers appear to be insensitive to the difference between social inclusion measures on the one hand, a minority rights framework that enhances minority identity on the other, and anti-discrimination measures protecting vulnerable groups. In particular, here the question will be whether 'Roma' refer to a social class, a race, an ethnicity or a national minority?

In social sciences and law, the purpose of typologies and classification is to help us understand the internal logic and substance of concepts and institutions. As shown before, *race* is a controversial category, and it is generally not considered to be a fruitful analytical concept in the social sciences, where it is widely understood to be a social construct rather than a biological trait without a theoretically or politically uniform definition (see, for example, Tajfel, 1981). Legal instruments for the most part identify race with physical appearance, and they put perception and external classifications in the centre when prohibiting discrimination or violence (on *racial* grounds). In this, race is rarely distinguished from *ethnicity*, and the two terms are often used interchangeably by lawmakers (and drafters of international documents) and most of all by judicial bodies. Ethnic minorities, however, are more complex groups. While many of their claims are grounded in the anti-discrimination rhetoric employed by racial minorities, some 'ethnically defined' groups, such as the Roma, might also have similar cultural claims (and protections) that national minorities might make. The international legal terminology habitually differentiates between the two groups on the grounds that ethnic minorities are different from national minorities in the sense that they do not have nation-states as national homelands (Hannum, 2000, 405–19). In this way, ethnic minorities are a sort of hybrid categorisation, blending, and often mirroring, the claims made by racial and national groups.

As for 'national minorities', the third group, the 1993 recommendation (No. 1201) of the Parliamentary Assembly of the Council of Europe in an additional protocol regarding the rights of national minorities in the European Convention on Human Rights holds: '"National minority" refers to a group of persons in a state who: reside on the territory of that state and are citizens thereof; maintain longstanding, firm and lasting ties with that state; display distinctive ethnic, cultural, religious or linguistic characteristics; are sufficiently representative, although smaller in number than the rest of the population of that state or of a region of that state; are motivated by a concern to preserve together that which constitutes their common identity, including their culture, their traditions, their religion or their language'. National minorities' claims for collective rights thus bypass the anti-discriminatory logic and seek recognition of cultural and political rights, especially autonomy and the toleration of various cultural practices that differ from the majority's and which often require formal exceptions from generally applicable norms and regulations.[6]

These conceptualisations cannot be separated from discussions concerning what concept of social justice and equality decision-makers are endorsing in regard to a given community. McCrudden (2005) suggests that there are at least four different meanings of equality, and what might be suitable in one context might not be suitable in another. First, what he calls the 'individual justice model' focuses on merit, efficiency and achievement and aims to *reduce discrimination*. Second, the 'group justice model' concentrates on outcomes and on the improvement of the relative positions of particular groups, with

---

[6] According to Will Kymlicka (2001), cultural minorities can be divided into nations and ethnicities. The former is a historical community, more or less institutionally complete, occupying a given territory or homeland, and sharing a distinct language or culture, while the latter is a group with common cultural origins but whose members do not constitute an institutionally complete society concentrated in one territory.

redistribution and economic empowerment at its core. Equality as the *recognition* of diverse identities is the third dimension because the failure to accord diversity is a form of oppression and inequality itself. Finally, the fourth conception of equality includes social dialogue and *representation*, in other words, the meaningful articulation of group priorities and perspectives.

Lost in the labyrinth?

As we will see, Hungarian Roma policies are rooted in the chaotic application of all of the above (for more, see Pap, 2019).

In Hungary, immigration figures are very low, and the overwhelming majority of immigrants are ethnic Hungarians from neighbouring states and who do not constitute a cultural minority (with an overall population of about 10 million, the immigration authorities recorded 213,000 foreigners living legally in Hungary in 2012 (Council of Europe & ERICarts, 2010)). According to the ERRC of Europe, about 7 per cent of the total Roma population lives in Hungary (2010), and the Roma constitute the largest minority group in the country. In the 2011 population census, about 3.2 per cent of the population, 308,957 people, identified as Roma (Hungarian Central Statistical Office, 2013), but the Council of Europe (2010) suggests that the real number might be closer to 700,000–1,000,000 people. In fact, the Roma are practically the only visible minority and have been present for centuries (Szuhay, 2003).[7]

In 1993, Hungary adopted a comprehensive law on the rights of national and ethnic minorities, which defined national and ethnic minorities as groups that have been present in the territory of Hungary for over hundred years and that 'constitute a numerical minority within the population of the country [...] and differ from the rest of the population in terms of their own tongue, cultures and traditions, and [...] aim at preserving all these and at articulating and safeguarding the interests of their respective historically developed communities'.

The act guarantees cultural and linguistic rights for thirteen recognised groups, and the Roma being one, and also establishes a unique Hungarian institution, the minority self-governments (MSGs). Funded by the local authorities or by the state where national-level bodies are concerned, MSGs

---

7 The Roma in Hungary are linguistically assimilated – practically all speak Hungarian, with some only speaking Hungarian and others being bilingual – and they do not differ significantly from the majority in terms of religious affiliation. Also, the Roma in Hungary live a sedentary lifestyle – unlike some Roma communities in Europe – and only a very small group of Sinti (estimated to be less than 1 per cent among the Roma population, some operating travelling carnivals/carousels) are semi-sedentary (Szuhay, 2003).

are elected bodies that operate at the local, regional and national level and that have special competences for protecting cultural heritage and language use; fixing the calendar for festivals and celebrations; fostering the preservation of traditions; participating in public education; managing public theatres, libraries and science and arts institutions; awarding study grants; and providing services for to the community (legal aid in particular). As Darquennes et al. (2012) point out, the function and design of MSGs are quite ambiguous: political representation and empowerment, cultural competences and a vague promise of social integration potential are bundled together. When it comes to the Roma, the function and design of the MSGs are quite controversial, as, even though this is what the community would most wish for, it cannot enhance social inclusion, because its mandate is limited to cultural autonomy. The language provisions are also not too helpful for a community that largely speaks Hungarian at home (Ram, 2014, 31). This lack of authority leaves MSGs as a 'half-way house' between a government institution and an NGO, with an undefined, underfunded mandate. As an OSCE report points out, 'While other minorities are primarily concerned with protection of cultural and linguistic autonomy, the Roma population faces an almost opposite challenge, needing more integration to combat segregated education, discrimination, unemployment, and problems with housing and healthcare' (NDI, OSCE/ODIHR, 2006, 5). Roma leaders repeatedly call for a redistribution-oriented, rather than a recognition-oriented, minority (Cahn, 2001; Molnár and Schaft, 2003).

In 2011, a new minority law was adopted (Act CLXXIX of 2011 on the Rights of Nationalities), preserving the earlier institutional and conceptual framework, yet bringing a change in terminology and changing 'national and ethnic minorities', to 'nationalities', making the philosophy of the law more straightforward. Surprisingly, Roma MSGs have formally been involved in social inclusion measures (e.g. as Annex 2 to the first version of the Hungarian National Social Inclusion Strategy (2011), Hungarian National Social Inclusion Strategy II (2014)),[8] creating an even more confusing hybrid, mutant model. The new legislation, thus, clearly signals that on the one hand the legislature conceptualises Roma issues foremost as issues of identity politics and uses cultural identity as a tool for social integration. This commitment is further explored in the field of law enforcement. In 2011, the chief of

---

8 For example, as Annex 2 to the first version of the Hungarian National Social Inclusion Strategy (2011), Hungarian National Social Inclusion Strategy II (2014), the government signed a framework agreement with the National Roma Self-Government, in fact, appointing it as one of the core implementing bodies of the strategy.

the national police issued two orders on policing multicultural communities and cooperation with Roma self-governments (and an adjacent methodological guideline in 2012).[9] These documents establish local liaisons (contact points) and working groups to facilitate crime prevention and to map deviance and criminal behaviour that arises from differing cultural norms of the majority and the minorities. By applying the term 'multicultural' communities and environment, the mandatory legal text blends cultural differences pertaining to religious communities, asylum seekers in refugee camps and the Roma, and singling out Roma self-governments as institutional partners for the force. The regulations include the prevention of victimisation as well as detecting criminality. Thus, culturally rooted target activity can include victimisation of minorities or refugees in hate crimes, as well as victims of harmful traditional practices, say honour crimes, when perpetrators are also members of the (culturally defined) minority community. A thorough reading of the texts shows that perpetrators and not victims are in the focus of the regulations, and in particular those who commit crimes against members of the majority, due to their special cultural norms, that are in conflict with national criminal law. The regulations identify three target communities: legal and illegal immigrants and asylum seekers, the Roma, and resident migrants and autochthonous (indigenous) national minorities who 'exhibit cultural, behavioral, religious or value patterns differing from the majority'. Given the practically ethnically homogenous nature of Hungarian society (apart from the Roma), no literature in anthropology or criminology shows the existence of such patterns or behaviour for either the indigenous or new immigrant groups (besides an essentialist and overbroad generalisation connecting terrorism with the miniscule Muslim community) (according to the latest 2011 census there were 5,579 Muslims in the country. http://www.ksh.hu/nepszamlalas/tablak_vallas), especially since the size of these communities is miniature. Generally, one can follow a bona fide and a more critical approach in trying to decipher the intent of the legislator. The former would imply that the chief of police simply wanted to implement international standards for policing multicultural communities (such as the European Code of Police Ethics (Recommendation (2001)) 10 adopted by the Committee of Ministers of the Council of Europe on 19 September 2001) or the Ljubljana Guidelines on Integration of Diverse Societies by the Organization for Security and

---

9 A multikulturális környezetben végrehajtott rendőri intézkedésekről szóló 27/2011. (XII. 30.) ORFK utasítás, a roma kisebbségi önkormányzatok közötti együttműködésről, kapcsolattartásról szóló 22/2011. (X. 21.) ORFK utasítás, (2012. január 19-én kelt.) 29000/126311/2012 ált. számú módszertani útmutató.

Cooperation in Europe (adopted in November 2012), both adopted around the same time) in a politically correct and harmless, cost-free fashion, even though such communities do not exist (for the time being). A more critical reading (and the author has no intention or proper methodological tools to guess or identify which reading is the actual, correct one, but argues that both are problematic) suggests that there is an essential, relevant link between potential criminality and being Roma. The term 'Gypsy Criminality' was coined by not the government, but by the extreme far-right party, Jobbik, and there is no straightforward commitment to this in government documents, yet this is what the logic of various legislative texts implies. A document for Roma inclusion issued by the government (Emberi Erőforrások Minisztériuma Szociális és társadalmi felzárkózásért felelős államtitkársága, 'Magyar nemzeti társadalmi felzárkózási stratégia II. Tartósan rászorulók–szegény családban élő gyermekek–romák (2011–2020)') repeatedly mentions the deep and robust cultural difference between the Roma and the majority, that needs to be tackled via law enforcement strategies: 'mutual acceptance and forming an alliance' between the majority and the Roma. (Special Roma liaisons are also to be appointed in prisons.) (Romaügyekért Felelős Tematikus Munkacsoport, https://emberijogok.kormany.hu/romaugyekert-felelos-tematikus-munkacsoport.) The workfare state propagated by Prime Minister Orbán also hints at canonising the 'culture of poverty', which can be linked to 'culturalism', 'new racism' (see, for example, Taguieff, 1990, 109–22), and essentialising, othering, marginalising and scapegoating discourses, where cultural specificities are used to explain criminality and poverty, which in turn allow for securitised policies and blatant 'correctional' segregation and paternalistic and patronising rhetoric and policies.[10]

Benevolent populism

The bottom line to the previous section is that even if the reason for the Hungarian legislation is not something like what Lynne Haney (2016) would call penal nationalism, a particularly vile form of penal populism, the benevolent form of populism, where the legislative initiative roots in a theatrical diplomatic gesture are equally problematic. Even more controversial than symbolic non-normative legislation, lawmaking that actually lacks an actual commitment for enforcement, pertaining to non-existing subject matters is a

---

10 It needs to be added that the European Roma Rights Center raised concerns about the regulations. 'Az Európai Roma Jogi Központ Aggódik a Rendőri Intézkedések Miatt', 2012. http://biztonsagpiac.hu/az-europai-roma-jogi-kozpont-aggodik-a-rendori-intezkedesek-miatt

form of desuetude, depreciation of law, which violates the integrity of the legal system and the principle of rule of law. This arguably can be conceptualised as a form of penal populism directed towards international organisations.

Arguably (see Bartha et al., 2020, 78)[11] this type of populism actually also characterises the entire conceptualisation of Roma as a (culturally defined) national minority. It has been widely discussed how the first right-wing conservative government elected after the political transition adopted an extremely generous model for accommodating multiculturalism for indigenous minorities – meaning traditional national minorities, and specifically those with homelands in the neighbouring states with large Hungarian minorities – in order to create an indirect tool to provide a politically marketable model and example for the neighbouring countries. As the OSCE noted: 'By developing the MSG system and other minority institutions, the government hoped to build leverage that it could use in bi-lateral negotiations with neighbouring states on guaranteeing the rights of Hungarians living abroad' (NDI, OSCE/ODIHR, 2006, 10). This explains the inadequateness of the legislative framework regarding the Roma.

It also needs to be added that by a thorough analysis of EU accession reports, Vizi (2005, 2013) showed that in terms of conceptualisation the European Commission turned out to be just as obtuse, blindfolded and conceptually disoriented as the Hungarian legislature. Even though annual accession progress reports and documents adopted by the European Parliament and the Commission discussed Roma-related issues under 'minority rights' labels, recommendations and concerns only focused on anti-discrimination, very broad social integration measures and complaints against the treatment of the Roma by the police and other authorities – none which actually have to do much with minority rights (Vermeersch and Vab Baar, 2017). Even the question of the parliamentary representation of minorities was seen as a tool for addressing social integration (Vizi, 2013).

Penal Populism Transformed: Anti-Roma Rhetoric and Action against the Roma

This section will show how the emergence of the COVID-19 pandemic brings a new angle to the scrutiny of benevolent penal populism, as it may

---

11 For a comprehensive methodology of populism, as applied in this research (conducted under the auspices of the DEMOS – Democratic efficacy and the varieties of populism in Europe H2020 RIA project, as well as the 129018, 129245 Hungarian National Research and Innovation Grants), see Bartha et al. (2020, 78).

awaken and transform into a powerful malevolent type and a tool for racist state oppression, as experienced (primarily not in Hungary but in Romania, Bulgaria and even Western Europe), as Roma are targeted and profiled in relation to curfew and social distancing measures, along a rhetoric that points to ethno-culturally rooted reasons for these actions. For example, claims that for Roma Easter was too important a family tradition to keep social distancing (see, for example, Berta, 2020) gave food for an essentialising rhetoric for targeted law enforcement action – and the novelty here is that for the first time, actual reference was found to identify 'Roma culture' as something mismatching the law and the majority (social and legal) norms. As argued before, ethnic culture-based policing is a relevant routine, if 'real', culture-based incompatibility of norms exists, for example in the case of certain harmful traditional practices like FGM and alike, but none of these were ever present in East Europe in lieu of the Roma.

The pandemic, hence, is used for marginalisation as cultural difference is utilised for scapegoating, offering a new rhetorical tool for far-right nationalism and an operationalising scheme for law enforcement action. Matache and Bhabha (2020) report 'a frightening escalation of populist and racist voices intent on blaming the Roma community for this pandemic', with local and national newspapers often raging racist, hateful and life-threatening campaign of anti-Roma propaganda, along with the appearance of dehumanising, degrading and deeply offensive fake posts and 'news' on Facebook, which remains unaddressed (Matache and Bhabha, 2020).

Available data is still scarce, and systematic data collection is impossible since the pandemic is far from being over at the time of the submission of the manuscript, hence it is early to draw valid conclusions, but sources confirm the emergence of language from politicians portraying Roma as a public health risk by labelling them as carriers of the coronavirus, and the moral panic created by this rhetoric leads to targeted law enforcement action and police violence. An overview and analysis of experiences of the first wave of the pandemic published by the European Roma Rights Centre (ERRC Report, 2020) documents the most egregious human rights abuses which occurred against Roma during the period from February to June 2020, in twelve European countries (Albania, Belgium, Bulgaria, Hungary, Italy, Moldova, North Macedonia, Romania, Serbia, Slovakia, Turkey and Ukraine). This report exposes how these exceptional circumstances exacerbated already existing institutional racism against Roma, resulting in an increase in human rights violations by state authorities, as 'the implementation of curfews, bans on public gatherings, and social distancing measures provided additional contexts for law enforcement with inflated powers to brutalise Romani people with relative impunity' (ERRC Report, 2020, 32). It shows that although the first wave of COVID-19 actually did not have a disproportionate impact on marginalised Romani communities in Europe in terms of numbers of infections, and Eastern and Central Europe in general was for most, spared and only had a tiny number of cases compared to Western Europe, yet 'whilst no one was looking, vulnerable Romani communities were being brutalised by racist police officers, forcefully evicted from their homes, scapegoated by the far-right [...] while a hostile media, starved of tabloid content, demonised them for cheap clicks. [...] Institutionally racist public institutions have both directly and indirectly caused additional suffering to Roma living on the margins of society in segregated neighbourhoods throughout Europe' (ERRC Report, 2020, 3).

Just to provide a few examples: the Bulgarian town of Yambol was fully quarantined and blockaded for 14 days and a helicopter sprayed nearly three thousand litres of detergent to 'disinfect' the Romani neighbourhood '(E. Tendayi Achiume Special Rapporteur on contemporary forms of racism, racial discrimination, xenophobia, and related intolerance, and Fernand de Varennes Special Rapporteur on minority issues expressed deep concern at the discriminatory limitations; ERRC Report, 2020, 9–10; United Nations Human Rights Office of the High Commissioner, 2020a)'. On the same day the National Assembly voted to declare a sense of emergency, Interior Minister Mladen Marinov told Parliament that Romani ghettos will be quarantined if necessary, should people 'lack self-awareness'; and that the ministry will exercise its powers 'to ensure compliance with quarantine'. The measures were found disproportionate, unrelated to actual infection rates and later acknowledged to have been largely ineffective (ERRC Report, 2020, 12).

In Edinet, Moldova, the mayor publicly voiced concerns that Roma returning from abroad and disrespecting quarantine measures constitute a public health hazard to the rest of the population (ERRC Report, 2020, 24). Soroca, the so-called Roma capital of Moldova, was quarantined by the government after a relative rise in the number of infections. Alongside the police, soldiers from the 22nd Peacekeeping Battalion and the Anti-Air Missile Regiment installed fixed checkpoints at the entrance and exit of three localities to monitor the movement of citizens and vehicles (ERRC Report, 2020, 28).

In Romania, 'broadcast and print media commentators amplified racist tropes about "Gypsy violence" and "Gypsy crime" when covering incidents involving Roma and law enforcement to turn essentially localized incidents into a full-blown safety and public health emergency', resulting in an 'outpouring over Romanian social media of hate-filled calls for anti-Roma violence, in some cases laced with approving references to Roma extermination during the Holocaust' (ERRC Report, 2020, 35). The report lists a number of violent police attacks on Romani communities, including a disproportionate use of force, tear gassing women and children, inhumane and degrading treatment of detained persons, and police attempts to prevent NGOs delivering humanitarian aid (ERRC Report, 2020, 35).

In Slovakia, where five entire Romani settlements were entirely quarantined, Jaroslav Polacek, the mayor of the major city, Kosice, posted a warning on social media that coronavirus can spread because of the behaviour of 'socially unadaptable people' in Romani settlements who do not respect emergency measures. Another mayor, in an open letter to the prime minister, called for the lockdown of all Romani settlements to prevent mass outbreaks of the virus (ERRC Report, 2020, 44). *CounterPunch* magazine reports (Rain, 2020) how speaker of the Slovak Parliament Boris Kollár, when asked how he would address the perpetual humanitarian crisis of the Romani in Slovakia, suggested purchasing 700,000 plane tickets to relocate them in the UK.

In response to events principally in Slovakia, Bulgaria and Romania, Council of Europe secretary general Marija Pejčinović Burić expressed concern at government measures that could result in further compromising the human rights of Roma (ERRC Report, 2020, 49; Council of Europe Newsroom, 2020).

As mentioned before, similar reports came from Western Europe as well. For example, Romani travellers in Belgium were the focus of increased police attention and harassment on the pretext of enforcing emergency social distancing measures vie lice operations targeting Romani communities and seizing caravans (thereby making families homeless without being offered any alternative housing solution, social aid or COVID-19 emergency support) (ERRC Report, 2020, 6–8).

As Jonathan Lee summarises, 'with coronavirus lockdowns in force across Europe, the continent's largest and most marginalised minority – the Roma – is at the mercy of racist and violent police officers seemingly accountable to no one. [...] Police officers from Slovakia to Ireland, who need little encouragement to terrorise the Roma even during normal times, are taking advantage of the unprecedented public health emergency we are currently facing to abuse, beat and harass vulnerable Roma men, women and even children with complete impunity. [...] In the past month in Romania alone, we have recorded at least eight incidents where police officers used disproportionate force against the Roma. *Video footage* from one of these incidents shows police officers beating eight handcuffed Romani men and one 13-year-old boy for allegedly having a barbecue outside one of their houses. Several policemen and gendarmes, in and out of uniform, take part in the collective punishment. Two officers are seen holding the arms of a Romani man screaming in agony, as a third whips the bare soles of his feet. Another officer is heard using racial slurs and threatening anyone who dares to report the incident. […] Today we are witnessing what happens when the structures that normally hold security forces accountable – the media, civil society, and judicial systems – are paralysed by a pandemic. With NGOs, activists, and journalists unable to work in the field because of state-imposed lockdowns and social distancing measures, the only resources we can rely on to bring abusive police officers to justice are witness accounts and a few videos secretly recorded by terrified people. […] Police violence against Romani communities does not occur in a vacuum. It comes as part of a bigger package, alongside Roma-only ghettos, segregated education, discrimination in employment and healthcare, and a lack of basic utilities and infrastructure in places where poorest communities live. This system is maintained and perpetuated by society's refusal to be confronted with the daily apartheid of Romani people, which is plain to see for anyone who just cares enough to look' (see Lee, 2020).

As Ioanida Costache argues, this rhetoric is borne of the biopolitical ideology of white supremacy in which Roma do not make up part of the nation, in fact, they threaten it, as a contagion, spoiling its purported homogeneity. Roma bodies have long been considered a 'biological threat to the health of the body politic' (Costache, 2020; for more, see Krasimirov and Tsolova, 2020; Rorke, 2020; Muller et al., 2020; Carstocea, 2020; Cheng and Barzakova, 2020; Vanecek et al., 2020; Sudbrock and Mihalache, 2020; D'Agostino, 2020).

Concluding Remarks

The aim of this chapter was to provide an interpretative framework for scapegoating anti-Roma rhetoric and over-policing targeting members of the Roma community throughout Europe, who are already disproportionally affected by virus (as many live without running water, find it difficult impossible to socially distance, are likely to lose their jobs as irregular workers, and lacking digital skills or online connectivity, face extreme difficulties navigating in a healthcare system that switched to online and telephone consultations). The case study was situated in the context of the American 'Black Lives Matter movement', and current debates on conceptualising and operationalising race and ethnicity, ethno-racial disparities in the effects of the COVID-19 pandemic, as well as various forms of penal populism and nationalism, and showed that the virus exacerbates social inequalities, but it is not the virus itself, but the social environment and institutions are to be blamed. And the proverbial truism (Fulwood, 2015) that 'when whites folks catch a cold, black folks get pneumonia' applies for all minorities worldwide.

References

Barnes, Ashleigh and McDonnel, Emilie. (2020). An Overview of Emerging International Human Rights Law Guidance: Promoting Human Rights Compatibility of Government COVID-19 Responses. Bonavero Riport No. 5/2020. 17 August. https://www.law.ox.ac.uk/sites/files/oxlaw/bonavero_report_5_of_2020.pdf.

Bartha, Attila, Boda, Zsolt and Szikra, Dorottya. (2020). When Populist Leaders Govern: Conceptualising Populism in Policy Making. *Politics and Governance* 8, no. 3: 71–81. DOI: 10.17645/pag.v8i3.2922.

Bernstein, Gregory, Guzman, Stephanie, Hadley, Maggie, Huff, Rosalyn M., Hung, Alison, Yandle, Anita N., Hoag, Alexis and Harcourt, Bernard E. (2020). COVID-19 and Prisoners' Rights. In *Law in the Time of COVID-19*, edited by Katharina Pistor. Columbia Law School. https://scholarship.law.columbia.edu/faculty_scholarship/2682.

Berta, Péter. (2020). Ethnicizing a Pandemic:COVID-19, Culture Blaming, and Romanian Roma. *Society for Romanian Studies Newsletter* 42, no. 1: 1–7.

Brubaker, Rogers. (2016a). The Dolezal Affair: Race, Gender, and the Micropolitics of Identity. *Ethnic and Racial Studies* 39, no. 3: 414–448. DOI: 10.1080/01419870.2015.1084430.

Brubaker, Rogers. (2016b). *Trans: Gender, Race, and the Micropolitics of Identity*. Princeton, NJ: Princeton University Press.

Busby, Mattha and Gidda, Mirren. (2020). BAME People Fined More Than White Population Under Coronavirus Laws. *The Guardian*, 26 May. https://www.theguardian.com/world/2020/may/26/bame-people-fined-more-than-white-population-under-coronavirus-laws.

Cahn, Claude. (2001). Smoke and Mirrors: Roma and Minority Policy in Hungary. *Der Donauraum* 41, no. 3. DOI: 10.7767/dnrm.2001.41.3.101.

CARE International. (2020). Girl-Driven Change. Meeting the Needs of Adolescent Girls During COVID-19 and Beyond. Accessed October. https://www.care-international.org/files/files/CARE-USA-Adolescent-Girls-and-COVID-19-FINAL-Report.pdf.

CARE International and International Rescue Committee. (2020). Global Rapid Gender Analysis for COVID-19. Accessed 31 March. https://www.rescue.org/report/global-rapid-gender-analysis-covid-19.

Carstocea, Andreea. (2020). Pandemics of Exclusion: The Scapegoating of the Roma in Romania. *ECMI Minorities Blog*, 11 May. https://www.ecmi.de/infochannel/detail/ecmi-minorities-blog-pandemics-of-exclusion-the-scapegoating-of-the-roma-in-romania.

Chanbonpin, Kim D. (2015). Between Black and White: The Coloring of Asian Americans: Passing in Colorism. *Washington University Global Studies Law Review* 14, no. 4: 637–663.

Cheng, Maria and Barzakova, Teodora. (2020). Some European Officials Use Virus as a Cover to Target Roma. *AP News*, 15 October. https://apnews.com/article/virus-outbreak-pandemics-police-discrimination-eastern-europe-2cbcdb5ee070578b73b1bc35ebdb426e.

Costache, Ioanida. (2020). "Until We Are Able to Gas Them Like the Nazis, the Roma Will Infect the Nation": Roma and the Ethnicization of COVID-19 in Romania. *DOR*, 22 April. https://www.dor.ro/roma-and-the-ethnicization-of-covid-19-in-romania/.

Council of Europe and ERICarts. (2010). Statistics. www.coe.int/t/dg3/romatravellers/default_en.asp.

Council of Europe Newsroom. (2020). 8 April, International Roma Day: "Step Up Human Rights Protection for Roma and Guarantee Their Access to Vital Services During COVID-19 Pandemic." 7 April 2020. https://www.coe.int/en/web/portal/-/8-april-international-roma-day-step-up-human-rights-protection-for-roma-and-guarantee-their-access-to-vital-services-during-covid-19-pandemic-.

Cultural Survival. (2020). 9 Ways Indigenous Rights Are at Risk During the COVID-19 Crisis. 20 May. https://www.culturalsurvival.org/news/9-ways-indigenous-rights-are-risk-during-covid-19-crisis.

D'Agostino, Serena. (2020). Anti-Gypsyism Under COVID-19 Pandemic. *Institute for European Studies*, 8 May. https://www.ies.be/content/anti-gypsyism-under-covid-19-pandemic.

Darquennes, J., Melis, A., Nelde, P. H., Salmasi, S., Tikka, M. and Weber, P. J. (2012). *Euromosaic III Presence of Regional and Minority Language Groups in the New Member States, European Commission: Directorate-General for Education and Culture.* Brussels: Katholieke Universiteit Brussel.

ERRC Report. (2020). *Roma Rights in the Time of Covid.* Brussels: European Roma Rights Centre. http://www.errc.org/uploads/upload_en/file/5265_file1_roma-rights-in-the-time-of-covid..pdf.

EU Roma Strategic. (2020). *A Union of Equality: EU Roma Strategic Framework for Equality, Inclusion and Participation for 2020–2030.* Communication from the Commission to the European Parliament and the Council, 7 October. Brussels.

Faleiro, Sonia. (2020). Britain's Ethnic Minorities Are Being Left for Dead. *The New York Times*, 22 May. https://www.nytimes.com/2020/05/22/opinion/britain-coronavirus-minorities.html.

FRA. (2018a). *Second European Union Minorities and Discrimination Survey Roma – Selected Findings. European Union Agency for Fundamental Rights (FRA).* Luxembourg: Publications Office of the European Union. DOI: 10.2811/189587. https://fra.europa.eu/en/news/2016/80-roma-are-risk-poverty-new-survey-finds.

FRA. (2018b). *A Persisting Concern: Anti-Gypsyism as a Barrier to Roma Inclusion.* European Union Agency for Fundamental Rights (FRA). Luxembourg: Publications Office of the European Union. DOI: 10.2811/423901. https://fra.europa.eu/sites/default/files/fra_uploads/fra-2018-anti-gypsyism-barrier-roma-inclusion_en.pdf.

Fulwood, Sam. (2015). When White Folks Catch a Cold, Black Folks Get Pneumonia. *Center for American Progress*, 28 January. https://www.americanprogress.org/issues/race/news/2015/01/28/105551/when-whites-folks-catch-a-cold-black-folks-get-pneumonia/.

Godzisz, Piotr. (2019). The Europeanization of Anti-LGBT Hate Crime Laws in the Western Balkans. *Crime, Law and Social Change* 71: 291–306.

Haney, Lynne. (2016). Prisons of the Past: Penal Nationalism and the Politics of Punishment in Central Europe. *Punishment & Society* 18, no. 3: 346–368.DOI: 10.1177/1462474516645686.

Hannum, Hurst. (2000). International Law. In *Encyclopedia of Nationalism*, First edition, edited by A. J. Motyl, 405–419. San Diego: Academic Press.

Hobbs, Allyson Vanessa. (2014). *A Chosen Exile: A History of Racial Passing in American Life.* Cambridge, MA: Harvard University Press.

Hungarian Central Statistical Office. (2013). http://www.ksh.hu/.

Hunter, Margaret. (2011). Buying Racial Capital: Skin-Bleaching and Cosmetic Surgery in a Globalized World. *The Journal of Pan African Studies* 4, no. 4: 142–164.

Ignatiev, Noel. (1995). *How the Irish Became White*. New York: Routledge.
Ignatiev, Noel and Garvey, John. (Eds.). (1996). *Race Traitor*. New York: Routledge.
Interpol. (2020). Threats and Trends Child Sexual Exploitation and Abuse. *COVID-19 Impact*. Accessed September 2020. https://www.interpol.int/content/download/15611/file/COVID19%20-%20Child%20Sexual%20Exploitation%20and%20Abuse%20threats%20and%20trends.pdf.
Izsák, Rita. (2015). *Comprehensive Study of the Human Rights Situation of Roma Worldwide, with a Particular Focus on the Phenomenon of Anti-Gypsyism, Human Rights Council Twenty-Ninth Session Agenda Item 3 Promotion and Protection of All Human Rights, Civil, Political, Economic, Social and Cultural Rights, Including the Right to Development General Assembly Distr.: General 11 May 2015.*
Jovanovic, Zeljko. (2020). To Recover from COVID-19, the EU Cannot Afford the Cost of Inequality. *The Brussels Times*, 20 May. https://www.brusselstimes.com/opinion/112518/to-recover-from-covid-19-the-eu-cannot-afford-the-cost-of-inequality/.
Kelly, Mary E. and Nagel, Joane. (2002). Ethnic Re-Identification: Lithuanian Americans and Native Americans. *Journal of Ethnic and Migration Studies* 28, no. 2: 275–289.
Kennedy, Randall. (2003). *Interracial Intimacies: Sex, Marriage, Identity, and Adoption*. New York: Pantheon.
Kolata, Gina. (2020). Many Medical Decision Tools Disadvantage Black Patients. *The New York Times*, 17 June. https://www.nytimes.com/2020/06/17/health/many-medical-decision-tools-disadvantage-black-patients.html.
Krasimirov, Angel and Tsolova, Tsvetelia. (2020). Bulgaria's Roma Say Some Coronavirus Measures Are Discriminatory. *Reuters*, 24 March. https://www.reuters.com/article/us-health-coronavirus-bulgaria-roma-idUSKBN21B355.
Kymlicka, Will. (2001). Western Political Theory and Ethnic Relations in Eastern Europe. In *Can Liberal Pluralism Be Exported? Western Political Theory and Ethnic Relations in Eastern Europe*, First Edition, edited by Will Kymlicka and Magda Opalski, 13–107. Oxford: Oxford University Press.
Lee, Jonathan. (2020). Police Are Using the COVID-19 Pandemic as an Excuse to Abuse Roma. 14 May. https://www.aljazeera.com/opinions/2020/5/14/police-are-using-the-covid-19-pandemic-as-an-excuse-to-abuse-roma/.
Matache, Margareta and Bhabha, Jacqueline. (2020). Anti-Roma Racism Is Spiraling During COVID-19 Pandemic. *Health and Human Rights Journal* 22, no. 1: 379–382. https://www.hhrjournal.org/2020/04/anti-roma-racism-is-spiraling-during-covid-19-pandemic/.
McCrudden, Christopher. (2005). Thinking About the Discrimination Directives. *European Anti-Discrimination Law Review*, no. 1: 17–23.
McCrudden, Christopher. (2020). Democracy, Protests, and Covid-19: The Challenge of (and for) Human Rights. *UK Constitutional Law Association*, 19 June. https://ukconstitutionallaw.org/2020/06/19/christopher-mccrudden-democracy-protests-and-covid-19-the-challenge-of-and-for-human-rights/.
Molnár, E. and Schaft, K. A. (2003). Preserving 'Cultural Autonomy' or Confronting Social Crisis? *Review of Sociology of the Hungarian Sociological Association* 9, no. 1: 27–42.
Motoc, Catrinel. (2015). The Roma in Europe: 11 Things You Always Wanted to Know But Were Afraid to Ask. 23 April. https://www.amnesty.org/en/latest/campaigns/2015/04/roma-in-europe-11-things-you-always-wanted-to-know-but-were-afraid-to-ask/hjkj.
Muller, Stephan, Tair, Fikrija, Ibishi, Bashkim and Gracanin, Dragan. (2020). Roma: Europe's Neglected Coronavirus Victims. *Balkan Insight*, 1 April. https://balkaninsight

.com/2020/04/01/roma-europes-neglected-coronavirus-victims/?fbclid=IwAR1hE kVMBuiMZD1GOK0EbuPBpQq85j0qSsagRaLgkeTXZn9Xx29YRCmtgUo.
NDI, OSCE/ODIHR. (2006). *The Hungarian Minority Self-Government System as a Means of Increasing Romani Political Participation: National Democratic Institute Assessment Report September/October 2006*. National Democratic Institute for International Affairs, Office for Democratic Institutions and Human Rights of the Organization for Security and Co-operation in Europe: 1–31.
Oppel, Richard A., Jr., Gebeloff, Robert, Lai, K. K. Rebecca, Wright, Will and Smith, Mitch. (2020). The Fullest Look Yet at the Racial Inequity of Coronavirus. *The New York Times*, 5 July. https://www.nytimes.com/interactive/2020/07/05/us/coronavirus-latinos-african-americans-cdc-data.html.
Orchid Project. Working Together to End Female Genital Cutting. (2020). Impacts of COVID-19 on Female Genital Cutting. Accessed September 2020. https://reliefweb.int/sites/reliefweb.int/files/resources/COVID_female_genital_cutting_FGC_policy_briefing_Orchid_Project_FINAL%20%281%29.pdf.
Overall, Christine and Rowan, John. (2004). Transsexualism and "Transracialism." *Social Philosophy Today* 20: 183–193.
Pap, Andras L. (2017). Ethno-Racial Identity (Politics) by Law: "Fraud" and "Choice". *Nationalities Papers* 45, no. 5: 968–987. DOI: 10.1080/00905992.2017.1311846.
Pap, Andras L. (2019). Policies for Whom? Roma as Ethnic and/or National Minorities – The Case of Hungary and the European Union. In *Implementation of EU Policies on Social Inclusion of Disadvantaged Populations in Former Socialist Countries*, edited by Ingrid Fylling, Elena Loreni Baciu and Janne Paulsen Breimo, 75–98. London: Routledge Press.
Pap, Andras L. (2020). Neglect, Marginalization, and Abuse: Hate Crime Legislation and Practice in the Labyrinth of Identity Politics, Minority Protection, and Penal Populism. *Nationalities Papers* 49, no. 3: 1–19. DOI: 10.1017/nps.2020.21.
Rain. (2020). Social Distancing with Tear Gas and Walls: The "Racist, Hateful, and Life-Threatening Campaign" Unleashed Against the Romani With Covid-19. 5 May. https://www.counterpunch.org/2020/05/05/social-distancing-with-tear-gas-and-walls-the-racist-hateful-and-life-threatening-campaign-unleashed-against-the-romani-with-covid-19/.
Ram, Melanie H. (2014). Europeanization and the Roma: Spreading the Norms of Inclusion and Exclusion. In *10th Biennial Conference of the European Community Studies Association-Canada*, 1–30.
Raterman, Elizabeth. (2020). A Health Justice Perspective of Asthma and COVID-19. *Human Rights Brief* 24, no. 1: Article 7. https://digitalcommons.wcl.american.edu/hrbrief/vol24/iss1/7.
Reuters. (2020). Moderna Vaccine Trial Contractors Fail to Enroll Enough Minorities. 6 October 2020. https://www.reuters.com/article/us-health-coronavirus-vaccine-moderna-ex/exclusive-moderna-vaccine-trial-contractors-fail-to-enroll-enough-minorities-prompting-slowdown-sources-idINKBN26R1SP.
Rorke, Bernard. (2020). Inequality, Anti-Roma Racism, and the Coronavirus. *EU Observer*, 19 March. https://euobserver.com/coronavirus/147759.
Save the Children's Resource Centre. (2020). Beyond the Shadow Pandemic: Protecting a Generation of Girls from Gender-Based Violence Through COVID-19 to Recovery. Accessed 17 July. https://resourcecentre.savethechildren.net/node/17911/pdf/sc_covid19_gbv_brief_english.pdf.

Sharfstein, Daniel J. (2007). Crossing the Color Line: Racial Migration and the One-Drop Rule, 1600–1860. *Minnesota Law Review* 91: 592–656.

Stack, Liam. (2020). Hasidic Jews, Hit Hard by the Outbreak, Flock to Donate Plasma. *The New York Times*, 12 May. https://www.nytimes.com/2020/05/12/nyregion/virus-orthodox-plasma-donation.html.

Sturm, Susan P., Pirani, Faiz, Kim, Hyun, Behr, Natalie and Hardwick, Zachary D. (2020). Linked Fate: Justice and the Criminal Legal System During the COVID-19 Pandemic. In *Law in the Time of COVID-19*, edited by Katharina Pistor. Columbia Law School. https://scholarship.law.columbia.edu/faculty_scholarship/2683.

Sudbrock, Christine and Mihalache, Isabela. (2020). Roma Part of #BlackLivesMatter. *The Brussels Times*, 9 July. https://www.brusselstimes.com/opinion/120784/roma-part-of-blacklivesmatter/.

Suzuki, Kazuko and Von Vacano, Diego A. (2018). *Reconsidering Race: Social Science Perspectives on Racial Categories in the Age of Genomics*. Oxford: Oxford University Press.

Szuhay, Peter. (2003). Ez egy eredeti cigányélet [An Authentic 'Gypsy' Life]. *Beszélő Online* 8, no. 5. http://beszelo.c3.hu/cikkek/%E2%80%9Eez-egy-eredeti-ciganyelet%E2%80%9D. Accessed 20 February 2018.

Taguieff, Pierre-André. (1990). The New Cultural Racism in France. *Telos: Critical Theory of the Contemporary* 83, 109–22. DOI: 10.3817/0390083109.

Tajfel, Henri. (1981). *Human Groups and Social Categories: Studies in Social Psychology*. Cambridge: Cambridge University Press.

Taylor, Derrick Bryson. (2020). For the Deaf, Social Distancing Can Mean Social Isolation. *The New York Times*, 4 June. https://www.nytimes.com/2020/06/04/us/coronavirus-deaf-culture-challenges.html.

The Economist. (2020). A Lack of Data on Race Hampers Efforts to Tackle Inequalities. 21 November. https://www.economist.com/leaders/2020/11/21/a-lack-of-data-on-race-hampers-efforts-to-tackle-inequalities.

Twohey, Megan. (2020). Who Gets a Vaccine First? U.S. Considers Race in Coronavirus Plans. *The New York Times*, 9 July. https://www.nytimes.com/2020/07/09/us/coronavirus-vaccine.html.

United Nations. (2020). Policy Brief: The Impact of COVID-19 on Older Persons. May 2020. https://unsdg.un.org/sites/default/files/2020-05/Policy-Brief-The-Impact-of-COVID-19-on-Older-Persons.pdf.

United Nations Human Rights Office of the High Commissioner. (2020a). Bulgaria/COVID-19 Response: "Stop Hate Speech and Racial Discrimination Against the Roma Minority" – UN Experts. 13 May. https://www.ohchr.org/EN/NewsEvents/Pages/DisplayNews.aspx?NewsID=25881&LangID=E.

United Nations Human Rights Office of the High Commissioner. (2020b). Disproportionate Impact of COVID-19 on Racial and Ethnic Minorities Needs to be Urgently Addressed – Bachelet. 2 June. https://www.ohchr.org/EN/NewsEvents/Pages/DisplayNews.aspx?NewsID=25916.

Vanecek, Anya, Seiler, Naomi K., Heyison, Claire and Horton, Katherine. (2020). The Risks of Criminalizing COVID-19 Exposure: Lessons from HIV. *Human Rights Brief* 24, no. 1. https://digitalcommons.wcl.american.edu/hrbrief/vol24/iss1/3.

Vermeersch, Peter and Van Baar, Huub. (2017). The Limits of Operational Representations: Ways of Seeing Roma Beyond the Recognition-Redistribution Paradigm. *Intersections: East European Journal of Society and Politics* 3, no. 4: 120–139. DOI: 10.17356/ieejsp.v3i4.412.

Vizi, Balazs. (2005). The EU and the Situation of Roma in Hungary in the Accession Process. *Central European Political Science Review* 6, no. 20: 66–91.
Vizi, Balazs. (2013). *Európai Kaleidoszkóp. Az Európai Unió és a Kisebbségek [European Kaleidoscope: The EU and the Minorities]*. Budapest: L'Harmattan Kiadó. http://real.mtak.hu/10041/1/15_nemnyilv.pdf.
Vyas, Darshali A., Eisenstein, Leo G. and Jones, David S. (2020). Hidden in Plain Sight – Reconsidering the Use of Race Correction in Clinical Algorithms. *The New England Journal of Medicine*, 17 August. DOI: 10.1056/NEJMms2004740.
Women Enabled International. (2020). COVID-19 at the Intersection of Gender and Disability: Findings of a Global Survey March to April 2020. 20 May. https://womenenabled.org/blog/covid-19-survey-findings/.
World Trade Organization News. (2020). The Economic Impact of COVID-19 on Women in Vulnerable Sectors and Economies. Accessed 3 August. https://www.wto.org/english/news_e/news20_e/info_note_covid_05aug20_e.pdf.

Chapter 5

ETHICS OF PERSONAL DATA COLLECTION IN BOSNIA–HERZEGOVINA (BIH)

Mary Kate Schneider

How ought one to conduct research in post-conflict spaces? The issue of ethical data collection becomes increasingly fraught when research takes place in settings that have experienced, or are currently experiencing, violent conflict. In addition to the usual considerations of human research subject protections – in particular, preserving the confidentiality of personally identifying information and minimising harm or the potential for harm to research subjects – researchers who study populations in settings that have experienced violence also must take into consideration the heightened vulnerability of these populations. For example, research participants may face grave threats to their physical security should their personally identifying information be exposed. Furthermore, participation in research may be triggering to participants who have experienced primary or secondary trauma as a result of the conflict. That is to say, these research participants face greater and different risks than research participants in other situations, and thus it is necessary to take special care when designing research in conflict and post-conflict spaces.

The Project

This project began as the subject of my doctoral dissertation, which aimed to assess secondary school students' attitudes towards different ethnic groups within BiH. The 1992–95 Bosnian War ended with the signing of the Dayton Peace Agreement (DPA), also known as the General Framework Agreement for Peace. The DPA introduced consociational democracy to BiH and consequently restructured all of the country's political institutions. The redesign of these political institutions included the administration of the Bosnian education system, and as a result, there are effectively three different models of primary and secondary education in BiH. My project was rooted in the suspicion that those different models of education would correspond with differences in students' attitudes towards different ethnic groups.

BiH holds the distinction of being the most ethnically mixed of the former Yugoslavia's six constituent republics. Unlike Slovenia, Croatia, Serbia, Montenegro and Macedonia, BiH could not be claimed by any one dominant ethnic group. Rather, BiH prior to the war was a republic in which three main ethnoreligious groups – Bosniaks (who were typically Muslim), Croats (who were typically Catholic) and Serbs (who were typically Orthodox) – lived together, with none of these groups able to claim an absolute majority of the population. It was not uncommon for members of different ethnic groups to intermingle in various ways, either professionally at work or school, or socially through interethnic friendships, marriages and families. This mixing resulted in BiH taking on a complex patchwork quilt of demographic geography. Its capital city, Sarajevo, served as the host of the 1984 Winter Olympics, which was attended by both the United States and the Soviet Union. This signalled to the world that if Yugoslavia was the world's most accessible communist country (owing in part to its non-aligned status and positioning at the crossroads of Europe), BiH was Yugoslavia's most cosmopolitan republic.

This is one reason why, when the war commenced in 1992, citizens of BiH found themselves blindsided.[1] What followed was a shocking campaign

---

1   On this, Yugoslav (Croatian) journalist Slavenka Drakulić writes: 'We, the citizens of Yugoslavia, were even more surprised. When I think about it, I am still angry with myself. Is it

of ethnic violence, centring around the issue of Bosnian independence vs. preserving the already-spiralling Yugoslav federation. On 25 June 1991, the Yugoslav republics of Slovenia and Croatia had declared independence. On 1 March 1992, BiH followed suit after a referendum – largely boycotted by Bosnian Serbs – yielded overwhelmingly in favour of independence. Sides were drawn along ethnic lines, and the conflict quickly escalated into a full-scale ethnic, cleansing campaign. Over the course of the war, families were routinely forced from their homes and expelled from cities, towns, villages and neighbourhoods that they had inhabited for generations. After more than three years of violence, the demographic map of BiH had been redrawn into more or less ethnically homogenous territories.

What followed the peace at Dayton was a climate of continuous ethnic insecurity. This pervasive ethnic insecurity hailed from two sources: first, the fact that the peace agreement was effectively the long-form version of a cease-fire and did not represent any meaningful remediation of the issues underlying the conflict; second, the international community – led by the United States – that was responsible for implementing the peace agreement, prioritised elections as a key component to establishing democracy in BiH. Thus, the country's first democratic elections were held in November 1996 – while more than eight hundred thousand people were still displaced from their homes and prior to the establishment of any general sense of physical security among most citizens (International Crisis Group 1997). Thus, and somewhat predictably, the parties that prevailed during these early elections were ethnic political parties that ran on platforms promising to promote ethnic – rather than civic – interests in the nascent democracy. These ethnic political parties remain the dominant political parties in BiH to this day.

The Dayton agreement effectively crystalised the territorial borders that were produced via ethnic cleansing, dividing BiH into two entities – the Federation of Bosnia–Herzegovina and Republika Srpska (RS). Administrative control over the federation was shared between Bosniaks and Croats, while Serbs retained administrative rights within the RS. Within the federation, the territory was further divided into ten cantons, seven of which were either Bosniak- or Croat-majority cantons and three of which were ethnically mixed. The Dayton Constitution devolved certain powers to local authorities, including within the areas of policing and education. This matters because education policy largely emanated from the entity-level (in the RS) or cantonal-level (in the Federation) Ministries of Education – and

---

possible that the war crept into our lives slowly, stealthily, like a thief? Why didn't we see it coming? Why didn't we do something to prevent it? Why were we so arrogant that we thought it could not happen to us?' (Drakulić, 2004, pp. 1–2)

those ministries were subject to the highly ethnicised politicking that has been the hallmark of post-war Bosnian democracy.

Party patronage largely determines political ascendancy in BiH. Since the dominant political parties in BiH are ethnic political parties, it stands to reason that patronage in service to ethnic interests – including the prolongation of ethnic insecurities so as to ensure the continued relevance of ethnic political parties – yields the greatest success in terms of securing a position within government, including within the education ministries. Thus, education policy in BiH is not only highly localised, but it is also highly ethnicised.

This system has led to the emergence of competing and often contradictory education policies in BiH. Primary and secondary public schools tend to follow one of three organisational models: ethnically integrated, ethnically segregated, or what I have termed 'the monoethnic default'. Ethnically integrated schools are those within which students of different ethnicities attend school together, at the same time, and study the same subjects. Segregated schools are also known as *dvije škole pod jednom krovom* ('two schools under one roof'). There are approximately just over fifty such schools in BiH, existing mainly in the three cantons in which both Bosniaks and Croats live in large numbers. These schools are segregated on the basis of ethnicity and may either organise students on different schedules or in different spaces. For example, in Busovača, Croat students attended school in the morning and Bosniak students attended school in the afternoon. In Žepče, Bosniak students attended school in one half of the building, while Croat students attended school using the other half of the building. Finally, there is the monoethnic default. The vast majority of schools in BiH follow this model, which reflects the ethnic composition of the communities that they serve. As a result of ethnic cleansing, many Bosnian communities that were once multi-ethnic are now predominantly populated by a single ethnic group.

Curriculum is another contentious issue within BiH. So-called national subjects include subjects such as language, history and religion. The specific national subjects that are taught at a given school reflect the type of school. An integrated school, such as Vaso Pelagić Gimnazija in Brčko, offers all three language options (Bosnian, Croatian or Serbian) for students to choose between.[2] Segregated schools will offer instruction in either the Bosniak set

---

2 A note on language: Bosnian, Croatian and Serbian are recognized as distinct languages. However, the differences between the three languages are somewhat analogous to the differences between British, American and Australian English. There are some variations in vocabulary (e.g. *hleb* (Serbian) vs. *hljeb* (Bosnian) vs. *kruh* (Croatian) for bread) and there are some differences in syntax, but the three languages are mutually intelligible. During my fieldwork, students would often tell me 'we all speak the same language', and in light of this, rather than referring to the

of national subjects or the Croatian set, but it would be unlikely (or in some cases, impossible) for a student of one ethnicity to crossover to study the other group's version of language or history. Finally, monoethnic schools offer instruction in the set of national subjects that reflect the dominant ethnic group for that school. The issue of national subjects is particularly challenging as each group's interpretation of history is not necessarily compatible with the others'. Rather, questions of guilt and blame for historical grievances (one well-known example is the notorious Jasenovac concentration camp during World War II) can have very different answers depending on who is answering them. What this means is that students' understanding of the histories of their country and their people can be quite different, depending upon where in the country they are learning.

This led me to question the impact of education on the peacebuilding process in BiH. If students are taught conflicting versions of history – or conflicting versions of civic identity – it struck me as unlikely that young people in BiH would relate to one another as members of the same group, working towards a common goal. Rather, I suspected that students might feel alienated from one another and would not see each other as co-citizens. Thus, I designed a research project to assess the interethnic attitudes of third- and fourth-year Bosnian high school students.

Design

I was particularly interested in understanding the attitudes of Bosnian youth because of the timing of my project. I defended my prospectus in December 2011, 16 years after the DPA had been signed. I conducted my field research in 2013 and 2014, working with students who were – on average – 17 years old. Thus, my research sampled a particularly unique population at a particularly unique moment in time – BiH's first post-war generation as they were just about to make the transition from childhood to adulthood. These were students who had no direct memory of the war and did not personally experience ethnic violence. But these students also had never experienced multi-ethnic Yugoslavia nor Sarajevo at its cosmopolitan heights. Thus, they had no first-hand knowledge of how good – or how bad – things could be.

---

language as either Bosnian, Croatian or Serbian, I would often say *vaš* (or *tvoj*) *jezik*, meaning 'your language'. The most obvious difference between the languages is the alphabet they use – Bosnian and Croatian are typically written using the Latin alphabet, while Serbian is typically written in Cyrillic. Although everyone can understand the spoken version of each language, not all students (particularly those in the Federation) learn to read Cyrillic, and so this can pose a barrier to understanding written Serbian – including things like street and shop signs in RS.

I hoped to be able to capture their opinions and form an accurate assessment of the situation by using a mixed methodology based on interviews, focus groups and surveys. My one-to-one interviews were mainly conducted with local and international elites, as well as with school administrators and teachers. I also conducted a series of focus groups in which high school students met in a small group to discuss issues related to ethnicity, schools and citizenship. Finally, the largest source of data for this project came from a written survey (n=1,228) that I administered in schools throughout BiH. The bulk of the discussion within this chapter will focus on ethical considerations surrounding this survey.

Survey questions addressed issues of identity, ethnicity, discrimination and social distance (Bogardus 1933). Social distance questions were informed by the contact hypothesis (Allport 1954), which suggests that under certain positive conditions, social contact between different groups can lead to an improvement in group relations.

Results

My findings revealed that, on the whole, the kids were (mostly) all right. Overall, most students reported high levels of interethnic tolerance under a variety of social situations. Many students reported that they felt misunderstood and somewhat marginalised, but for the most part this reflected dissatisfaction with the institutional paralysis that characterised the Bosnian government and not a fundamental sense of alienation from other ethnic groups within their country.

However, approximately 20 per cent of Bosnian high school students surveyed reported attitudes of intolerance towards other ethnic groups. Additionally, the type of school that students attended mattered. Students who attended segregated or monoethnic schools reported, on average, less tolerant attitudes than students who attended integrated schools.

Furthermore, there were significant within-group differences. Serbs from the RS were significantly less tolerant than Serbs from Brčko District, an integrated region of the country.

Focus groups revealed additional layers of complexity within students' lives. For example, at one focus group I held in Vareš,[3] I asked students what would happen if a new federal policy took effect that mandated the integration of

---

3 In Vareš, elementary schools are segregated by ethnicity between Bosniaks and Croats, but the secondary school is integrated. National subjects are taught, but language is simply called *maternji jezik* or 'mother tongue'.

schools, both in terms of curriculum and students. One student volunteered, 'There would be a lot of verbal fighting between our parents.' This reflected two things: first, that it was not the younger generation of Bosnians who were responsible for perpetuating ethnic politics within the country, and second, that there was little appetite for a return to physical violence.

In all, the data I collected painted a picture largely characterised by interethnic tolerance and a desire among students to be a part of a multi-ethnic democracy that is not hyperfocused on the ethnic identities of its citizens. The data also suggested that there were differences in students' attitudes that varied in conjunction with the type of school that they attended (monoethnic, segregated or integrated). Given the limitations of my research design, it is not possible to state conclusively that school type can accurately predict student attitudes (in large part because it is not possible to extricate the effects of family and community – two major determinants of social attitudes – from school type); however, the data do show regional variations in student attitudes and, as such, I can draw the conclusion that students attending school in Banja Luka see themselves and their country very differently than students attending school in Sarajevo. This matters in terms of institutional design and democratisation. As noted, the political institutions of BiH are rooted in the entrenchment of ethnic political parties whose longevity relies on ongoing ethnic insecurities. Thus, if those institutions have produced a system of competing and contradictory education policy and practice, then this suggests that the extant political institutions of BiH are hindering, rather than helping, the consolidation of democracy in BiH. They also appear to be inhibiting the cultivation of an inclusive civic national identity to which all Bosnian citizens can ascribe.

Sensitive Data

Throughout this project I encountered sensitive data that challenged me to think critically about how to most ethically collect these data and – more importantly – to most ethically engage with my research subjects. In particular, these included issues surrounding trauma (including collective trauma and trauma triggers) and the somewhat fraught nature of collecting demographic information.

Trauma

It is important to note that just because an individual has not directly experienced violence, war or other traumatic events, this does not preclude the possibility of that individual experiencing trauma themselves. Furthermore, trauma felt at the collective level is often a key element of national or other group identity. Collective trauma, often referred to interchangeably as chosen trauma, can be defined as 'the shared mental representation of a massive trauma that [a] group's ancestors suffered at the hands of an enemy' (Volkan 2001). Thus, even though my research population – that is, Bosnian high school students – was born after the war and, thus, did not directly experience the violence that it entailed, that does not exclude this group from feeling the very real and direct traumas that were inflicted on their parents and other members of older generations. Indeed, as per a recent report from the Balkan Investigative Reporting Network, 'many post-war children have adopted the trauma of their parents and internalised ethnonationalist discourses via family upbringing' (Buljubasic 2020).

In light of this collective trauma, I had to be careful in considering the wording of questions and conversation topics so as to avoid triggering trauma responses in my research participants. I did not ask questions about direct or indirect exposures to violence and refrained from making any reference to the war. Rather, I modelled my questions on the European Social Survey, which had been conducted in neighbouring Croatia (a state that also had recently experienced violent conflict along ethnic lines) in 2010. Finally, each survey also included an informed assent statement that informed respondents of the nature of the questions that would be asked by the survey.

Demographics

Despite the fact that I avoided directly raising trauma-related issues, I did need to ask questions about the ethnic and religious identity of respondents, as well as the language(s) that they spoke at home. Although this type of demographic data collection can be fairly quotidian in some places, in BiH, demographic information can be quite sensitive, if it directly informs the distribution of political power throughout the country. Furthermore, the collective narratives that are attached to ethnic and religious identities in BiH do not always align with individuals' narratives and experiences. As such, I had to exercise care in how I disseminated and collected written surveys.

I administered the survey personally to students within their own classrooms with the express permission of the school's pedagogue (head administrator) and the verbal permission of each teacher whose classroom I entered. Because I was entering the students' classrooms and speaking from a position of authority (i.e. from the front of the classroom), I was sensitive to the fact that some students may have felt pressured into responding to the survey. I emphasised – both verbally, as I introduced myself in front of the classroom, and in writing within the assent statement – that participation was absolutely voluntary and that there would be no penalty for lack of participation. I told students that if they did not wish to complete the survey, they could simply turn in a blank survey when it was time to collect them. To preserve confidentiality, no personally identifying information was collected from the survey respondents. Students were explicitly instructed not to write their name on the survey.

Demographics – and in particular, ethnic and religious identities – influence the distribution of political power in BiH due to the structure of BiH's political institutions. The Dayton Constitution affirmed the notion of 'constituent peoples' in BiH; that is, it effectively enshrined Bosniaks, Croats and Serbs as the only groups with full access to political power within BiH. The institutionalised marginalisation of ethnic minorities by the Dayton Constitution is beyond the scope of this chapter, but it is important to understand that in BiH, access to power is largely influenced by ethnicity. One key example of this is the tripartite presidency of BiH, in which three individuals – a Bosniak member, a Croat member and a Serb member – form the country's executive branch. Eligibility to run for this office is determined by ethnicity (e.g. a Bosniak may not run for president in the RS because the RS is only eligible to vote for the Serbian member of the presidency). Thus, access to power is largely influenced by one's ethnicity in BiH, and questions in which survey respondents reveal their ethnicity could potentially expose respondents to discrimination should the confidentiality of their responses be breached.

The sensitivity surrounding demographic data in BiH is illustrated by the 2013 census and the issues that impeded the release of official census data. The 2013 census was the first official census of the citizens of BiH since 1991, and the administration of the 2013 census was hotly contested by members of the ethnic political parties that dominate Bosnian politics (Irwin 2013). Census data was collected in October 2013 but was not released publicly for almost three years, June 2016, and only after intense pressure from the European Union (Recknagel 2016).

Trust

Finally, in light of the issues associated with the collection of sensitive data, it is important to discuss the role of trust in human subjects research. Trust is critical to human subjects research. This applies not only to trust between the researcher and research subjects but also to trust between the broader research community and research population; between the researcher's institution and other institutions; and between sponsors, institutional review boards (IRBs) and the general public (Resnick 2018). Furthermore, the researcher also must be able to trust the research subjects to provide honest and truthful responses to the researcher's inquiries, just as the research subject must be able to trust that the researcher will protect personal data and will not harm the research subject. In short, trust must flow in all directions, and the importance of trust is heightened in research settings involving vulnerable populations.

Researchers working in these settings must avoid any sense of entitlement to subjects' personal data. Rather, researchers should remain cognizant of the fact that research subjects are effectively doing a service to the researcher and to the broader research community by being willing to share their personal data – which might better be described as their lived experiences. Therefore, researchers who are working with human subjects – in post-conflict spaces and otherwise – must continually strive to foster trust.

Trust can be achieved in any number of ways, from providing a credible guarantee of confidentiality, to offering a detailed consent statement, to demonstrating a personal commitment to the local community on the part of the researcher or researcher's institution (Resnick 2018). For this project, I sought to establish trust between myself and my research participants by obtaining, and then demonstrating, my deep familiarity with the local community. Rather than relying exclusively on local research assistants for translation and context, I learned the local languages and familiarised myself with the history and culture of BiH. Moreover, I had made many trips to the region prior to conducting my research, and I assured my research subjects that I would return to BiH and share my results with them once the analysis was complete.

Ethical Challenges

Beyond the necessity of avoiding triggers and protecting sensitive data, this project also offers a host of more generalisable ethical issues for discussion. These include issues surrounding permission; consent; implicit bias; 'outsider' status of the researcher; neutrality; objectivity; the question of who, exactly, benefits from research and finally, the impact that public health crises such as the COVID-19 pandemic may have on field-based research in the social sciences.

Permission

In order for me to conduct this research, I had to secure formal written permission from various administrative bodies. Of course, the first hurdle to clear was my own institution's IRB, which reviewed the English-language version of my survey and assent statements. Once inside BiH, I then needed to secure a letter of permission from each of the ministries of education for each of the cantons within which I would be collecting data from within the federation, as well as from the ministries in the RS and Brčko District. This was easier said than done. I wrote letters to each of the ministries, explaining the purpose of my research and enclosing a copy of my survey. Some of the ministries responded quickly via email or post, either providing permission outright or requesting additional information. However, some of the ministries did not respond at all, while other ministries issued an outright denial.

This undoubtedly influenced my sample, as I was only able to conduct research in places where I had received explicit permission. As a foreign researcher, I felt deeply obligated to adhere to local research protocols, not only because I wanted to respect the rules of the country in which I was a guest, but also because I recognised that as a foreign researcher my position was one of great privilege. I was personally removed from the situation, and I could choose to leave the narrative at any time. My research subjects could not. As such, when considering how one ought to ethnically conduct research in post-conflict spaces, I would argue that it is exceptionally important to follow the rules and regulations that govern research in that community.

Consent

Consent was another area for special concern. Because I was working with minors, my research subjects could not technically consent to participate in my research. Furthermore, as discussed earlier in the chapter, I had concerns that students would feel pressured to complete the survey or to participate in focus groups because they were told (or asked) to do so from someone who was standing the front of their classroom – a position of authority. Therefore, it is important to go beyond the perfunctory requirement of a written assent statement and to make a point to verbally emphasise – in the primary language spoken by the research subjects – that participation is wholly voluntary and that there will be no negative repercussions for declining to participate. In saying this, it is also important to disclose the purpose of the research, if possible. This allows research participants to make better-informed decisions regarding whether they wish to participate.

These considerations apply to all human subjects research, but especially for research conducted with minors in a classroom setting.

Implicit bias

When constructing survey instruments or scripts for focus groups or interviews, it is essential to consider the risk of implicit bias. For example, survey questions should not imply favouritism on the part of the researcher towards any one party. Equally important is the avoidance of any implicit bias or favouritism towards the researcher's own background.

'Outsider' status

Often, researchers are not members of the research populations they study. This does not necessarily render the researcher incapable of conducting a sound and robust analysis of the population of interest – rather, in many ways, this can be an advantage to preserving objectivity and impartiality or neutrality. In my research in BiH, I was often asked by students, 'Why do you care about our situation?' Researchers should be able to answer this question readily and genuinely. As mentioned earlier in this chapter, research subjects do not owe researchers their participation. If the researcher is an outsider (in the local language in BiH, I was a *strankinja* – literally, a stranger), incentives for participants to trust the researcher are low. If the researcher has a compelling reason why they are interested in the local situation despite the fact that they are an outsider, this can improve trust between both parties, and thereby improve the validity (and perhaps also the volume) of the data collected.

Neutrality

Social science researchers have long attempted to maintain neutral orientation towards their data and research subjects, in part because this has allowed social scientists to mimic the patterns of inquiry typically associated with the physical sciences (Horowitz 1962). However, social scientists are far more likely than physical scientists to confront moral ambiguities and ethical obstacles to maintaining their neutrality.

In post-conflict spaces or otherwise contentious research settings, the researcher may experience implicit or explicit pressure from research subjects to side with one group over another. This pressure can be particularly difficult to navigate in settings where the prevailing local attitude differs from the researcher's own perspective on the situation. Nevertheless, it is essential for researchers to avoid revealing their own personal opinions to research subjects; rather, researchers must maintain a position of detached and neutral inquiry.

One instance that challenged my neutrality during this research project in BiH was when I visited a secondary school in Banja Luka, the administrative capital of the RS. In one of the classrooms there, I was met with a portrait of Bosnian Serb Gen. Ratko Mladić hanging above the blackboard. At the time, Mladić was on trial at the International Criminal Tribunal for the Former Yugoslavia in The Hague for crimes against humanity, including responsibility for the Srebrenica genocide. Although I was struck by the fact that the likeness of a man who had called for Bosnian Serb forces to 'bomb [Sarajevans] to the edge of madness' (Off 2000, 294), and who would ultimately be found guilty of the crime of genocide, was hanging in a classroom where children were educated, I could not reveal my reaction.

Although the researcher may maintain his or her own internal personal opinion about who is right and who is wrong, the researcher must also maintain his or her own outward neutrality when collecting data in post-conflict spaces and other contentious research settings. This is to avoid jeopardising trust as well as to avoid swaying research participants' responses. The researcher's role is not to arbitrate but, rather, to understand.

Objectivity

Objectivity is an ethical challenge that is related to – but not synonymous with – the challenge of neutrality. Scientific research demands objectivity on the part of the researcher if that research is to generate valid conclusions. However, objectivity and neutrality are not interchangeable. Furthermore, objectivity is not to be confused with truth. Instead, objectivity can be defined as 'an attitude toward the truth value of propositions' (Harding 1977).

Objectivity as an attitude suggests that the researcher must maintain a sense of openness to the data they are collecting. This can be particularly difficult to negotiate when having frank conversations with research subjects about painful or traumatic experiences. In most cases, it is essential for the researcher to maintain a position of compassionate detachment during these conversations, separating the details of the event(s) that happened from the actor(s) who perpetrated the action. After the fact, the researcher may then evaluate, analyse and synthesise all of the narratives that have been presented to form a scholarly assessment of the situation – but at the moment of data collection, it is essential that the researcher maintain a sense of objectivity and receptiveness to all of the information they can compile. By accepting the potential truthfulness of the full array of available information, the researcher maximises the possibility that they will be able to generate a more accurate and more complete analysis.

This is, admittedly, exceptionally difficult. As such, issues of preserving neutrality and objectivity are perhaps some of the most pressing ethical challenges associated with conducting research in post-conflict spaces.

Who benefits from this research?

It is important to consider who will benefit from any given research project. Research that is undertaken for the sole benefit of the researcher or the researcher's home research community is not as compelling as research that will benefit the research subject(s) in some way. Before undertaking any research project, researchers ought to think critically about what both parties stand to gain (and perhaps lose) from the research project.

Unfortunately, I could not promise any direct benefits to my research participants beyond the chocolate bars that I often brought to focus group meetings. However, I did tell my participants that I hoped that my research would be used to inform policy, which might ultimately strengthen the democratic institutions in BiH. Moreover, I also made sure to tell my research subjects that I would share my experiences in BiH with my students in the United States, and so, in a sense, they were contributing to the broader long-term project of fostering mutual understanding between BiH and the United States. Admittedly, these benefits may not have resonated deeply with the Bosnian teenagers who submitted survey responses and participated in focus groups, but nevertheless I presented them for their consideration.

Implications of COVID-19

Finally, the COVID-19 pandemic has perhaps irrevocably altered the way that social science research using human subjects – and in particular, minor human subjects – can take place. Therefore, it is necessary to consider what ethical research in post-conflict spaces might look like when public health concerns raise complications.

For this specific project, having access to a large number of research subjects within a classroom setting was essential to collecting survey responses. Had I attempted this research in spring 2020, I would not have been able to collect data from within schools, as they had been shuttered due to the pandemic. This would have dramatically impeded my ability to measure student attitudes, as I would not have been able to gain access to that population. As schools began to transition to online courses, it would have been theoretically possible to survey students remotely through distance education channels. However, it would have been much more difficult to preserve the validity of the survey data, as I would not have been able to visually confirm that the students themselves were completing the survey and that they were doing so without feedback or input from anyone else in their homes. As such, sometimes face-to-face interaction with research subjects is essential. In the case of research designed to measure the interethnic attitudes of Bosnian high school students, it would not have been possible to adapt this research design to a virtual or remote version.

COVID-19 will pose long-lasting challenges to researchers in post-conflict spaces. States have reasserted control over their international borders, and it is now difficult or impossible to travel between countries. Moreover, in many states, this control extends to the local level as states such as France, Italy and Spain have restricted the travel of their own citizens to relatively small radii. Furthermore, research involving close contact between individuals and groups – for example, interviews and focus groups – must now be conducted virtually via telephone or videoconference rather than in person. The loss of the in-person element potentially compromises the collection of sensitive data as it lessens the human connection between researcher and research subject – an essential element of trust-building. Absent a trusting relationship between these two parties, it is less likely that research subjects will be entirely candid in their responses.

Thus, public health crises such as the COVID-19 pandemic pose dual threats to the ethical conduct of research in post-conflict spaces – first, in terms of limiting access to research subjects, and second, in terms of inhibiting trust between the researcher and research subjects.

Conclusion

This chapter uses a research project on interethnic attitudes among Bosnian youth as a case study illustrating the ethical considerations and challenges associated with data collection in post-conflict spaces. Ultimately, the question of how one ought to conduct research in post-conflict settings is one that should be answered by first developing a deep familiarity with the case in question. Some specific ethical issues that may arise in each situation – especially those challenges related to issues of permission, consent, implicit bias, outsider status, neutrality, objectivity and the question of who benefits from research – will be idiosyncratic to the case at hand. These should be assessed and considered carefully.

Nevertheless, consideration of the broader issues discussed in this chapter – namely, questioning whether and which personal data should be deemed sensitive and thinking critically about specific ethical challenges to the case at hand – will provide a strong starting point for scholars to conduct research in post-conflict spaces.

Bibliography

Allport, Gordon W. 1954. *The Nature of Prejudice*. Reading, MA: Addison-Wesley.
Bogardus, E. S. 1933. "A Social Distance Scale." *Sociology and Social Research* 17: 265–271.
Buljubasic, Mirza, and Barbora Holá. 2020. "Next Generation: Enemies Inherited and the Bosnians Trying to Resist." *Balkan Investigative Reporting Network (BIRN)*. July 30. Accessed July 30, 2020. https://balkaninsight.com/2020/07/30/next-generation

-enemies-inherited-and-the-bosnians-trying-to-resist/?fbclid=IwAR3iaFbdBaL-bQEwyQF2aE7s8BXm6H5wYbBDf6TlRZtwryHqMYVqwFr4WxY.

Drakulić, Slavenka. 2004. *They Would Never Hurt a Fly: War Criminals on Trial in The Hague*. New York: Viking Penguin.

Harding, Sandra G. 1977. "Does Objectivity in Social Science Require Value-Neutrality?" *Soundings: An Interdisciplinary Journal* 60(4): 351–366.

Horowitz, Irving Lewis. 1962. "Social Science Objectivity and Value Neutrality: Historical Problems and Projections." *Diogenes* 10(39): 17–44.

International Crisis Group. 1997. *Refugees and Internally Displaced Persons in B-H*. April 30. Accessed July 31, 2020. https://www.refworld.org/docid/3ae6a6d20.html.

Irwin, Rachel, Dzenana Halimovic, Drazen Huterer, Meja Bjelajac, and Mladen Lakic. 2013. *Bosnian Census Risks Deepening Ethnic Rifts*. December 12. Accessed July 31, 2020. https://www.opendemocracy.net/en/opensecurity/bosnian-census/.

Off, Carol. 2000. *The Lion, the Fox, & the Eagle: A Story of Generals and Justice in Rwanda and Yugoslavia*. Toronto: Random House Canada.

Recknagel, Charles. 2016. *Bosnia Erupts in Feuding Over New Census Data*. June 30. Accessed July 31, 2020. https://www.rferl.org/a/bosnia-census-results-spark-feuding/27831183.html.

Resnick, David B. 2018. *The Ethics of Research with Human Subjects: Protecting People, Advancing Science, Promoting Trust*. Cham, Switzerland: Springer.

Volkan, Vamik D. 2001. "Transgenerational Transmissions and Chosen Traumas: An Aspect of Large-Group Identity." *Group Analysis* 34(1): 79–97.

PART III

Chapter 6

LESSONS FROM THE EBOLA EPIDEMIC IN SIERRA LEONE: THE IMPORTANCE OF STATE, INGO, AND LOCAL NETWORK ACTORS

Thynn Thynn Hlaing and Emilie J. Greenhalgh

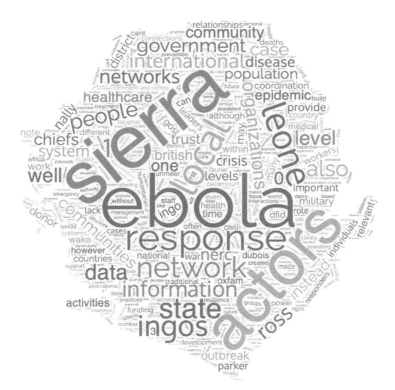

Introduction

On 31 March 2020, Sierra Leone reported its first case of COVID-19. Meanwhile, the rest of the world was already implementing curfews, quarantines and contact tracing to try and prevent the novel coronavirus from continuing to spread. Sierra Leone was experienced in implementing similar measures, being one of the three contiguous West African countries that suffered from the worst outbreak of Ebola Virus Disease (EVD) in history, from 2014 to 2016. Sierra Leone was finally deemed Ebola-free in March 2016, after 14,124 probable cases and 3,956 deaths out of 11,325 deaths worldwide (CDC, 2019).

Sierra Leone's experience and lessons learned fighting Ebola are relevant today, as COVID-19 is present in nearly every country on earth. How did Sierra Leone manage to curb the spread of Ebola when the Centers for Disease Control and Prevention (CDC) projected that up to 1.4 million people would succumb to the disease? Not only did Sierra Leone rank 180 out of 187 on the UN Human Development Index in 2014, but it was also ranked among the world's 10 poorest countries (World Bank, 2011). When Ebola hit, the country had only recently emerged from an 11-year civil war and local trust in the government was low. It had one of the weakest healthcare systems in the world, with an average life expectancy of 52.37 years (World Bank). The number of doctors for the population was dangerously low and rural roads were in such poor condition, with clinics so far away, that it made it nearly impossible for people to seek healthcare – and they might be unwilling to go anyway, given the rumours circulating about Ebola. Some believed that the disease was introduced by the ruling political party to kill their rivals. Others simply believed that Ebola was a death sentence: if you went to an Ebola treatment unit (ETU) you would die and the doctors would not return your body to your family for a traditional burial, despite its cultural importance. The high death rate was also tragically reflected in the number of local healthcare workers who succumbed to the disease: out of the 307 who were infected in Sierra Leone, 221 died (Raven et al., 2018).

During the Ebola crisis, the Government of Sierra Leone (GoSL), led by President Ernest Bai Koroma, relied heavily on support and guidance from its former coloniser, Great Britain, as well as on technical expertise provided by the myriad of international humanitarian and development non-governmental organisations (INGOs) that responded to the crisis. Ineffective and in denial at the beginning of the epidemic, under the advisement of the British, the GoSL eventually adopted a militarised command-and-control framework that attempted to organise the various actors in an efficient and effective manner, with mixed results. This framework was the National Ebola Response Centre (NERC), led by the Minister of Defence. This framework was necessary because the United Nations (UN) decided not to declare Ebola a Level-3 humanitarian emergency due to political concerns, despite the potential magnitude of the epidemic. This classification would have taken away the sovereignty of government in regard to the management of the crisis and turned it over to the UN Office for the Coordination of Humanitarian Affairs (OCHA). OCHA would have activated a formal cluster system that would have allowed networks of INGOs working on similar activities to officially coordinate with each other, strategically plan and would have provided streamlined monitoring and evaluation tools (Humanitarianresponse.info, accessed 2020).

Without the cluster system, INGOs in Sierra Leone were struggling to obtain accurate and up-to-date data on who was doing what, where. While the government's command-and-control system slowly became operational, INGOs relied on information from the UK's development donor arm, the Department for International Development (DfID), their own actors in the field and on each other. Organisations that typically worked in development were pressured to go beyond their comfort zones and work on emergency health projects while pausing their traditional programming.

While the government was establishing its command-and-control system and the INGOs were struggling to find direction, Sierra Leoneans on the ground were beginning to respond to the crisis as well. Initially, they were sceptical of the outbreak but eventually, after witnessing the destruction Ebola could bring to their communities, grudgingly complied with strict containment strategies that were often developed by their own local leaders.

This chapter considers the three most salient levels of analysis during the Ebola crisis in Sierra Leone: the state, the network of INGOs and the local community networks of individuals, analysing how these different levels interacted or did not interact with each other – and how these interactions helped or hindered the Ebola response. It will consider these interactions through the lens of Anne-Marie Slaughter's theory put forward in *The Chessboard and the Web*, determining that the role of state actors as inherently self-interested is critical, but networks of INGOs and local actors are equally as relevant, especially in a post-colonial, post-conflict context. While the lessons from the Sierra Leone Ebola response may be unique, they demonstrate the importance of network actors in a pandemic response, which is applicable to COVID-19 today.

International Relations Theory

In her book *The Chessboard and the Web*, Anne-Marie Slaughter notes the importance of both traditional Waltzian realist international relations theory, which gives primacy to states, powered by human nature and operating in a chaotic international system (the 'chessboard'), but also network theory, which suggests that in a rapidly globalising age with continuous improvements to technology, networks of actors are equally important in international relations (the 'web'). She notes that the neoliberal theory of complex interdependence put forth by Robert Keohane and Joseph Nye in their seminal work *Power and Interdependence* is 'the extreme case of the web world', but that their work 'describes the web world, but does not give us web strategies' (Slaughter, 2017, 27–28). This more classical liberalism also gives priority to states as the preferred level of analysis, as well as considering state-driven international institutions, such as the UN, as the main mode of cooperation. However, Slaughter then brings in Andrew Moravcsik's neoliberalist assertion that individuals and groups within a state have an essential impact on both the states where they are based as well as on foreign individuals, groups and states (Slaughter, 2017, 29), which is what we will see in our analysis of the Ebola response in Sierra Leone.

A unique element of Slaughter's framework is her focus on the importance of actors across different levels of analysis. When scholars analyse what happened during a particular political event or crisis, they typically deem one level of analysis most important: the state, international organisations or individuals. Slaughter argues, 'It is important that we see power and interdependence, states and people, structure and agency, stasis and dynamism, all at the same time' (2017, 59). To her, web actors are not just 'determinants of state behavior, [but] global actors in their own right' (2017, 29).

Networks are found somewhere between markets, where interactions are not repetitive or particularly complex, and hierarchies, where interactions are formal, inflexible, repetitive and require some level of investment of time, human resources and people (Williamson, 1975, 1985). Some of the key characteristics of a network are its relational nature, its emphasis on reciprocity, its interdependence and its allowance for expressing complementary strengths (Powell, 1990). Networks can still be hierarchical and indeed, sometimes it can be difficult to determine whether an organised group of people is operating in a hierarchy or a network. But one of the important differences is that in a network, there is an 'ability of actors to increase their power by enhancing and exploiting their network positions' and also the unique 'fungibility of network power' (Hafner-Burton et al., 2009, 3). This ability to increase or decrease one's power in a network, as opposed to a more static power structure in a hierarchy, is one of the key differences.

A focus on networks and the individual actors within them, instead of just on the 'black box' of the state, is particularly relevant in the case of Sierra Leone. Like most African countries, the borders of Sierra Leone were artificially created by a colonial power, the British, in 1895, and the local vassals who interacted with the British government did not necessarily have the typical legitimacy found in home-grown states, which, especially in the Western world, determine their own borders and governments. The artificial creation of a state along with a government that lacks complete legitimacy in the eyes of its people suggests that a simple focus on the state as the most important actor is inappropriate in this context.

This is further demonstrated by the fact that the country only emerged from a brutal 11-year civil war in 2002. The civil war was largely driven by perceived and real corruption at the state level, but also external regional factors, competition for access to natural resources, and poverty and lack of opportunity, particularly for the country's youth population. The civil war saw child soldiers across all ethnic groups and over national borders swept up in the violence. The war left in its wake a generation of people who lacked education, proper healthcare, trust in government and were traumatised by the events that had rocked their country for more than a decade. Therefore, it would be simplistic to only consider the state's actions when looking at any events that have occurred in recent Sierra Leonean history.

Sierra Leone achieved independence from Great Britain in 1961, and post-colonial elements, namely, an inherent belief that the former coloniser can 'do it better' and that external solutions to local problems will produce the optimal results, are also major factors to consider when analysing the Ebola response in Sierra Leone (Inayatullah and Blaney, 2004). These post-colonial aspects are prevalent in the GoSL's ongoing relationship with the British, for 'connections were not just based on money, but were built on good individual relationships and were even "cultural" in nature or encompassing "deference to the British"' (Harris and Conteh, 2020, 10). The belief in the superiority of the British's ability to handle the Ebola response went both ways: both the British and the Sierra Leoneans seemed to believe the British were better equipped to handle the crisis – or at least had the money to do so. 'A common phrase heard during the Ebola crisis was "Papa don cam fo save pikin", meaning "Father has returned to save his children" and mostly in reference to the British intervention' (Harris and Conteh, 2020, 13). The United States, primarily through the CDC, was also a prominent actor, although its focus was Liberia, also due to former colonial ties. Yet, while the British were seen by some as a saviour, the capabilities of the local population to respond to the outbreak were mostly ignored or denigrated (Parker et al., 2019; Thomas, 2014). This negative perception of the local communities was reflected by international news coverage, the actions of both the government and the international community and is still present in much of the post-epidemic literature.

In addition to the difficulty of throwing off colonial vestiges simply because the dominion of OECD countries is baked into international institutions (Persaud and Sajed, 2018), Sierra Leone's government struggles to assert its primacy on the international stage because it is highly dependent on foreign aid to meet its budget requirements (Kargbo, 2012). Aid money poured in after the civil war ended and the UK government stepped in to provide hands-on guidance and support to the government. For the Ebola response in Sierra Leone, Guinea and Liberia, governments, international organisations and NGOs donated over $3.2 billion (CDC, 2016), with the United States as the biggest donor and the UK the biggest donor in Sierra Leone.

In addition to the multitude of development and humanitarian organisations already operating in Sierra Leone when Ebola hit, countless others arrived in the country to assist with the response. One organisation that was present in Sierra Leone since 2002, engaged primarily in longer-term Water, Sanitation, and Hygiene (WASH) work, was Oxfam. At the time, it was led by Thynn Thynn Hlaing in Sierra Leone, who is the primary author of this chapter. Hlaing's experience leading Oxfam in Sierra Leone during the epidemic is relevant to this analysis as it was similar to many other INGOs present in the country at the time and shows how the power and influence of INGO network actors can ebb and flow, based on various factors.

The existing literature on the Ebola response typically focuses on the role of state actors, international organisations such as the UN and INGOs – and their management systems. This lens, while demonstrating important lessons learned that might apply to the organisational aspects of future epidemic responses, does not take into consideration individual network actors at the district and village levels. The literature mostly notes that the management structure of the response and the coordination between state and INGO actors were inefficient and ineffective in the beginning but then slowly improved, eventually resulting in a group of actors that worked well together (Mobula et al., 2018; NERC, 2015; Olu et al., 2016; Ross et al., 2017). Interestingly, the outbreak reportedly peaked before the management systems were finally effective, again begging the question of what created the turning point in the fight against the disease, as both the World Health Organization (WHO) and CDC predicted far greater numbers of cases and deaths than occurred. While it may be difficult to pinpoint one particular factor that finally stopped the disease, it is important to acknowledge the significance of relevant actors at the state, INGO and individual network levels and how they interacted with one another – not just the command-and-control structure put in place by the GoSL under the recommendation of DfID.

Finally, a few chapters within the literature consider the importance of individual networks by way of an anthropological lens (Abramovitz et al., 2014;

Chandler et al., 2015; Goguen and Bolten, 2017; Oosterhoff and Wilkinson, 2015; Parker et al., 2019; Richards et al., 2015). These chapters note how the government simultaneously disempowered the local population by making top-down decisions about information sharing, containment and treatment while also putting out information campaigns blaming them for the 'wasted [first] seven months' in the fight against the disease (Oosterhoff and Wilkinson, 2015, 1). The literature also brings in case studies of how remote individual villages used their own trial-and-error strategies, honed during other disease outbreaks, and trust in local actors to curb Ebola's advance without external medical interventions (Parker et al., 2019; Richards et al., 2015). It further explores how the state and INGO's lack of understanding of trade, school and family networks made the EVD jump more quickly in certain areas of the country (Richards et al., 2015, 9). However, there are gaps regarding the interactions between the powerful local network actors, the state and the INGO community and the mechanisms by which one network actor influenced another.

In this chapter, we argue that hierarchical networks exist at the three different levels of the state, INGOs and local individuals, and occasionally actors in one network overlap into another, creating opportunities for increased efficiency and information sharing. We will consider state actors to be anyone working for a country's government, anyone in the military and somewhat uniquely, the WHO and UNMEER (UN Mission for Ebola Emergency Response), which seemed, in this case, to act purely based on the interests of their member countries and not as impartial bodies. State representatives are included down to the level of the 149 paramount chiefs in Sierra Leone's 14 districts. However, as these chiefs are the highest existing level of traditional authority in the country (Richards et al., 2015, 4), they may also be considered as a part of local networks, operating as important hubs connecting the local population with the central government and transmitting information.

For this analysis, international NGOs (including locally employed staff), local NGOs and Western medicine-trained healthcare workers are included at the INGO level. International NGOs are heavily influenced by the states from which they receive funding and are often unable to make timely, autonomous decisions based on the information from their networks. Instead, they are forced to comply with the more hierarchical and bureaucratic state structures. Local NGOs are also affected by the decisions of the international NGOs, for whom they often subcontract. The locally employed staff in international organisations may also straddle the INGO and local levels, as many are from the districts in which they operate, speak the local languages and still have ties to traditional leaders. Western medicine-trained healthcare workers straddle both the INGO and local levels as well, as they may be from the communities in which they serve. However, healthcare workers were frequently mistrusted and ostracised during the crisis (Miller et al., 2018).

Finally, at the local level, in which there are chiefdoms comprised of villages, there are speakers, section chiefs, councils of elders, village chiefs, religious leaders, secret societies, mammy queens (female leaders) and traditional healers – with the paramount chiefs operating as the highest level of traditional authority and the lowest level of administrative authority.

Background on the Ebola Outbreak and Response in Sierra Leone

The first reported case of Ebola that launched the outbreak in West Africa was a young boy in Guinea in December 2013. The case likely occurred from contact with an infected bat, but most of the cases that followed were from human-to-human transmission. By March 2014, the disease had spread to neighbouring Liberia. In preparation for a potential outbreak, Sierra Leone's Ministry of Health and Sanitation (MOHS) established a National Ebola Task Force in late March 2014, whose role was to launch awareness campaigns and provide surveillance in border regions (Ross et al., 2017). Sierra Leone reported its first case of Ebola in late May 2014, which was traced to a traditional healer who had treated patients from Guinea (Ross et al., 2017).

Of the four known strains of Ebola that affect humans (Zaire, Sudan, Taï Forest and Bundibugyo), the epidemic was the Zaire strain, which has the highest mortality rate (Kadanali and Karagoz, 2015). All strains of Ebola are spread by bodily fluids from an ill or dead person, with the disease transmitted through broken skin or the mucus membranes in the eyes, nose or mouth. It is a social disease, in that people typically catch it from caring for the sick or engaging in traditional burial practices that involve washing the body. The symptoms of this deadly haemorrhagic fever are bleeding, vomiting and chronic diarrhoea. It is highly contagious, particularly within close quarters, with family transmission rates of up to 74 per cent (Ribacke et al., 2016). At the time of the outbreak, there was no EVD vaccine and no proven treatment. Thus, the only way to manage the Ebola epidemic was to isolate infected individuals and provide rehydration.

Much of Sierra Leone's infrastructure and public systems were destroyed during its civil war, and its health system, in particular, was abysmal. In Sierra Leone, Liberia and Guinea – the most affected countries – 'systemic weaknesses in [their] health systems and services – including insufficient funding, an inadequate workforce, poor infrastructure, shortages of medicines and supplies, and weak health information and disease surveillance systems – all contributed to the spread of Ebola and undermined efforts to respond' (DuBois and Wake, 2015, v). In Sierra Leone, in particular, there were not enough quality healthcare workers, limited access to healthcare centres especially for the rural population, poor communication among the local and national healthcare levels, and inadequate funding (Denney and Mallett, 2015). The WHO asserts that countries should have one healthcare worker per 439 people. In Sierra Leone, there was one worker per 5,219 people (Save the Children, 2015). Furthermore, the population did not have confidence in the healthcare system and would often choose traditional and/or private methods of healthcare instead (Denney and Mallett, 2015). Although donors provided funding for projects to help Sierra Leone achieve the Millennium Development Goal targets, which helped make major strides in access to basic health services for women, new mothers and children under five, these siloed projects neglected to strengthen the overall healthcare system (Denney and Mallett, 2015).

When Ebola finally arrived in Sierra Leone, both the MOHS and the WHO were ill-prepared and slow to act. Although the National Ebola Task Force met daily, 'the meetings were "long and ineffective. The early coordination lacked leadership, focus and there was a lot of flailing around. There was a real issue around gripping the size of the problem"' (Ross et al., 2017, 7). By July 2014, with Ebola in-country for more than a month already, the MOHS dissolved the task force and established an Ebola Operations Centre (EOC) as the first iteration command-and-control system (Ross et al., 2017). This response mechanism was also rife with issues. 'Data sharing was a significant problem. Figures quoted by the MOHS were not matching WHO's, nor what responders were reporting for the field. [...] WHO was not playing an independent role, and no one in authority wanted to admit to President Koroma how bad the situation was' (Ross et al., 2017, 7). The president had to personally witness the ineffectiveness of the EOC before he elected to change the response mechanism for the third time in four months. On 30 July, the president declared a national emergency, viewed by many as late, and established the Presidential Task Force on Ebola. It too was ineffective. The MOHS did not have a clear mandate to hold other ministries or the military accountable for the response, and by August 2014, the disease had spread to all but two of the country's 14 districts (National Ebola Response Centre, 2015). By the end of August, the president had decided to fire the Minister of Health and Sanitation, Miatta Kargbo, who was not qualified for the job anyway (Thomas, 2014). The UN also decided to replace the WHO country representative (Ross et al., 2017).

By September, deeming the Ebola outbreak a national security threat, the UK decided that it would step up support to Sierra Leone (Govt. UK, 2014).

The UK's prominent role in the Ebola response may be traced to its long history with Sierra Leone. Sierra Leone, subject to the slave trade in the sixteenth and seventeenth centuries, became a colony for freed slaves from the UK, Nova Scotia and Jamaica and was the British's hub to fight the trans-Atlantic slave trade after 1807. Freetown became the capital of British West Africa, with Sierra Leone's modern borders established by the British in 1895. The British ruled indirectly through paramount chiefs until Sierra Leone's independence in 1961. Post-independence, the colonial ties remained strong, with the UK acting as a key player in providing military support to end the civil war, followed by ongoing support and training to the military in order to promote peace and stability (Ucko, 2015). The UK remains the largest bilateral donor to Sierra Leone (Harris and Conteh, 2020).

In September 2014, the UK, in collaboration with the WHO, determined that the British military would be best suited to help with the Ebola response in Sierra Leone (Global Ebola Response, 2015). This was closely followed by the UN's creation of UNMEER, the first-ever UN health emergency mission combining health, humanitarian response and security. As previously mentioned, President Koroma declined a UN Level-3 humanitarian crisis designation, which would have activated the OCHA cluster system. This system would have imposed a more ordered response with a globally understood structure and systems for reporting and accountability. However, this designation would have taken away the response authority from the GoSL and put it officially into the hands of the international community. Despite the lack of official responsibility given to the UN or bilateral actors, because of their epidemiological, organisational, military and logistical expertise, as well as significant amounts of funding, these major post-colonial donors had more power and influence than officially recognised. Two days after the creation of UNMEER, the UK launched Operation Gritrock, a civilian–military task force that would end up leading the international operational Ebola response (Ross et al., 2017, 5).

Meanwhile, without the leadership and official networks created by the cluster system, many INGOs were without direction. For many, the first few months of the epidemic were marked by fear for the well-being of their staff, resulting in the decision to pause traditional development activities. As UK involvement ramped up, DfID started to push the INGOs to engage in work outside their areas of expertise. Most of these organisations called on their networks, both in the local community and within other organisations, to try and better understand what was happening on the ground while also searching for guarantees that their staff could receive adequate medical treatment should they contract Ebola (Adams et al., 2015).

As the outbreak unfolded, the network of INGOs expanded to incorporate newly arriving organisations and their roles evolved as different activities were prioritised. These changes may have led to some being ignored by the main hub actors, such as DfID or the GoSL, who had the money and authority to back up their decisions and were not initially concerned with listening to the recommendations of organisations, even if they had deep operational experience on the ground. Yet finally, after the worst of the epidemic had passed, the INGOs, including Oxfam, reached a more comfortable state of power and interaction within their networks. Over time, their knowledge of the context and connections with the community were finally valued by the main network hubs (Adams et al., 2015).

In October 2014, with the epidemic nearing its peak, President Koroma decided to reconfigure the national response strategy one last time. With a clear recommendation from DfID, the president formed the NERC, headed by the Minister of Defence. The NERC's 'situation room' was charged with data collection, analysis and information management, with the goal of driving decisions around the response strategy (Ross et al., 2017). The NERC, at the national level, was followed by a roll-out of 14 District Ebola Response Centres (DERCs) at the district level in late October, which ran parallel to the existing regional government structures. The DERCs were made up of politically appointed district coordinators and district medical officers, as well as epidemiologists, a DFID command team and NGOs operating in the region (Ross et al., 2017). Within both the NERC and the DERCs, work was organised in eight technical pillars: case management, burials, alerts, surveillance, quarantine, labs, social mobilisation and psychosocial support. Notably absent was a WASH pillar, although Ebola is transmitted through bodily fluids and simple sanitary measures can prevent new cases. Also of note is that although the command-and-control structure was officially rolled out by the end of October, with both donors and NGOs complaining about its initial ineffectiveness and saying that it was 'building the plane while flying it' (DuBois and Wake, 2015, 27), the number of cases in Sierra Leone peaked by late November. This would suggest that other factors apart from the command-and-control system contributed to the slow in cases.

While the GoSL and DfID managed the command-and-control mechanisms, bringing in the British military to assist with logistics, the INGOs were far more implicated in the eight technical pillars. Because the OCHA cluster system was not activated, these organisations decided to create their own coordination structures to share information and decide who would do what. Fifteen international organisations headed by the International Rescue Committee (IRC) formed the Ebola Response Consortium (Ebola Response Consortium, 2015), while five organisations created the Social Mobilisation

Action Consortium (SMAC). These groups were not inclusive of all organisations operating in the country, so coordination and coverage were not comprehensive.

Interestingly, because the outbreak required flexible information sharing and coordination, the telltale signs of a web structure (Slaughter, 2017, 49), the response community created an informal Skype group that had, 'At its peak [...] a total of 232 active users from 92 organisation (Waugaman and Fast, 2016, 92). Oxfam had been the lead organisation in the Freetown WASH Consortium funded by DFID and maintained these relationships, as well as engaging daily through SMS, WhatsApp groups and emails with a variety of actors. The creation of these types of groups demonstrates the flexible, web-like nature of the network of international and local organisations in the face of a rapidly evolving situation – and also suggests that they were not receiving adequate data from the UN and the NERC. These informal groups contrasted with the militarised top-down state response, which often held up decision-making. Ross et al. note that when the NERC was in its early days, DfID would often go directly to the DERCs to speed things up. Furthermore, once the NERC became more effective, there were reported clashes of character between the NERC and DfID, not to mention between the NERC and the MOHS, which was upset about its authority being usurped. With so many structures in place and inconsistent leadership, each actor sought to follow their interests and the strategy they thought was best (Adams et al., 2015, 20; Ross et al., 2017).

Meanwhile, local community networks, being on the front lines, were heavily involved in the Ebola response. The paramount chiefs were one of the more important network hub actors, straddling the local and state levels to channel information and enforce rules. As previously noted, Sierra Leone was made up of 14 districts during the time of the epidemic. Every district has a paramount chief although 'paramount chiefs, and the chiefly system associated with them, is an introduced hybrid of customary and formal institutions' (Parker et al., 2019, 444). One paramount chief per district also holds parliamentary seats in the national government (Richards et al., 2015, 4). The paramount chiefs have held a contentious role in Sierra Leonean history since colonisation when they 'were appointed from a small pool of elite families, and they were expected to exercise sole authority over local government, with mentoring and support from British officials' (Parker et al., 2019, 442). During this time, the chiefs acted as middlemen between the British and the local population to promote their own best interests. Interestingly, this included fighting the British's attempts to control a smallpox outbreak in 1905 and again a smallpox and Spanish flu outbreak from 1915 to 1919 (Rashid, 2011). Leading up to the civil war, the paramount chiefs were known for their abuses of power and for not allowing dissenting views (Keen, 2005). The Ebola crisis provided an avenue by which they could again play a mediation role between the state and the local population. A more in-depth discussion of how the paramount chiefs operated during the epidemic is found in the coordination section below.

The Role of Trust

Slaughter (2017) notes that a network ceases to exist if no information is passed among its nodes. It is these repeated interactions that build up the resilience and effectiveness of a network. Repeated interactions can also build or erode trust, depending on their quality. And while networks of similar actors organically form, it can be more difficult for different networks to interact with one another, even if cooperation may be in their best interest. The networks of state actors, INGOs and within the local communities were unable to effectively integrate during the Ebola response in Sierra Leone due to a tremendous lack of trust between the levels. 'Trust consists of placing valued outcomes at risk of others' malfeasance, mistakes, or failures' (Tilly, 2005, 12), and in this case, the valued outcome was the health of the members of each network. Because of past interactions, the different network actors did not believe that outsiders could be trusted to value their best interests, not take advantage of them or simply protect them.

This lack of trust was exacerbated by the fear that surrounded Ebola. With a high mortality rate, dying healthcare workers, sensationalised media, local conspiracy theories and a need to don something akin to a spacesuit when around Ebola patients (personal protective equipment, or PPE), the Ebola outbreak caused significant fear at all levels – from the local communities to world leaders. Fear caused airlines to stop flights to and from West Africa, insurance companies to refuse to insure responder organisations and normally ready emergency responders to think twice about volunteering for an assignment in Sierra Leone, Guinea or Liberia. This underlying fear made it ever more difficult to have the regular interactions that are necessary to bolster a functioning network.

State level

The local population did not trust the government's stewardship of their healthcare for good reason – there was proven corruption in the health sector right before the Ebola outbreak (GAVI, 2013). In order to receive regular healthcare services, 48 per cent of surveyed patients reported needing to pay bribes (DuBois and Wake, 2015, 11). Furthermore, an audit post-Ebola showed that a third of GoSL-managed private funding for Ebola was not properly accounted for, with the corruption from high levels down to the levels of local leaders (O'Carroll, 2015). Understandably, the local population suspected that 'money-making – by governments, ghost workers collecting hazard pay and NGOs – has been a central theme' (Oosterhoff and Wilkinson, 2015, 3). Bilateral donors to Sierra Leone seemed to be aware of this corruption but also to accept it to a certain extent, noting that 'some level of corruption is "tolerated" in order to maintain access [to the government]' (Harris and Conteh, 2020, 18).

The recent civil war had been waged in part to fight against elite capture. The communities needed to rely on each other to stay safe during that time, since the government, embroiled in the fight between the Revolutionary United Front and the National Patriotic Front of Liberia, failed to protect them. When Ebola first arrived in Sierra Leone, its path was eerily similar to that of the civil war conflict, and 'commentators pushed the war analogy to highlight the inadequacy of the government's response in ways which recalled state failure, complacency and protracted violence' (Wilkinson and Fairhead, 2017, 20). After the first three national response mechanisms failed to control the outbreak, the Minister of Health was sacked for her incompetence and inaction after infamously 'blaming those suffering from Ebola for their own demise' (Thomas, 2014). Moreover, 'top-down communication sidelined the communities whose engagement was essential in enabling people to protect themselves and others from infection; reduce fear and mistrust of and resistance to health authorities and stigmatization; prevent transmission of the disease; develop safe, supportive practices of care for the ill or those at risk of infection; and develop safe and supportive burial practices' (DuBois and Wake, 2015, v).

This lack of trust came to a head in the first six months of the Ebola response, in the hard-hit eastern city of Kenema, with riots that could only be dispelled with tear gas and live rounds. People in Kenema believed that Ebola was a ploy to wipe out opposition supporters, sell body parts or receive money from the international community (Wilkinson and Fairhead, 2017). There were even rumours that healthcare workers at a government hospital in Kenema administered lethal injections to Ebola patients (Wilkinson and Fairhead, 2017, 21). Fortunately, this was the worst of the violence in Sierra Leone – in Guinea a team of eight healthcare workers, local leaders and journalists were murdered in a village, possibly because the villagers suspected them of spreading the disease (BBC, 2014b).

There seemed to be a double perception by the local population that the government had created or invented Ebola for political ends and also that it did not act swiftly enough to contain the outbreak. The many iterations of the response architecture, the refusal of the Level-3 crisis designation and the belated declaration of a national emergency are all pointed to as reasons for not trusting the government's actions in the early days of Ebola.

Interestingly, although there were initial riots in Sierra Leone, they were eventually quelled and many people ended up grudgingly complying with authoritarian Ebola prevention measures, including quarantines. Wilkinson and Fairhead hypothesise that the 'explanation for Sierra Leone's turnaround lies in the synergistic relationship between national and local politics, and the way the Ebola response was able to embed public health responsibilities in locally trusted institutions' (2017, 21). That is, because the local population mostly trusted the paramount chiefs, who were also working with the GoSL, they were willing to comply with strict measures that occasionally went against important cultural practices. The National Council of Paramount Chiefs played an important role in developing by-laws governing local behaviour around Ebola, including promoting safe burials, reporting suspected cases and prohibiting traditional healers from treating suspected cases (By-laws, 2014). The GoSL decided to make these by-laws mandatory for all chiefdoms, threatening fines or removal of chiefs who did not comply (Voors and Van de Windt, 2019; Wilkinson and Fairhead, 2017, 21).

Another salient point is that while the local population had a general lack of trust for the government, it mostly trusted the military. 'Several interviewees in [Sierra Leone] stated how proud they were of their military, noting that they had undergone significant reform as part of post-conflict reconstruction efforts at the end of the civil war' (Kamradt-Scott et al., 2015, 18). The UK military had worked to reform the Sierra Leone military and they were widely regarded as professional and respectful.

The INGO community did not inherently trust the government either. Corruption was a real concern, and funds destined for frontline healthcare workers and burial teams were diverted to ghost workers, eventually leading to strikes at one point (BBC, 2014). INGOs had varying relationships with the GoSL but interacted most frequently with government officials at the district level. The typical district-level coordination bodies were not used for the Ebola response and some of them stopped functioning altogether. However, because there was so much funding made available to the INGOs, many found themselves in direct informal interactions with higher levels of government. For example, during the response, the sister of the First Lady of Sierra Leone sent a wish list of project priorities to Oxfam, followed by an email to Oxfam's headquarters when the demands were not met.

Organisations like Oxfam had direct contact with their donors, such as DfID or USAID, but limited contact with UNMEER and the NERC. The interactions were top-down, with DfID inviting Oxfam to meetings to provide updates on certain programming, but then dismissing recommendations from Oxfam on WASH activities. The UK government was the most trusted actor within the state network, making it the node that received the most information from most other actors. As noted before, this is due to its expertise, the amount of funding it was willing to provide, its recent history in post-conflict reconstruction and the post-colonial perception that it was there to save the day.

INGO level

Sources note that as well as suspecting the government for introducing Ebola for political gains, the local population also did not trust the INGOs (Kamradt-Scott et al., 2015). Rumours spread that these organisations had made up Ebola to get additional funding for themselves, going so far as to say that 'Ebola had been intentionally introduced to depopulate West Africa for its mineral resources, with some suggesting the national governments were in league with this plan' (Kamradt-Scott et al., 2015, 12).

It is also clear that these organisations, along with state actors, provided ineffective informational campaigns to the population that did not integrate cultural considerations in their recommendations. People viewed the medical care centres as dangerous places where sick people went and never returned. Moreover, because neither the government nor the INGOs considered the importance of local burial practices, they ended up happening in secret and were a significant way by which the disease was transmitted. Because the local population did not trust the healthcare centres, or they were too far away, people often chose to care for their sick loved ones at home, which significantly increased the risk of transmission as well. Individual local healthcare workers were also not trusted by the local communities. '[Community Healthcare Workers'] association with health facilities, the government, and international organisations, and their engagement as Ebola responders, resulted in significant fear, mistrust, and rejection by communities' (Miller et al., 2018, 10). Moreover, there was 'concern that medical personnel were spreading the disease; [these deaths] fanned fears of the disease ("if even the doctors are dying [...]")'; and they drove medical personnel to fear and shun patients, thereby essentially denying medical care for non-Ebola ailments' (DuBois and Wake, 2015, 14). In a way, it was the position of healthcare workers as network actors who communicated across networks that made the local communities mistrust them. This breakdown of trust had the dual impact of making networks of local actors and frontline healthcare workers more insular, as well as potentially causing negative health outcomes for diseases other than Ebola.

During the Ebola crisis, UNMEER and the UK government came up with 'hard' targets: constructing a certain number of ETUs with a certain number of beds, providing ambulances, training safe burial teams, constructing community care centres (CCC) as a holding place for suspected cases, and so on. These targets focused on treatment instead of prevention and did not take into account the historical or cultural context in Sierra Leone. INGOs tried to promote these 'softer' program priorities, focusing on community engagement and prevention. Because of the donor–client relationships, giving the power to the donor, the INGO priorities were often dismissed. In fact, MSF (Doctors Without Borders) had been trying to warn the international community about the severity of the crisis without success, because the GoSL and the WHO had initially downplayed it.

Local level

Richards et al. (2015, 15) found in their research that within communities, trust is highest among immediate and extended family members, with distrust increasing when someone is born outside of the community. This is particularly relevant when considering how to roll out any response programming in the 14 districts. 'People listen to people they trust, which places a tactical emphasis on employing insiders (i.e. members of the community) rather than outsiders, especially outsiders accompanied by PPE-clad colleagues' (DuBois and Wake, 2015, 29). Because of the history of distrust towards anyone outside of their immediate communities, it became essential for prevention and treatment information, as well as rules that prevented important cultural practices, to be communicated by people within the community. In most cases, as the response wore on, it was the place of paramount chiefs as trusted hubs in the local network that made people have confidence in their messages, leading people to comply with burial practices and limit contact with people who had fallen ill (Miliband and Piot, 2015; Richards et al., 2015).

Burial practices were a particularly contentious topic that was exacerbated by the lack of trust. Twenty per cent of Ebola cases reportedly occurred from traditional burials (WHO, 2014), but in their attempt to shut down the practice, the GoSL and INGOs clumsily impinged on this important cultural practice without considering its significance. 'Safe burial' teams were established and groups of young men clad in PPE were sent to collect the bodies of patients who had died in the ETUs, CCCs or the home and put them in black body bags, forbidding their families to touch them and not allowing them or their religious leaders to witness the actual burial. Not only were black body bags culturally taboo, but there was also special significance to families washing and kissing a body – which unfortunately was a prime way to spread Ebola. In addition to the cultural reasons for washing a body, marriages in Sierra Leone often involve land and other assets, and their post-mortem division may not be completed until a body is buried (Richards et al., 2015). The prioritisation of 'safe burials' without consulting local government, civil society or religious leaders to better understand the nuanced cultural and economic implications is a prime example of the international community not understanding or trusting what the communities needed – and the communities rejecting a purely medically focused practice because it was rigidly introduced by actors whom they did not trust. To make it worse, at one point, the burial teams even went on strike because they had not been paid and bodies piled up in the streets of Freetown (Rush, 2015). These disorganised and culturally unacceptable realities led many people to flout the burial requirements, which was recognised as a major challenge by the government and the international community. It took the government finally allowing pastors or imams to pray at the gravesite while the family looked on from a distance, in tandem with the by-laws imposed by the paramount chiefs requiring safe burials, to finally get people to start complying with the requirements (Parker et al., 2019).

Apart from the complexities surrounding burial practices, both the state actors and the INGOs generally looked down on the local population for being 'backward and paranoid', which was exacerbated by the international news media (DuBois and Wake, 2015, vi). When the government established task forces for the Ebola response, instead of looking within the country, they brought back elite from the diaspora. Most of the Ebola containment strategies did not rely on knowledge of local customs or networks. Belatedly, to better understand what motivated the local communities and perhaps trust them further, many INGOs decided to bring in anthropologists – although it was likely too late in the game to really affect the quality of the response. One benefit of their presence was to shine a light on how much work was being done at the local levels to curb the advance of the disease. One interesting case documented by Parker et al. (2019) highlights how the local population in the village in Mathaineh, Sierra Leone, managed Ebola. Through their own trial and error, the villagers isolated and cared for their sick Ebola patients, developed their own PPE and strict hygienic practices, and carried out what they deemed to be safe burials. In the case of this village, the patients who were treated there had a similar survival rate to those that went to an ETU (Parker et al., 2019, 444–47). While this is an isolated case, it shows that the local communities can develop the capacity to understand and treat Ebola effectively, even without outside help.

Data Flows and Information Sharing

Collecting and sharing up-to-date data during the Ebola crisis posed some logistical and then ethical considerations. Because the OCHA cluster system was not activated, there were no standard tools shared for monitoring and evaluation. Case information and the geographic locations of emerging hot spots were essential for decision-making, and the typical medical confidentiality could not always be practised in the field. Furthermore, the government, the network of INGOs and the local communities all collected different types of data, used different platforms and shared it in different ways. There was no harmonisation of norms, methods or common platforms. Because of the risk of contagion, frontline health workers had to come up with complicated and time-consuming ways to share patient information without contaminated forms leaving the red zone (Waugaman and Fast, 2016, 55). The severity of the outbreak and the sheer number of actors involved led to a complex data-sharing situation where most data was communicated within networks (state, INGO and local) and mostly went up the command-and-control structure, instead of back down to the people on the front lines (Waugaman and Fast, 2016, 92). It was through the informal networks, such as the Skype group, that actors learned of emerging hot spots across the country and were able to prepare for what was next.

Data illiteracy is a chronic issue in developing countries where most of the population receives limited years of schooling and does not yet have access to technology. Across the networks of state, INGO and local actors, limited proficiency in collecting and understanding data hampered the Ebola response efforts. Ross et al. note that data collection at the level of the NERC dramatically improved when a Situation Room Academy was offered, training more than 600 people from 20 ministries on information management (2017, 21). INGOs struggled to find the quality staff to collect and manage data and did not adequately integrate information management into their activities, which is an issue with development organisations worldwide even under normal circumstances. The local population did not receive up-to-date information on how Ebola was evolving in the country and thus often relied on word of mouth and, inevitably, rumour.

State level

Given the complexity of the EVD response and the multiple iterations of the state's response framework, it is important to note that its ability to generate, consolidate and communicate accurate, up-to-date data changed over time. The first three drafts of the government response framework were not only inefficient, they could not provide accurate data. Ross et al. note, 'One of the reasons for the establishment of the NERC was that data from the MOHS and WHO were inconsistent and unreliable. Getting data from the field was a major challenge during the NERC's first few months, and a lot of time was spent trying to find out what was happening in the districts' (2017, 21).

One of the primary organs of the NERC was the Situation Room, which was made up of staff from the MOHS and the Sierra Leone military who were then connected mainly with bilateral international actors representing foreign state interests, such as the CDC or British military. The Situation Room's main function was to acquire and analyse data so that it could inform the NERC's decisions (Ross et al., 2017).

Because the UN cluster system was not activated for the response, a standard mechanism for the network of INGOs to interact with the network of state actors was not in place. This meant that the critical experiences of organisations that had knowledge of the context were not always considered. It also made it more challenging to track who was doing what, where – avoiding duplication of efforts and ensuring that gaps in coverage were addressed (Waugaman and Fast, 2016). Politics also tended to influence data sharing. One Ross et al. interviewee noted, 'MOHS wouldn't share data with the NERC, but they would share it with WHO. We would only get the top-level data from MOHS, but not the granularity that was needed. WHO would publish its data. That had a material effect on the credibility of our data; people didn't trust the data coming out of the NERC and the President was asking DFID and [the Africa Governance Initiative] for data' (2017, 22).

Initially, the NERC had 160 key performance indicators for the Ebola response. However, once the NERC became fully operational it held a meeting with all of the INGOs that were collecting data and cut the number of indicators down to 41 (Ross et al., 2017). After its establishment in mid-October, the NERC was finally collecting reliable data by January.

One innovative data-collecting approach developed by the GoSL was to create a national phone number, 117, for people to report suspected Ebola cases and any deaths. People were informed about the number via radio and discussions with community leaders and it received 350,000 complete, non-prank calls during the epidemic (Alpren et al., 2017). Yet, a lack of connectivity in rural areas likely hampered the effectiveness of this initiative, as the responders were only able to follow up with 60 per cent of reported cases and 70 per cent of the reported deaths (Alpren et al., 2017). Importantly, deaths were more likely to be reported than potential cases, likely because the local population did not want to inform on their family members and have them whisked away to a treatment facility, possibly to never be seen again.

INGO level

Like the other NGOs active in the Ebola response, Oxfam produced and consumed as much data as it could, with mixed results. Although the NERC had a list of primary indicators driving its data collection, Oxfam's monitoring, evaluation, accountability and learning (MEAL) activities were mostly driven by donor reporting requirements. There were three groups of Oxfam personnel managing information: program managers, the MEAL staff and the communications team, although people tended to work in silos, and thus the information collected was not strongly linked. A public evaluation report of Oxfam's response to Ebola notes, 'In Sierra Leone, a great deal of raw data was produced on programme activities, but little in the way of understandable and useable information. [...] Some of the most understandable information was not produced for programme management, but for internal communications (e.g. for briefing the CEO when he visited in January 2015) and for donor reporting' (Adams et al., 2015, 23). Organisational MEAL databases were used as repositories of data that could be used for donor reporting, but did not produce summarised conclusions that could drive program priorities. The report also notes that the data did not make it possible to evaluate the overall impact of Oxfam's Ebola programming in either Sierra Leone or Liberia. While this is a harsh pronouncement, it does not appear to be unique to the Oxfam experience. Without the strong leadership found in a formal cluster system, organisations like Oxfam struggled to find their place in the broader response framework and put in place MEAL systems that would allow them to measure the impact of their activities.

This lack of coordination also meant that different actors required different information. For example, DfID may have had demands for different information than the CDC or the NERC. A USAID report on data collection during the West Africa Ebola crisis notes that many interviewees complained about having to report data to multiple sources, whom all had different requirements (Waugaman and Fast, 2016, 51). Each actor implementing the response had their own priorities and targets. This significantly added to the workload of the responder organisations, which were caught in the middle between the state and the local population at a time when timely data was necessary to save lives.

Local level

Perhaps the most important role of the local population in terms of data collection was in contact tracing. Contact tracing maps out whom an infected person may have had contact with so that they may be monitored, quarantined and treated if necessary. For example, in the Southeastern district of Pujehun, the first district declared Ebola-free in Sierra Leone, 'the youth community played an essential part in implementing a robust case-searcher model (physically tracing all known contacts of an individual who tested positive for Ebola and monitoring these contacts for symptoms, for a period of 21 days) and set up informal screening checkpoints to protect the community' (Hitchen, 2015). Depending on the district, the paramount chiefs worked with the local communities and INGOs to gather this information and communicate it to the DERCs. However, this sharing of data was almost always one way: the community networks fed information into the state-run DERC hubs, and then that information disappeared into the NERC. 'One can imagine how contextualized data, returned to the point of data origin – such as a rise in Ebola caseload in a neighboring district – might have empowered health workers with important situational awareness that could have improved local preparation and decision-making' (Waugaman and Fast, 2016, 92).

Communications and information campaigns to local communities are also relevant for discussion. The state and INGOs needed to better adapt their communication strategies towards the local level over time, as the local communities' understanding of the disease evolved. First, there was initial doubt over the outbreak, which promoted an 'Ebola is real' communication campaign. However, communities quickly learned that Ebola was, in fact, real because they witnessed it first-hand. Secondly, there was a focus on preventing people from eating bushmeat, which was how Ebola first made the jump to humans. However, it would have been much more relevant to communicate that Ebola was more likely to jump from person to person, especially when caring for sick family members or preparing a body for burial. Finally, early communications materials were said to instil unnecessary fear in the local population, convincing them that catching Ebola was a death sentence, leading people to hide cases from the authorities. Instead, it would have been more helpful to demonstrate how to safely care for sick family members while they waited for treatment at a CCC or ETU, as well as show that people can recover – and should be reintegrated into villages without stigmatisation. The issues that arose in these information campaigns likely come from a lack of data and information sharing between networks. Case data was transmitted from the local levels up to the state, but data on Ebola knowledge was not prioritised.

Coordination/Working Together during the Response: What Worked and What Was a Missed Opportunity

The complexity of the Ebola response, both in Sierra Leone and the region in general, creates challenges in understanding who was in what network, how the networks worked together and what could have been improved. The plethora of actors also seems to have created a collective action problem at the beginning of the epidemic. Who was really responsible for the response? The GoSL or perhaps the WHO? What about the post-colonial donors who provided the majority of budget support to each country? One USAID team leader bluntly said, 'Whose crisis is this? If you can't answer that question in beginning, you're getting off to a rocky start' (DuBois and Wake, 2015, 16). Yet, as previously noted, while the state and INGOs may have been responsible for putting in place the infrastructure for treating cases, the paramount chiefs at the local level were responsible for implementing the by-laws that may have slowed the spread of the disease at the village level.

Despite several months of confusion at the beginning of the response, military, medical and humanitarian personnel mobilised from a variety of countries to supplement what was happening domestically, and 'the intervention successfully created a web of networks that spanned nations, allowing information to be disseminated village by village' (DuBois and Wake, 2015, 17). The response ultimately relied on existing networks, such as the state actors within the GoSL and UK, the INGOs who had been operating in Sierra Leone since the end of the civil war and the local leaders at the district level and below. As the magnitude of the epidemic became clearer, these networks expanded to include new members: at the state level the CDC demonstrated its technical capacity and manpower, while UNMEER struggled to become relevant in a network where key actors already had strong relationships; non-health-focused INGOs lost some of their authority while the focus shifted to INGOs with medically trained staff and with an ability to manage emergencies; and paramount chiefs regained some of the legitimacy they had lost during the civil war, developing high levels of what Slaughter (2017) calls 'betweenness centrality', sitting at the intersection of the shortest paths between the state and the local population.

Because bilateral donors funded the INGOs directly, they also communicated with them directly, bypassing the NERC. Donors like DfID had direct influence over the NERC, had staff embedded in the DERCs and were able to dictate the actions of INGOs, who were unable to effectively exercise collective bargaining over DfID's program demands. During the EVD epidemic, Paramount Chief did not have such direct influence at the local level (traditionally, the paramount chiefs were influential since colonial time), allowing the chiefs to finally develop their own home-grown legitimacy, although there were still some cases of distrust for chiefs who had been appointed by the ruling political party or lived overseas (Parker et al., 2019).

State level

The state of Sierra Leone seems to behave somewhat like a network and less like a static hierarchy. Personal relationships are more important than formal meetings and 'most access to government was said to be on a personal basis, often with the President or his Chief of Staff or sometimes ministers, and as long as there were personal connections access could be arranged at any time' (Harris and Conteh, 2020, 11). The president was the most powerful node, but the power of different ministers ebbed and flowed based on their relationships and effectiveness – demonstrated by the sacking of the health minister and the president's decision to have the Minister of Defence lead the NERC.

The NERC was an example of a formalised coordination mechanism, made up of operational and medical arms staffed by members of the GoSL and advised by the UK and UNMEER. Unlike the MOHS, the NERC was able to convene all actors and make decisions that were respected by a variety of stakeholders, although it took some time for this new node to generate and transmit information to other network actors. Although the British recommended the structure of the NERC, there were personality clashes between the GoSL and the British, with the British wanting to maintain their role as the post-colonial saviour. 'DFID, particularly in 2015, was variously seen as "arrogant", "bullying", "resented" and not a "team-player", and as having "solved" the Ebola crisis' (Harris and Conteh, 2020, 22). The British also held their own decisional meetings and communicated directly with the DERCs, bypassing the NERC. 'This didn't just slow things down. It completely altered the shape of the response in line with how they thought it should go, ignoring the host nation machinery that was supposed to be the coordination mechanism that everybody bought into' (Ross et al., 2017, 23). Interestingly, this behaviour shows the British, on one hand, behaving more like a network node, seeking out information from another actor directly as opposed to respecting a hierarchy. On the other hand, the British were invalidating the authority of the very structure they had pushed for, demonstrating a post-colonial role driven by their own interests.

Created in September 2014, UNMEER was the first-ever combination of UN health and humanitarian mission, although it seemed to operate almost exclusively at the state level: both the author's personal experience and various chapters confirm that neither the network of INGOs nor the local population understood its mandate, which was to scale up the response and establish unity of purpose among responders. Indeed, instead of working with these networks, it worked almost exclusively with the GoSL and DfID in closed-door weekly meetings (DuBois and Wake, 2015). This disconnect – with the UN, DfID and the GoSL on one side and the INGOs and the local communities on the other – meant 'the actual implementers did not see a place for themselves at the coordination table or a representative there' (DuBois and Wake, p. 28). Perhaps the lack of trust between the three levels led to this lack of coordination, but it resulted in disorganisation, a lack of direction and a clear ignorance on the part of UNMEER of what was happening on the ground. UNMEER completed its mandate in July 2015, before Sierra Leone was deemed Ebola-free. Given that it took some time for UNMEER to become fully operational after its creation in September, the short life of this mission reinforced the perception that it was not an essential actor in the response – and not an essential node in the state network.

In addition to the creation of UNMEER, 'more than 5,000 military personnel were deployed from the USA, UK, China, Canada, France, and Germany' to Sierra Leone, Guinea and Liberia (Kamradt-Scott et al., 2015, 1). The military intervention was positively portrayed in the international news media and was lauded by the local population (Ross et al., 2017). However, most troops did not arrive in-country until October and November 2014, as the outbreak was reaching its peak. The British and Americans sent the largest number of troops but they were not authorised to provide clinical assistance based on fear of contracting the disease (Kamradt-Scott et al., 2015). Instead, they assisted with logistics, built ETUs and trained healthcare workers. They also created a hospital meant to treat international response workers, as insurance companies would not guarantee medical evacuation for INGO staff that contracted Ebola.

The British and Sierra Leonean militaries worked particularly well together due to the British history of military training and reconstruction in Sierra Leone after the civil war (Ross et al., 2017). The Sierra Leonean military was highly respected for their professionalism by the local communities (Kamradt-Scott et al., 2015). However, the INGO networks were typically against the militarisation of the response as well as the top-down decision-making that came with it, being more accustomed to consensus-based planning and action during a humanitarian crisis (Ross et al., 2017).

Although the military was helpful during the response, its role may have had the unintended consequence of minimising the importance of local and INGO network actors in curbing the epidemic. And the success of the military element of the response reinforces the primacy of states that wish to demonstrate that their interests are paramount to those of the individual. DuBois and Wake caution, 'the securitisation of Ebola also pitted the human rights of individuals against the security of a public or nation and introduced a hierarchy whereby the security of some individuals would be protected at the expense of the rights and freedoms of others' (2015, vi). In this context, the individuals who are protected are those from the post-colonial nations, which is reinforced by how the WHO downplayed the crisis in early months, and the UK and the United States only mobilised significant assistance after the epidemic started threatening their borders.

Finally, although the NERC, its international advisers and the military ended up effectively coordinating late in the Ebola response, there was a significant missed opportunity for regional coordination and collaboration. Staff from UNMEER in Sierra Leone did not collaborate with their counterparts in Liberia or Guinea (DuBois and Wake, 2015, 28). Even the UNMEER headquarters was in Accra, Ghana – not any of the affected countries. It is also unlikely that the state actors charged with the Ebola response in each of the three affected countries coordinated with one another, despite likely having helpful lessons learned to share.

INGO level

The politically fraught decision of the UN to not activate the cluster system created many missed opportunities for collaboration and coordination within the network of INGOs, as well as denying them a formal pathway to communicate up to the state level. 'The assessment, planning and data collection, and analysis it would also have triggered may have released early and substantial funds. [...] Without [the clusters], many non-health NGOs found it difficult to know when, how or where to engage' (DuBois and Wake, 2015, 27). This was true for organisations such as Oxfam, which ended up joining the response relatively late, with Ebola response teams not arriving until October. Adams et al. note that this late start to Oxfam's response meant that they did not have a strong role or much credibility within different coordinating bodies until their activities ramped up, despite normally having strong ties with network nodes within the GoSL and the UN (2015, 58).

Many of the non-health development organisations already present in Sierra Leone had been working on long-term development programs under strict funding agreements. When EVD hit, many organisations, including Oxfam, went into 'hibernation mode', pausing programming in order to protect their staff from catching the disease. As with the state level, Oxfam had initial difficulty deciding how it would be organised for the response, finally mobilising emergency teams in both Sierra Leone and Liberia right after the British deployed their civilian–military task force and as the GoSL was putting in place the NERC.

When the response finally ramped up, there was a scramble at both the state and INGO level to find qualified staff because Ebola incited such fear, leading to airlines cancelling their flights to West Africa and insurance companies unwilling to provide medical evacuations. There was insufficient local healthcare staff for the population before the epidemic, as well as insufficient international medical crisis responders. This dearth of qualified people and organisations caused donors to demand organisations like Oxfam to build and operate health centres. In order to ensure their success, non-medical INGOs would usually partner with medically focused INGOs. For example, Oxfam worked with IRC, Partners in Health, Médecins du Monde and MedAir to run CCCs. These partnerships are an example of a good coordination practice that may improve Sierra Leone's resilience to future health crises – combining the health response capabilities of certain INGOs and operational abilities of others.

With the British deployment and the NERC finally in place, it became infinitely more difficult for non-medical INGOs to negotiate program priorities based on their expertise and contextual knowledge. Adams et al. lament, 'Oxfam could have been stronger in negotiating with donors for funding for its proposed programmes and areas of strength at earlier stages. […] There were a number of implementing agencies saying the same thing, so a more collaborative approach including beyond the NGO sector and especially with public health specialists could have resulted in a more persuasive argument' (2015, 19). This demonstrates a breakdown in the network coordination tendencies of INGOs as the response ramped up. Under normal circumstances, Oxfam ran the Freetown WASH consortium coordination meeting in Sierra Leone. As Ebola is transmitted via bodily fluids and many poor Sierra Leoneans do not have access to potable water or plumbing, a focus on WASH to prevent the disease, instead of on care facilities to treat it, could have slowed its advance. Oxfam tried and failed to have the government add a WASH technical pillar to the NERC, and the value of WASH activities was not recognised until much later (Adams et al., 2015, 15). This demonstrates that the fear generated from the disease, along with the establishment of the command-and-control structure, caused the traditional INGO network to pause network operations along with their programming. Non-medical INGOs had to reorganise themselves, connecting to new network nodes and building new relationships to regain their positions of legitimacy and influence.

The overall shift of priorities caused new INGO network hubs to emerge during the crisis. Medical and emergency-focused INGOs took on a bigger role in the response due to their combination of technical expertise and logistical capacity. For example, MSF was one of the first organisations responding to the outbreak and is partially attributed with finally getting the attention of the international community after publishing a chapter announcing the severity of the crisis – when the WHO had consistently downplayed it. Further, the IRC played a leading role in the SMAC, likely due to their experience in emergency settings. These emergency responders were able to act more quickly and take on leadership roles as hubs in the network of organisations, while the non-medical development organisations fought to catch up, slowly adapting their role to be of use in a more nimble environment.

INGOs have been criticised for furthering their agendas and being too risk-averse during the epidemic (DuBois and Wake, 2015), but many had been operating in the country at least since the end of the civil war, employing local staff and engaging in participatory needs assessments with communities in order to better understand local requirements. There was a missed opportunity to utilise these organisations' community connections, as well as their areas of expertise, to determine what was needed on the front lines. Instead, donors like DfID and the Office of Foreign Disaster Assistance (OFDA) within USAID ended up pressuring INGOs to adopt programming outside of their areas of expertise that was based on a containment strategy generated by the WHO. This strategy focused primarily on treatment and was criticised for its lack of focus on community engagement and inability to keep up with the evolving needs of the crisis. One INGO official noted, 'To get the grant with OFDA, we needed to build Community Care Centers (CCCs), but we didn't want to build more [because we knew the outbreak was changing]' (DuBois and Wake, 2015, 26). Moreover, it takes away from the autonomy of the INGOs as actors with mandates to serve the poor. 'Compromising humanitarian independence in this way reinforces the practice of NGOs being used as "force multipliers" in support of the strategic security interests of donor governments' instead of responding directly to the needs of the communities they serve (DuBois and Wake, 2015, 44).

Finally, similarly to the state actors at the regional level, INGO network actors also did not have a platform by which they could share information with their regional counterparts. Medical personnel involved in the response did not have a network platform by which they could share best practices. The lack of a cluster system for INGOs meant that information management was not streamlined, making it challenging to communicate among themselves and also with similar organisations operating in the region. As Ebola does not recognise borders, strengthening the regional networks of healthcare responders, local leaders and logisticians could have helped improve the quality of the response.

Local level

The paramount chiefs operated as an important hub in the local network of actors, also acting as the frontline state network hubs. They often held enough political and social capital in the villages to explain and enforce rules, working with influential local actors such as religious leaders and youth groups.

They held the keys to important and up-to-date data on the ground that the DERCs and then the NERC needed to make relevant decisions. In fact, 'the Ebola epidemic had the effect of re-invigorating the chieftainship system. National and international Ebola responses worked in collaboration with paramount chiefs, often in ways that replicated strategies adopted under British protectorate rule' (Parker et al., 2019, 443). This is an interesting development, as, during colonisation, the paramount chiefs did not necessarily have legitimacy in the eyes of the people. However, post-civil war and during a crisis when other links to the local communities were weak, the paramount chiefs took advantage of the need for information and on both sides, as well as the fear of Ebola, and increased their power in the network. 'Paramount chiefs were locally more believable than politicians or medical experts in addressing the disease as a "family problem". […] Chiefs could explain the risks of the disease in a way that was believable to even the most skeptical of villagers' (Richards et al., 2015).

The relevance of the paramount chiefs in the Ebola response was initially not recognised at the state level, and the chiefs had to petition the president to be included in the DERCs at the district level (Ross et al., 2017). However, once they were included, this coordination provided opportunities for more efficient collaboration on both sides.

Once again, because the cluster system had not been activated, it wasn't always clear which INGOs were operating where and what activities they were doing. The chiefs and other local leaders were active in their districts, engaging in contact tracing and disseminating information to the local population, as were the INGOs. INGOs worked often with DERCs, but the DERCs did not always coordinate with the local leaders, sometimes not including them in social mobilisation activities even late in the response (Ross et al., 2017). The number of parallel structures and networks without effective coordination necessarily led to gaps or duplication of efforts and the comparative advantages of different network actors were not fully exploited.

Building Resilience for Future Outbreaks

In *The Chessboard and the Web*, Slaughter writes, 'In the human environment, trust has proved critical in resilient systems. Resilience demands cooperation during a crisis; cooperation requires a basic level of trust. Trust, in turn, requires repeated human interaction, building a reservoir of social capital that supports the propensity of human beings who know and like one another to self-organize into groups and associations' (2017, 67). Therefore, as previously discussed, improving the trust among the state, INGO and local network actors is critical to cooperation, and cooperation leads to greater resilience.

Across the three levels of the state, INGOs and local communities, connecting similar network actors across the region would also build resilience against future outbreaks. As previously noted, the borders between Sierra Leone, Guinea and Liberia were not determined by their indigenous peoples, but instead by outside actors. All three countries have a variety of ethnic groups and religions. They may have more in common with people on the other side of an international border than they do with people within their own country. Fostering network connections among traditional leaders, medical personnel, INGOs and state actors at the regional level could help establish early warning systems, share best practices and even ensure the continuation of a functioning healthcare system or economy, should a future health crisis shut down certain parts of the region.

State level

Multiple chapters note that Sierra Leone's health system must be strengthened if it wants to effectively respond to future epidemics, as opposed to focusing on siloed international standards of development (Abramovitz et al., 2014; Denney and Mallett, 2015; DuBois and Wake, 2015; Moon et al., 2015). However, there is also a focus on the international security implications of a pandemic, which will inherently give priority to the interests of the donor countries who provide budget support to Sierra Leone. Unfortunately, these actors will likely dictate the direction of Sierra Leone's health system strengthening, ultimately choosing initiatives that will likely provide more security to the donor than necessarily to the people of Sierra Leone.

In *The Chessboard and the Web*, Slaughter makes an idealistic suggestion that in order to create a mesh network so that different key hospital nodes do not become major disease transmission hubs during an epidemic, parallel systems should be created and maintained. 'Ebola […] or other tropical viruses, must be treated through this parallel distributed system, which can be active all the time or can be activated as soon as such a virus emerges' (Slaughter, 2017, 71). While this sounds like a good idea in theory, in a country such as Sierra Leone that cannot maintain even the most basic healthcare system to reach the majority of its population, it seems unlikely – and frankly yet another post-colonial interest-driven goal that would help stem the global spread of an infectious disease instead of prioritising the strengthening of Sierra Leone's entire healthcare system.

The resilience of the health system is not the only system that must be strengthened to bolster Sierra Leone against future epidemics. The way that UNMEER operated during the epidemic focused primarily on its health implications, but there were many other detrimental humanitarian side effects of the epidemic. Agriculture, private sector growth and cross-border trade were severely affected by EVD, with an estimated $2.2 billion in the GDP lost for Sierra Leone, Guinea and Liberia (CDC, 2019). Students were out of school for 39 weeks, unable to attend remote classes because of a lack of connectivity (UNDP, 2015). Because people did not have regular access to healthcare for other ailments during the Ebola outbreak, the CDC estimates that an additional 10,600 lives were lost to HIV, malaria and tuberculosis during that time (CDC, 2019).

In preparation for future epidemics, Sierra Leone can re-enact its command-and-control system but should improve community engagement to promote prevention before the focus shifts to containment and treatment. As witnessed with the EVD response, 'the speediness and size of an epidemic response depends directly on the funding priorities set by considerations of the Global North' (Ripoli et al., 2018, 9) and so the government must act independently in case the international community does not act quickly or provide adequate funding. The ability of the government to act depends on its repeated interactions with local leaders – strengthening the network connections between state and local levels.

Finally, these networks are only as good as the information they produce and transmit. Standardised early warning systems need to be put in place and made accessible to people with low levels of data literacy. Waugaman and Fast (2016) recommend standardising indicators and objectives as early as possible in a health and humanitarian crisis and DuBois and Wake (2015) note that INGOs may find themselves sidelined while state actors take the reigns. This implies that the UN cluster system may not be activated as frequently in the future. However, if this is the case, then states must define their own standards for data collection and information sharing that can hopefully be shared across regions.

INGO level

To improve their resilience to future epidemics, non-medical INGOs should continue their partnerships and information sharing with medical INGOs, rather than competing for funding or reinventing the wheel. This will allow both types of organisations to better plan for the humanitarian effects of a health crisis, such as food insecurity or loss of employment.

Unfortunately, it seems as if INGO behaviour will continue to be largely influenced by their donors and state governments, as opposed to being driven by their areas of expertise or ability to understand what the local communities need. However, if the INGOs continue to strengthen their existing network ties to other INGOs, they should be able to exert increased collective bargaining for priority areas during a crisis. Moreover, if they increase their communications with local communities and try and improve transparency, the local communities are more likely to trust them – instead of thinking that they've manufactured the crisis to receive additional funding. On all levels, building relationships and providing transparent information is key to building the resilience needed for future outbreaks and crises.

Local level

As previously noted, when Ebola hit, the local communities were still in the process of recovering from the civil war. Health and education systems were poor. Life expectancy was low. Infrastructure was damaged or non-existent. Insular community ties were strong, and communities discovered that they could mostly rely on their paramount chiefs to provide guidance to help curb the epidemic. However, often neglected in the discussion is how the 2014–16 Ebola epidemic disrupted daily life and the economy, reducing the resilience of subsistence farm and non-farm workers even more. The Global Hunger Index found that during the disease outbreak in 2015, Sierra Leone communities had 'alarming' hunger levels, with the country scored 113 out of 117 countries (von Grebmer et al., 2015). As prices of commercial goods rose along with unemployment, approximately two hundred eighty thousand people were in danger of starvation within the first year of the health emergency alone (FAO, 2014). As a consequence, poor people were not only afraid of dying by contracting the Ebola virus, they were also afraid of dying from hunger – not to mention AIDS, malaria and other endemic illnesses that were often left untreated during the epidemic.

Economic recovery has been slow following Ebola and the resilience of the local communities was severely tested so soon after the end of the civil war. And although Sierra Leone has not been hit as hard by COVID-19 as other countries, it will still feel the effects of lockdowns, quarantines and a global recession. These crises have the effect of making communities insular and more self-reliant, not necessarily trusting anyone outside of whom they know can help them during difficult times. The case of the village of Mathaineh in Moyamba district, studied by Parker et al. (2019), is again particularly salient in demonstrating the self-reliance of community networks. Based on similar experiences with cholera, the villagers isolated sick individuals and rehydrated them. They created their own PPE, never using it more than one time. Their efforts resulted in similar survival rates to more formal healthcare systems (Parker et al., 2019, 444–50). While this is an individual and perhaps unique case, it demonstrates how networks of community actors can build their resilience, cooperate during crises and trust each other. Any future response should endeavour to utilise these networks.

Conclusion: Lessons Learned Involving All Actors

Many chapters have been written reflecting on the command-and-control management system during the Ebola response, the politics of the response, the necessity to strengthen health systems and, more recently, the anthropological considerations that may have been the true drivers of the denouement of the epidemic. International organisations have developed lists of recommendations on how to prepare for the next pandemic. There has been, however, a paucity of work done to bring together actors across the three levels to carry out a collective reflection on how they could strengthen their network connections to improve trust, streamline data collection and information sharing, establish norms for cross-collaboration and improve resilience. And, while academics and researchers develop information to be shared internally within their organisations, little actionable material exists to drive policy. Instead, the interests of donor countries still dominate budget support to Sierra Leone and other recipient countries.

The overall lack of preparedness was witnessed worldwide with the outbreak of COVID-19 and the preference for developed countries is evident: predominantly affecting the United States and Europe, COVID-19 dominates the news. In contrast to what happened with Ebola, the news media does not blame the backwardness or lack of education of the people for the spread of COVID-19. Moreover, these developed countries are also receiving the majority of the PPE and now the vaccines. Sierra Leone has quietly managed to keep its COVID-19 caseload at low levels but has not been consulted by world leaders for advice – although it has had recent experience in containment, and far fewer deaths, from Ebola.

This serves as a reminder that epidemics are one of the most pressing threats of our time. State actors are important and must be well-organised and agile. INGOs can play an important role if they work together, complementing expertise instead of competing for funding. And perhaps most importantly, it is the network actors on the front lines of the response – the trusted community leaders who understand the people with whom they work, such as paramount chiefs and religious leaders – who can make the biggest difference. We should ensure that these actors with high levels of betweenness centrality can make even more connections: with actors in their extended networks across the world with whom they can share relevant information for the future.

References

Abramovitz, S., Hoffman, D. J., Liebow, E., Lubkemann, S., Moran, M. H., Shepler, S., Batty, F. J., Benton, A., Bolton, C., Faye, S. L. and Fosher, K. (2014) 'Strengthening West African Health Care Systems to Stop Ebola : Anthropologists Offer Insights'.

Workshop Recommendations, American Anthropological Association. Available at: /paper/Strengthening-West-African-health-care-systems-to-%3A-Abramovitz-Hoffman/607c8be9ca21db4697c3d077aa39a89c5ca730e6 (Accessed 15 January 2021).

Adams, J., Lloyd, A. and Miller, C. (2015) *The Oxfam Ebola Response in Liberia and Sierra Leone: An evaluation report for the Disasters Emergency Committee*. Oxfam. Available at: https://policy-practice.oxfam.org/resources/the-oxfam-ebola-response-in-liberia-and-sierra-leone-an-evaluation-report-for-t-560602/ (Accessed 15 January 2021).

Alpren, C., Jalloh, M. F., Kaiser, R., Diop, M., Kargbo, S. A., Castle, E., Dafae, F., Hersey, S., Redd, J. T. and Jambai, A. (2017) 'The 117 Call Alert System in Sierra Leone: From Rapid Ebola Notification to Routine Death Reporting'. *BMJ Global Health*, 2(3), p. e000392. DOI: 10.1136/bmjgh-2017-000392.

BBC News (2014a) 'Ebola Crisis: Sierra Leone Health Workers Strike'. 12 November. Available at: https://www.bbc.com/news/world-africa-30019895 (Accessed 10 January 2021).

BBC News (2014b) 'Ebola Outbreak: Guinea Health Team Killed'. 19 September. Available at: https://www.bbc.com/news/world-africa-29256443 (Accessed 12 January 2021).

BCG Global (no date) 'Smarter Ways to Fight Ebola'. Available at: https://www.bcg.com/capabilities/social-impact-sustainability/smarter-ways-fight-ebola (Accessed 11 January 2021).

Bedson, J., Jalloh, M. F., Pedi, D., Bah, S., Owen, K., Oniba, A., Sangarie, M., Fofanah, J. S., Jalloh, M. B., Sengeh, P. and Skrip, L. (2020) 'Community Engagement in Outbreak Response: Lessons From the 2014–2016 Ebola Outbreak in Sierra Leone'. *BMJ Global Health*, 5(8), p. e002145. DOI: 10.1136/bmjgh-2019-002145.

Blaney, D. L. (2004) *International Relations and the Problem of Difference*. London: Routledge. DOI: 10.4324/9780203644096.

Broadbent, E. (2012) 'Research-Based Evidence in African Policy Debates, Case Study 4: Chieftaincy Reform in Sierra Leone'. *Evidence-Based Policy in Development Network*, p. 55.

Bylaws for All Chiefdoms of Sierra Leone (2014) Available at: https://www.humanitarianresponse.info/sites/www.humanitarianresponse.info/files/documents/files/by-laws.pdf (Accessed 10 January 2021).

Centers for Disease Control and Prevention (2019) 'Cost of the Ebola Epidemic Error Processing SSI File'. Available at: https://www.cdc.gov/vhf/ebola/history/2014-2016-outbreak/cost-of-ebola.html (Accessed 10 January 2021).

Chandler, C., Fairhead, J., Kelly, A., Leach, M., Martineau, F., Mokuwa, E., Parker, M., Richards, P. and Wilkinson, A. (2015) 'Ebola: Limitations of Correcting Misinformation'. *The Lancet*, 385(9975), pp. 1275–1277. DOI: 10.1016/S0140-6736(14)62382-5.

Cowell, A. (2000) 'The World: Britain in Africa; Colonialism's Legacy Becomes a Burden (Published 2000)'. *The New York Times*, 11 June. Available at: https://www.nytimes.com/2000/06/11/weekinreview/the-world-britain-in-africa-colonialism-s-legacy-becomes-a-burden.html (Accessed 25 November 2020).

'Data Sharing During the West Africa Ebola Public Health Emergency: Case Study Report' (2018) Georgetown University Medical Center, Center for Global Health Science and Security. Available at: https://www.glopid-r.org/wp-content/uploads/2019/07/data-sharing-during-west-africa-ebola-public-health-emergency-case-study-report-georgetown.pdf (Accessed 15 January 2021).

Denney, L. and Mallett, R. (2015) 'After Ebola: Why and How Capacity Support to Sierra Leone's Health Sector Needs to Change'. *Overseas Development Institute*, Report 7. Available at: https://www.odi.org/publications/9679-after-ebola-why-and-how-capacity-support-sierra-leone-s-health-sector-needs-change (Accessed 15 January 2021).

Dhillon, R. S. and Kelly, J. D. (2015) 'Community Trust and the Ebola Endgame'. *New England Journal of Medicine*, 373(9), pp. 787–789. DOI: 10.1056/NEJMp1508413.

DuBois, M. and Wake, C. (2015) *The Ebola Response in West Africa: Exposing the Politics and Culture of International Aid*. ALNAP. Overseas Development Institute. Available at: https://www.alnap.org/help-library/the-ebola-response-in-west-africa-exposing-the-politics-and-culture-of-international (Accessed 15 January 2021).

Ebola Virus Disease|Audit (2014) 'Sierra Leone Has Failed to Properly Account for a Third of Ebola Funds Between May and October'. Auditors Report. Available at: https://www.scribd.com/document/255896806/Auditors-report-Sierra-leone-has-failed-to-properly-account-for-a-third-of-Ebola-funds-between-May-and-October (Accessed 2 January 2021).

Food and Agriculture Organization (FAO) (2014) *Ebola Leaves Hundreds of Thousands Facing Hunger in Three Worst-Hit Countries*. Food and Agriculture Organization (FAO). Available at: http://www.fao.org/news/story/en/item/272678/icode/.

GAVI Review of Health System Strengthening in Sierra Leone (2013) Available at: https://www.gavi.org/news/media-room/gavi-review-health-system-strengthening-sierra-leone.

Goguen, A. and Bolten, C. (2017) 'Ebola Through a Glass, Darkly: Ways of Knowing the State and Each Other'. *Anthropological Quarterly*, 90(2), pp. 423–449.

GOV.UK (no date) 'The End of the Ebola Epidemic'. Available at: https://www.gov.uk/government/news/the-end-of-the-ebola-outbreak (Accessed 8 January 2021).

Hafner-Burton, E., Kahler, M. and Montgomery, A. (2009) 'Network Analysis For International Relations'. *International Organization*, 63, pp. 559–592. DOI: 10.1017/S0020818309090195.

Harris, D. and Conteh, F. M. (2020) 'Government–Donor Relations in Sierra Leone: Who is in the Driving Seat?'. *The Journal of Modern African Studies*, 58(1), pp. 45–65. DOI: 10.1017/S0022278X19000569.

HumanitarianResponse (no date) 'What is the Cluster Approach?' Available at: https://www.humanitarianresponse.info/en/coordination/clusters/what-cluster-approach (Accessed 8 January 2021).

Inayatullah, N. and Blaney, D. (2003) 'International Relations and the Problem of Difference'. *International Relations and the Problem of Difference*, pp. 1–272. DOI: 10.4324/9780203644096.

Kadanali, Ayten, and Karagoz, Gul. (2015) 'An Overview of Ebola Virus Disease'. *Northern Clinics of Istanbul*, 2, pp. 81–86. DOI: 10.14744/nci.2015.97269.

Kamradt-Scott, A., Harman, S., Wenham, C. and Smith, F., III. (2015) *Saving Lives: The Civil-Military Response to the 2014 Ebola Outbreak in West Africa* (Final Report). DOI: 10.13140/RG.2.1.4659.5288.

Kamradt-Scott, A., Harman, S., Wenham, C. and Smith, F. (2016) 'Civil–Military Cooperation in Ebola and Beyond'. *The Lancet*, 387(10014), pp. 104–105. DOI: 10.1016/S0140-6736(15)01128-9.

Kargbo, P. M. (2012) 'Impact of Foreign Aid on Economic Growth in Sierra Leone'. 2012(44).

Keen, D. (2003) 'Greedy Elites, Dwindling Resources, Alienated Youths the Anatomy of Protracted Violence in Sierra Leone'. *International Politics and Society*, 2, pp. 67–94.

Keen, D. (2005) *Conflict & Collusion in Sierra Leone*. Oxford: James Currey Publishers.

National Ebola Response Centre (NERC) (no date) 'Lessons From the Response to the Ebola Virus Disease Outbreak in Sierra Leone: May 2014–November 2015'. Summary Report. Available at: https://www.afro.who.int/sites/default/files/2017-05/evdlessonslearned.pdf (Accessed 8 January 2021).

Lévy, Y., Lane, C., Piot, P., Beavogui, A. H., Kieh, M., Leigh, B., Doumbia, S., D'Ortenzio, E., Lévy-Marchal, C., Pierson, J. and Watson-Jones, D. (2018) 'Prevention of Ebola Virus Disease Through Vaccination: Where We Are in 2018'. *The Lancet*, 392(10149), pp. 787–790. DOI: 10.1016/S0140-6736(18)31710-0.

Lipton, J. (2017) 'Black' and 'White' Death: Burials in a Time of Ebola in Freetown, Sierra Leone: 'Black' and 'White' Death. *Journal of the Royal Anthropological Institute*, 23(4), pp. 801–819. DOI: 10.1111/1467-9655.12696.

Miller, N. P., Milsom, P., Johnson, G., Bedford, J., Kapeu, A. S., Diallo, A. O., Hassen, K., Rafique, N., Islam, K., Camara, R. and Kandeh, J. (2018) 'Community Health Workers During the Ebola Outbreak in Guinea, Liberia, and Sierra Leone'. *Journal of Global Health*, 8(2). DOI: 10.7189/jogh-08-020601.

Mobula, L. M., Nakao, J. H., Walia, S., Pendarvis, J., Morris, P. and Townes, D. (2018) 'A Humanitarian Response to the West African Ebola Virus Disease Outbreak'. *Journal of International Humanitarian Action*, 3(1), p. 10. DOI: 10.1186/s41018-018-0039-2.

Mokuwa, E. Y. and Maat, H. (2020) 'Rural Populations Exposed to Ebola Virus Disease Respond Positively to Localised Case Handling: Evidence From Sierra Leone'. *PLoS Neglected Tropical Diseases*, 14(1), p. e0007666. DOI: 10.1371/journal.pntd.0007666.

Moon, S., Sridhar, D., Pate, M. A., Jha, A. K., Clinton, C., Delaunay, S., Edwin, V., Fallah, M., Fidler, D. P., Garrett, L. and Goosby, E. (2015) 'Will Ebola Change the Game? Ten Essential Reforms Before the Next Pandemic. The Report of the Harvard-LSHTM Independent Panel on the Global Response to Ebola - The Lancet'. *The Lancet*, 386, pp. 2204–2221.

Nuesiri, E. (2019) 'Ebola and Chiefs in Sierra Leone'. *Africa at LSE*, 28 June. Available at: https://blogs.lse.ac.uk/africaatlse/2019/06/28/ebola-chiefs-sierra-leone-research/ (Accessed 5 January 2021).

O'Carroll, L. (2015a) 'A Third of Sierra Leone's Ebola Budget Unaccounted for, Says Report'. *The Guardian*. Available at: http://www.theguardian.com/world/2015/feb/16/ebola-sierra-leone-budget-report (Accessed 2 January 2021).

O'Carroll, L. (2015b) 'Sierra Leone Investigates Alleged Misuse of Emergency Ebola Funds'. *The Guardian*, 17 February. Available at: http://www.theguardian.com/world/2015/feb/17/sierra-leone-investigates-alleged-misuse-of-emergency-ebola-funds (Accessed 25 November 2020).

Olu, O. O., Lamunu, M., Chimbaru, A., Adegboyega, A., Conteh, I., Nsenga, N., Sempiira, N., Kamara, K. B. and Dafae, F. M. (2016) 'Incident Management Systems Are Essential for Effective Coordination of Large Disease Outbreaks: Perspectives From the Coordination of the Ebola Outbreak Response in Sierra Leone'. *Frontiers in Public Health*, 4, p. 254. DOI: 10.3389/fpubh.2016.00254.

Oosterhoff, P. and Wilkinson, A. (2015) *Local Engagement in Ebola Outbreaks and Beyond in Sierra Leone*. Practice Paper in Brief 24. Institute of Development Studies. Available at: https://opendocs.ids.ac.uk/opendocs/handle/20.500.12413/5857 (Accessed 15 January 2021).

Oxfam (2016) 'Ebola Funds Impossible to Track'. Oxfam International, 31 January. Available at: https://www.oxfam.org/en/press-releases/ebola-funds-impossible-track (Accessed 29 November 2020).

Parker, M., Hanson, T. M., Vandi, A., Babawo, L. S. and Allen, T. (2019) 'Ebola and Public Authority: Saving Loved Ones in Sierra Leone'. *Medical Anthropology*, 38(5), pp. 440–454. DOI: 10.1080/01459740.2019.1609472.

Persaud, R. and Sajed, A. (2018) *Race, Gender, and Culture in International Relations. Postcolonial Perspectives.* London: Routledge.

Piot, Peter and Miliband, David (2015) 'Fighting Ebola Requires a Culture Change in the West, as Well as West Africa'. *The Guardian.* Available at: http://www.theguardian.com/commentisfree/2015/mar/03/ebola-culture-change-west-africa-communities (Accessed 6 January 2021).

Powell, W. (1990) 'Neither Market Nor Hierarchy: Network Forms of Organization'. *Research in Organizational Behaviour*, 12, pp. 295–336.

Rami, E. (2017) 'Colonialism, Civil War, and Ebola: Historical Perspectives on Contemporary Healthcare in Sierra Leone'.*Yale Global Health Review*, 14 May. Available at: https://yaleglobalhealthreview.com/2017/05/14/colonialism-civil-war-and-ebola-historical-perspectives-on-contemporary-healthcare-in-sierra-leone/ (Accessed 25 November 2020).

Rashid, I. (2011) 'Epidemics and Resistance in Colonial Sierra Leone During the First World War'. *Canadian Journal of African Studies/Revue canadienne des études africaines*, 45(3), pp. 415–439. DOI: 10.1080/00083968.2011.10541064.

Raven, J., Wurie, H. and Witter, S. (2018) 'Health Workers' Experiences of Coping With the Ebola Epidemic in Sierra Leone's Health System: A Qualitative Study'. *BMC Health Services Research*, 18. DOI: 10.1186/s12913-018-3072-3.

ReliefWeb(no date) 'UK to Increase Support to Sierra Leone to Combat Ebola - Sierra Leone'. Available at: https://reliefweb.int/report/sierra-leone/uk-increase-support-sierra-leone-combat-ebola (Accessed 8 January 2021).

Ribacke, Kim J., Brolin, Dell D., Saulnier, Anneli Eriksson and Von Schreeb, Johan (October 2016) 'Effects of the West Africa Ebola Virus Disease on Health-Care Utilization – A Systematic Review'. *Frontiers in Public Health*,4, pp. 1–11. DOI: 10.3389/fpubh.2016.00222.

Richards, P., Amara, J., Ferme, M. C., Kamara, P., Mokuwa, E., Sheriff, A. I., Suluku, R. and Voors, M. (2015) 'Social Pathways for Ebola Virus Disease in Rural Sierra Leone, and Some Implications for Containment'. *PLoS Neglected Tropical Diseases*, 9(4), p. e0003567. DOI: 10.1371/journal.pntd.0003567.

Richards, P., Bah, K. and Vincent, J. (no date) 'Social Capital and Survival: Prospects for Community-Driven Development in Post-Conflict Sierra Leone'. p. 78.

Ripoll, S., Gercama, I., Jones, T. and Wilkinson, A. (no date) *Social Science in Epidemics: Ebola Virus Disease Lessons Learned.* Institute of Development Studies, p. 53.

Ross, E., Welch, G. H. and Angelides, P. (2017) *Sierra Leone's Response to the Ebola Outbreak.* Chatham House: The Royal Institute of International Affairs, p. 50.

Roy, M., Moreau, N., Rousseau, C., Mercier, A., Wilson, A. and Atlani-Duault, L. (2020) 'Ebola and Localized Blame on Social Media: Analysis of Twitter and Facebook Conversations During the 2014–2015 Ebola Epidemic'. *Culture, Medicine, and Psychiatry*, 44(1), pp. 56–79. DOI: 10.1007/s11013-019-09635-8.

Rush, J. (2015) 'Bodies of Ebola Victims 'Left in the Streets' as Burial Teams Go On Strike'. *The Independent.* Available at: https://www.independent.co.uk/news/world

/africa/ebola-outbreak-bodies-victims-left-streets-burial-teams-go-strike-9781499.html (Accessed 5 January 2021).

Sandvik, K. B. (2015) 'Evaluating Ebola: The Politics of the Military Response Narrative - Global Interagency Security Forum'. *The Global Interagency Security Forum*, 16 March. Available at: https://gisf.ngo/blogs/evaluating-ebola-the-politics-of-the-military-response-narrative/ (Accessed 6 January 2021).

Save the Children (2015) *A Wake-Up Call: Lessons From Ebola for the World's Health System*. London: Save the Children. Available at: https://www.savethechildren.org.uk/content/dam/global/reports/health-and-nutrition/a-wake-up-call.pdf.

Slaughter, A.-M. (2017) *Chessboard and the Web*. New Haven, CT: Yale University Press. Available at: https://yalebooks.yale.edu/book/9780300215649/chessboard-and-web (Accessed 15 January 2021).

The Secretariat (2015) *Ensuring WHO's Capacity to Prepare for and Respond to Future Large-Scale and Sustained Outbreaks and Emergencies*. EBSS/3/3. Geneva: World Health Organization. Available at: https://apps.who.int/iris/bitstream/handle/10665/251731/EBSS3_3-en.pdf?sequence=1&isAllowed=y (Accessed 6 January 2021).

Thomas, A. R. (2014) 'Health Minister Miatta Kargbo Sacked'. *Sierra Leone Telegraph*, 29 August. Available at: https://www.thesierraleonetelegraph.com/health-minister-miatta-kargbo-sacked/ (Accessed 8 January 2021).

Thompson, L. (2016) 'In Sierra Leone, Perceived Corruption Rises, Public Trust and Leaders' Job Approval Drop'. *Afrobarometer Dispatch 103*. Available at: https://afrobarometer.org/publications/ad103-sierra-leone-perceived-corruption-rises-public-trust-and-leaders-job-approval (Accessed 29 November 2020).

Tilly, C. (2005) *Trust and Rule*. Cambridge: Cambridge University Press.

Transparency International (2015) 'Ebola: Corruption and Aid – News'. Available at: https://www.transparency.org/en/news/ebola-corruption-and-aid?token=0-6DEP8J9gsvrwbDFWOEJICG4YkpcWjn (Accessed 25 November 2020).

Ucko, D. (2015) 'Can Limited Intervention Work? Lessons From Britain's Success Story in Sierra Leone'. *Journal of Strategic Studies*, 39, pp. 1–31. DOI: 10.1080/01402390.2015.1110695.

UN Mission for Ebola Emergency Response (UNMEER) (2014) 'Global Ebola Response'. Available at: https://ebolaresponse.un.org/un-mission-ebola-emergency-response-unmeer (Accessed 10 January 2021).

UNDP Regional Bureau for Africa (2015) Socio-Economic Impact of Ebola Virus Disease in West African Countries a Call for National and Regional Containment, Recovery and Prevention. DOI: 10.13140/RG.2.2.29620.04481.

von Grebmer, Klaus, Bernstein, Jill, de Waal, Alex, Prasai, Nilam, Yin, Sandra and Yohannes, Yisehac. (2015) *Global Hunger Index: Armed Conflict and the Challenge of Hunger*. Bonn, Germany; Washington, D.C. and Dublin, Ireland: Welthungerhilfe; International Food Policy Research Institute (IFPRI) and Concern Worldwide. DOI: 10.2499/9780896299641.

Voors, M. and Van der Windt, P. (2019) 'Traditional Leaders and the 2014–2015 Ebola Epidemic'. *The Journal of Politics*, 82. DOI: 10.1086/708777.

Waugaman, A. and Fast, L. (2016) *Fighting Ebola With Information: Learning From Data and Information Flows in the West Africa Ebola Response*. Washington, DC: USAID, p. 140. Available at: https://www.usaid.gov/sites/default/files/documents/15396/FightingEbolaWithInformation.pdf.

WHO (no date) *Ebola Response Funding*. Geneva: World Health Organization (WHO). Available at: http://www.who.int/csr/disease/ebola/funding/en/ (Accessed 8 January 2021).

WHO|New WHO Safe and Dignified Burial Protocol (no date) *Key to Reducing Ebola Transmission*.Geneva: World Health Organization (WHO). Available at: https://www.who.int/mediacentre/news/notes/2014/ebola-burial-protocol/en/ (Accessed 6 January 2021).

WHS Effectiveness Theme Focal Issue Paper 5: Accountability - World (no date) *ReliefWeb*. Available at: https://reliefweb.int/report/world/whs-effectiveness-theme-focal-issue-paper-5-accountability (Accessed 15 January 2021).

Wilkinson, A. and Fairhead, J. (2017) 'Comparison of Social Resistance to Ebola Response in Sierra Leone and Guinea Suggests Explanations Lie in Political Configurations Not Culture'. *Critical Public Health*, 27(1), pp. 14–27. DOI: 10.1080/09581596.2016.1252034.

Williamson, O. E. (1975) *Markets and Hierarchies: Analysis and Antitrust Implications: A Study in the Economics of Internal Organization. SSRN Scholarly Paper ID 1496220*. Rochester, NY: Social Science Research Network. Available at: https://papers.ssrn.com/abstract=1496220 (Accessed 8 January 2021).

Williamson, O. E. (1985) *The Economic Institutions of Capitalism: Firms, Markets, Relational Contracting*. New York: Free Press.

Chapter 7

THE DIGITAL 'MARKETPLACE OF IDEAS': THE NEED FOR A HUMAN RIGHTS-CENTRED, MULTI-STAKEHOLDER APPROACH TO CYBER NORMS

Laura Salter

Introduction

The study of international relations has long focused on the strategic interactions of governments – games of war and treatises of peace. But increasingly in today's globalised world, collective action crosses national boundaries and critical decisions that affect the world of politics fall to non-state actors, be they individuals, terrorist groups, grassroots movements or corporations. As Anne-Marie Slaughter describes in her apt analysis, practitioners and students of international affairs would benefit from seeing the world not as a chessboard of strategy games between statesmen, but as a web of networks, overlapping and intersecting worldwide and online (2017, 5–7). To understand action and reaction in the twenty-first century, one must now grapple with an entirely new space where neither state nor non-state actors exercise full control: the internet, whose infrastructure increasingly determines how information is consumed and decisions are made. This chapter discusses new challenges to the exercise of democracy and human rights in the international arena, brought on by the increasing ubiquity of online fora where modern public discourse takes place.

Freedom of expression is a key component of both democratic and human rights frameworks. Its regulation online has become subject of great discussion, both because of non-democratic regimes that seek to limit dissent and information online, and due to increasingly concerning disinformation and hate speech within social networks worldwide. Foundational to the liberal principle of free speech is the oft-invoked image of a 'marketplace of ideas'. The concept dates back to nineteenth-century political philosophers like John Stuart Mill, who argued that in an unfettered space where the public could freely debate and weigh competing ideas without interference, rational human behaviour would allow the 'best' ideas to be chosen and exercised in society (see Mill, 1989, Part 2). Yet many scholars, including Mill himself, have discussed the imperfections of such an image, as the marketplace can be distorted by real-life conditions that create 'market failures', such as censorship, human bias towards the status quo and the historical evidence that the rationality of a human mind is not infallible (Ingber, 1984, 4–6). Distortions alter the ability of a rational individual to identify and act on an objectively best option or identify truth. Still, the ideal type of a 'marketplace of ideas' remains the philosophical foundation for freedom of expression, creating a useful paradigm to analyse how new distortions present themselves in the global communications landscape and inform individuals' very perceptions of reality.

In modern society, the internet plays host to an unprecedented amount of daily life – it permeates our financial transactions, interpersonal connections and access to news and information. Yet these 'spaces' are not truly public spheres; ultimately, they are products of profit-driven corporations. The structure of these platforms has granted sudden and unprecedented power to a few technology giants over the flow of data, information and ideas, creating virtual spaces that are as critical to day-to-day life for much of society as the physical world. As a result, policymakers must now grapple with whether and how to regulate the 'marketplace of ideas' without treading on the rights of its inhabitants.

This chapter attempts to address this issue. First, it illustrates the risk of violence and human rights violations sparked by an anarchic cyberspace, as digital hate speech and disinformation can lead to offline and large-scale violence. For this, the chapter briefly examines the ethnic cleansing of the Rohingya in Myanmar. This case study illustrates the supposition that the algorithmically driven and anarchical space of social media can act as a catalyst for unmonitored, targeted disinformation campaigns, as the distorted 'marketplace of ideas' allows extremist views to flourish. The case also demonstrates the risks of employing an ad hoc approach to content moderation in cyberspace. Additionally, datasets are ever-growing and evolving, informing corporate practices, government policy, healthcare and education – and as a result, the relatively new field of data technology has created a number of ethical challenges that would not have traditionally fallen into the purview of computer scientists. These issues, too, will be touched on further in the 'Discussion' section.

While technology itself is intended to be ideologically neutral, it clearly has far-reaching effects on how communication takes place within societies. It is evident from the literature that the use of social media can have mobilising and polarising effects on connected communities, especially in populations with low digital literacy. Consequently, the introduction of Information and Communication Technologies (ICTs) can be considered a force multiplier or a catalyst in the outbreak of violence. It's clear, then, that there must be more discussion of cyberspace in terms of its users' human rights. The social network Twitter aspired to be the new 'public town square', a forum for ideas and perspectives to be shared (Perez, 2019). Social networks began to fill this role rapidly; just as rapidly, they were faced with questions of how to manage (mis) information about elections, which content to flag as hate speech, with whom to share users' personal data and whether to censor a sitting US president. The ethical and legal challenges facing a handful of global tech corporations cannot be understated. The decisions they make can alter foreign policy, compromise personal information, mobilise social movements and spark genocide. A dynamic system of networked decision-making that centres the full exercise of human rights, both online and offline, is critical.

Ultimately, this study attempts to address how the international community can mitigate those risks brought on by the effects of online polarisation, echo chambers and disinformation. The chapter argues the strengths of a multi-stakeholder approach to norm development with regard to cyberspace, paying particular attention to personal data collection and content moderation on social media platforms. The development and integration of such norms globally can be demonstrated to be a practical and ethical necessity.

Key literature

A growing subset of sociological literature concerns the introduction of ICTs into networks of social contact. As Ralph D. Berenger writes, 'Every technological innovation in the field of communication has caused disruption in how members of societies relate to each other, and each has resulted in a paradigm shift in civil discourse and behavior, sometimes with unintended consequences' (2013, 7). Much of the early literature surrounding this topic in relation to politics and international affairs focused on the perceived positive benefits of ICTs in empowering previously repressed populations by giving voice to marginalised actors, with reference to these technologies' prominent role in the Arab Spring. However, more recent case studies have also illuminated the role that the digital space can play in fomenting violent narratives and extremism.

This chapter frequently references Dennis Broeders and Bibi van der Berg's volume *Governing Cyberspace: Behavior, Power, and Diplomacy*, which provides a comprehensive look at the nascent development of cyberspace governance. The volume's authors consider the challenges of applying international law to the internet, introducing the polarising perspectives on internet regulation by different regime types. The compendium frequently points out the challenge that the infrastructure of the internet, and therefore any regulation of its space, does not fully fall into the realm of governmental control, as industry and civil involvement are also critical to the execution of any venture (Broeders and Van der Berg, 2020, 152). To this end, Jacqueline Eggenschwiler and Joanna Kulesza's chapter considers actions that individual and groups of tech corporations have taken to develop responsible norms and guidelines around behaviour in cyberspace (p245). By suggesting that non-state actors, like Microsoft, can themselves act as norm entrepreneurs in the cyber domain, Eggenschwiler and Kulesza introduce an important shift in the discussion of international norm-making: the debate extends beyond traditional diplomatic and state actors. With this in mind, the theme of a 'multi-stakeholder' approach to international norm entrepreneurship becomes clear throughout the volume. These themes and topics are expanded on in many of the individual chapters and are recommended further reading.

Analysis also extends to the more intentional side of narrative manipulation within the digital space. The Computational Propaganda Research Project lays out the variety of strategies employed in the digital space to influence opinions and disseminate narratives (Bradshaw and Howard, 2017). The use of disinformation campaigns is increasingly relevant in the promotion of violent nationalist movements, and many of the strategies explored in the report can be applied to analysis of such contexts.

Another element to consider in this domain is that of 'dangerous speech', a term coined by Susan Benesch to describe any form of expression 'that can increase the risk that its audience will condone or participate in violence against members of another group', intended to be a less vague phenomenon to address than the comparable concept of 'hate speech' (Benesch et al., 2018). The Dangerous Speech Project determines several key strategies that are employed in the dissemination of dangerous speech, including dehumanisation, the promotion of fear and a threat to group purity. Identification of dangerous speech is intended to serve as an early indicator of communal violence, which allows steps to be taken to proactively counter this form of speech.

Case Study: Myanmar

To provide a fully comprehensive historical background leading up to Myanmar's current socio-political context would be a lengthy undertaking. This section instead lays out the historical precursors of the country's divisions, followed by an analysis of the outbreak of violence.

The context

Myanmar gained independence from Britain in 1948 and, in 1962, began decades of rule under a military dictatorship during which heavy international sanctions were imposed. In 2011, Myanmar began to open to the outside world after decades of isolation, commencing a period of rapid social and political change. The heralded 'democratic transition', deemed necessary for long-term development by the state's ruling leaders, created relief from sanctions and opened the door to foreign investment, market expansion and trade relationships. However, this liberalising period coincided with communal violence reaching previously unattained scales of organisation and severity. Ultra-nationalist Buddhist groups organised anti-Muslim campaigns that drew on long-held fears of Islam, primarily targeted against the Rohingya ethnic group.

In Myanmar, Muslims had long been associated with foreign intrusion and economic exploitation by the native population (Gravers, 2015, 7). The

Rohingya, specifically, are associated with Bengal immigrants, creating their image as foreign intruders in the nation (Keck, 2016, 66). As in other colonies, the British ruled Burma by administering the population through a system of ethnic classification; the concept of 'race' was introduced as the primary tool of social organisation (Cho, 2018, 43). Consequently, early conceptualisations of the indigenous nation to the territory came to be based on the majority Burmese Buddhist ethnic group, and strict divisions between groups were established in the national consciousness. Throughout the nation-building process, ethnic violence occurred frequently and was often invoked strategically by leaders. The Rohingya, specifically, faced structural violence as well; the 1982 Citizenship Law deprived the Rohingya of citizenship rights, institutionalising their statelessness (Human Rights Watch, 1996, 26).

With political and economic liberalisation came newfound freedoms of communication and telecommunications reform. Under military rule, access to information and freedom of expression were closely controlled by the government. Public discussion was directed through a central provision of propaganda, while heavy censorship measures limited the role of an independent media (Simpson et al., 2018, 4). Throughout military rule, internet access was limited to those who were trusted by the government; even SIM cards were kept at an artificially high price in order to limit mobile access to friends of the state apparatus (McCarthy, 2018, 92). Prior to liberalisation in 2011, Myanmar's population was only reported to have a 2.6 per cent mobile penetration rate, according to the International Telecommunications Union. As a result, the democratic reforms introduced in 2011–12 revolutionised the flow of information in several key ways.

First, prepublication censorship measures were repealed in 2012, freeing publishers to expand public information and debate. Opposition leaders, such as Aung San Suu Kyi, were given new license to publish articles and opinion pieces (Hlaing, 2012, 202). Simultaneously, the population of Myanmar received access to internet-enabled technology for the first time. The globalised market's newfound access to Myanmar led to the rapid expansion of Telenor from Norway and Ooredoo from Qatar, each of whom established internet networks that collected millions of new users. Over forty-three million SIM cards had been sold by mid-2016, demonstrating a dramatic increase in private internet access and a significant reformatting of the country's information ecosystem. As Facebook came preloaded on most cell phones, it quickly emerged as the primary platform and source of information. Its prominence was so noted that analysts have stated that 'Facebook is the internet in Myanmar', used nearly universally as a main source of news, community and communication by its users (McCarthy, 93).

The escalation of violence

Anti-Muslim campaigns led by ultra-nationalist Buddhist monks took form in the early twenty-first century. The 969 Movement, and its de facto leader U Wirathu, promoted a radical Buddhist nationalist agenda that mobilised anti-Muslim sentiment among the general population. The 969 Movement emerged initially to promote a 'buy Buddhist' campaign, in order to boycott Muslim businesses and protect the Burmese race and religion (Kyaw, 2016, 185–95). The movement actively reignited a commonly held idea that Buddhism was under threat by Islam in Myanmar, requiring urgent action. Radical monks associated with the campaign produced sermons, videos and pamphlets that were distributed, often incorporating stories of forced marriage of Buddhist women to Muslims and conspiracy theories about Islamisation (185).

Prior to 2012, relations between the Rakhine Buddhist and Rohingya populations of the Rakhine State were reportedly positive and symbiotic (United Nations Human Rights Council, 2018a, 5). However, riots erupted in the Rakhine State in June and October of 2012, framed as a reaction to the rape and murder of a Buddhist Rakhine woman by Muslim men. Reports by state media sensationalised images of her body (Van Klinken and Aung, 2017, 359). Riots in June were largely spontaneous mob activity, while October's violent acts were more highly coordinated. Violence then spread across the country, in a geographic scope that was unprecedented since 1948 (Kyaw 2016, 183). Framing of the conflict in the state media claim that Muslims provoked the conflict and that the illegal Rohingya were the primary perpetrators.

Reuters journalists were present in Myanmar to report on the events that followed. According to their reports, Buddhist mobs led by monks were seen with machetes and swords, perpetrating mob violence in at least 14 villages of central Myanmar. Killings were witnessed and ignored by the police. Violence was perpetrated in both directions, but the motivating ideology that sparked the initial riots was found in the rhetoric promoted by the 969 monks (Szep, 2013). Human Rights Watch reported that the riots transformed into a coordinated campaign to drive Muslims from the land, stating that the attacks in October 'were organised, incited, and committed by local Arakanese political party operatives, the Buddhist monkhood, and ordinary Arakanese, at times directly supported by state security forces' (Human Rights Watch, 2013, 4). Prior to these attacks, monks and political party leaders actively demonised the Rohingya, called for their removal from the country or denying their existence. These tactics of public messaging and framing of the conflict resulted in mass mobilisation towards violence. As a result of these attacks, 125,000 Rohingya were displaced.

The Arakan Rohingya Salvation Army (ARSA) emerged in October 2016, organised with the purpose of fighting for the rights of the Rohingya (MacGregor, 2017). On 9 October 2016, the militant group attacked border police in the Rakhine State. In response, Myanmar's security forces enacted brutal campaigns justified as counter-insurgency measures or 'clearance operations' against the entire Rohingya population.

In the aftermath of the October attacks, a team commissioned by the Office of the United Nations High Commissioner for Human Rights (OHCHR) conducted interviews with Rohingya who had fled to Bangladesh following the violence. Statistics drawn from testimonies of witnessed and experienced violations were examined, followed by qualitative reports detailing Buddhist Rakhine villagers who participated in the violence and/or sexual abuse after having been armed and integrated into the security forces, either in uniform or in civilian dress (2017, 9–13). Violations included gang rape; sexual violence; psychological torture; and innocent civilian deaths, including of children, by systematic, indiscriminate attacks, regardless of affiliation with ARSA. Upon return, villages were found to be completely burnt. The OHCHR concluded that this evidence indicated the likely commission of crimes against humanity.

On 25 August 2017, ARSA conducted attacks on 30 police and security force outposts in the Rakhine State. The attacks were conducted by minimally trained militants and untrained villagers and resulted in the deaths of 12 security personnel. Within hours of these attacks, the crimes against humanity documented in October 2016 were initiated once again as security forces began a campaign of violence in the Rakhine State, again termed counterterrorism 'clearance operations' by the Tatmadaw. Amnesty International recounted a disproportionate degree of violence levelled against the Rohingya, as the entire population was targeted in multiple villages 'on the basis of their identity', regardless of affiliation with ARSA militants (2017, 99). The report concludes that the indiscriminate shooting into houses and fields, torture, gang rape and burning of villages by security forces and vigilantes have constituted crimes against humanity (p. 88). According to interviews, killings were conducted by soldiers as well as Rakhine civilians. In her statement, Special Rapporteur Yanghee Lee concluded that the events in the Rakhine State 'bear the hallmarks of genocide' (United Nations Human Rights Council, 2018b, 15). An estimated 725,000 Rohingya refugees were forced to flee into Bangladesh.

Myanmar's 'Marketplace of Ideas'

Under the strictures of military rule, information was passed by word of mouth and often incorporated rumours as a means of community building and to create a common frame of reality (Schissler, 2017, 220). Without the benefit of an independent press or reputable sources of information, rumour-sharing played a critical social function. For many years, the marketplace of ideas existed within this communal practice of information sharing. When this communication structure was transmuted to the digital space, a similar pattern of communication naturally evolved, but was augmented and segmented by the algorithmically driven function of the platform.

Early anticolonial nationalism had sparked slogans like 'Burma for Burmans' and 'Master Race We Are, We Burmans', planting the roots of ethno-nationalist activism and inherently emphasising the threat to the state posed by non-Burmans (Gravers, 2015, 8). These early instances of the anti-Muslim movement instrumentalised tactics and myths, such as the threat to the nation's women or pollution through intermarriage, that would continue to be used through the process of scapegoating in the decades that followed.

Although democratic reforms were introduced and did partially restrict the powers of the military, and despite the fact that the state underwent significant reforms as a result, the reality shows that the marketplace of ideas remained under the effective control of the military. Only those reforms that were amenable to the military's continued role as the protector of the nation were enacted, so while elections were held and communications restrictions were lifted, the space for expression itself was kept highly illiberal and encouraged a culture of hate speech and exclusion (United Nations, 2018a, 14).

The capacity of political and religious elites for mythmaking in the modernised marketplace of ideas was expedited. The substance of these ideas, however, drew on familiar symbols, stories and experiences within the national consciousness. While the 'clearance operations' conducted in the Rakhine State were organised and perpetrated primarily by security forces, public sentiment that supported these actions was rooted in pre-existing socio-economic grievances, the moral authority held by religious organisations, and the spread of familiar myths through communication networks.

One such myth is the belief that Muslims reproduce at a much faster rate than Buddhists in the nation (which has been debunked by researchers) and that they aim to either rape or force Buddhist women into marriage (Carstens, 2018, 131–32). The circulation of this form of myth, in particular, is likely to provoke a violent response. While organised attacks by Muslim militants provoke security responses by the Tatmadaw, rapes or attacks on Buddhist individuals spark the formation of civilian militias. Vigilante justice is then undertaken through rioting and attacks on Muslims (Banyan, 2012). This occurs because of what sociologists call 'frame alignment'. Framing, which is defined as 'conscious strategic efforts by groups of people to fashion shared understandings of the world and of themselves that legitimate and motivate collective action', is a clear element of the rise of identity-based violence in this case study (McAdam et al., 6). Frame alignment occurs when proof is presented of pre-existing fears. When a story or image is spread in the community that confirms an unsettling belief, a passive threat becomes salient and requires action in response (Van Klinken and Aung, 362).

Facebook was brought under international scrutiny for its role in this process following the 2017 violence in Myanmar, when it was observed that the network's sudden introduction to the country's public played a vital role in disseminating and amplifying disinformation and hate speech (Stevenson, 2018). In response to these allegations, the company commissioned the Business for Social Responsibility (BSR) to conduct an independent human rights impact assessment on the case. The BSR analysis of the context begins by describing Myanmar's crisis of digital literacy, caused by the country's rapid liberalisation and opening of the telecom sector: 'A large population of internet users lacks basic understanding of how to use a browser, how to set up an email address and access an email account, and how to navigate and make judgments on online content. Despite this, most mobile phones sold in the country come preloaded with Facebook' (2018, 12).

As the BSR report describes, Facebook itself was viewed as synonymous with the internet. In some ways, the network played a democratising role by introducing its users to information on human rights and democracy, connecting them to their elected officials, and creating a new space for free speech where there had previously been none. However, in a state where information was customarily passed communally, and where a lack of digital literacy decreased the public's ability to verify content or real news, the platform was easily abused for the purposes of spreading disinformation and extremist content.

The BSR report observes that women reported being harassed or extorted; rural people and those with lower education and/or income were more vulnerable to hate speech and misinformation; older users were more likely to subscribe to extremist nationalist content; and shopkeepers who sold the mobile devices were known to sell devices having pre-set Facebook accounts, which could then be used to extort customers (14). The report also analyses Myanmar's existing legal framework, which limits true freedom of expression by establishing that one's freedom of speech 'exists only when the views are not contrary to the laws of the country' (17).

Attention has been drawn to Facebook's role in such violent situations in cases beyond Myanmar, such as Sri Lanka and the Philippines. But as the BSR report points out, its role in this case is unique in that it is nearly the sole source of information for a majority of users. The first instance of this connection was in July 2014, when communal violence and rioting broke out in Mandalay following a nationalist monk's Facebook post reporting the rape of a Buddhist woman by a Muslim man (Schlissler, 211). This was the same year as Ooredoo and Telenor's massive investment in telecommunications infrastructure, following communications reform in Myanmar.

A *New York Times* investigation revealed that senior members of Myanmar's military used the social network, concealing their identities and spreading fear-mongering posts about Muslims and stories about the rape of Buddhist women (Mozur, 2018). Using troll accounts and pop culture pages on Facebook, these political elites spread support for the military's ultranationalist campaign, posting photos of corpses attributed to Rohingya killers and spreading anti-Islamic memes, while also collecting intelligence on government critics. According to the investigation, the military's Facebook propaganda campaign had begun several years earlier. Yet its most dangerous tactic was employed in 2017. Rumours were spread directly via Facebook Messenger to both Muslims and Buddhists, stating that attack from the other was imminent, simultaneously utilising 'news' sites and celebrity fan pages around the anniversary of the 11 September 2001, attacks to foment an environment of fear. Given their relationship to the existing institutional power structure, these military leaders fall into the category of 'cyber troops', as defined by the Computational Propaganda Research Project: government or political actors tasked with manipulating public opinion online (Bradshaw and Howard, 2017, 4). Facebook's lack of protocol to provide content moderation that removes hate speech or misinformation in Myanmar allowed this content to go viral within echo chambers, understood to be truth and motivating retributive violence.

Snyder and Ballentine have argued that a complete governmental monopoly over the press is not the most dangerous condition for nationalist mythmaking, because this context creates a sceptical audience (2001, 14). Yet with digitally enabled distortions to the marketplace of ideas, a monopoly on information is able to be disguised through fake accounts and false identities, based on existing popular culture and news identities – a clear indication that the digital space is able to amplify and disguise extremist speech.

The result of these distortions to the marketplace of ideas is that violent extremism emerges as a rational choice based on self-defence and frame alignment.

Discussion

A broad view of the case study reveals that violence was not solely caused by the presence of Facebook; indeed, the country's story of ethnic and religious division was already well written. A digital platform does not, itself, construct violence. However, the case study also illustrates the heightened role that digital platforms now play in manufacturing crises, with possible dire ramifications. The manipulation of an unfiltered platform, whose algorithm can intentionally create echo chambers and which is capable of targeting personalised disinformation, can easily act as a catalyst for offline violence and human rights violations. So we return to the original question posed in this research: How can we mitigate the risks of human rights violations and the spread of misinformation in a distorted 'marketplace of ideas'? What global actions could be considered ethical and necessary?

The case study exemplifies the role that ICTs now play in structuring the information flow of a society and catalysing the spread of extremism and misinformation. The distortions present in the marketplace of ideas, caused by a profit-centred and data-driven business model, can allow bad actors to manipulate the flow of ideas, aligning new information with pre-existing fears and anxieties in a tailored call to action. The case study clearly demonstrates that this manipulation was uniquely effective and destructive in the post-2011 context in Myanmar, and the effects could easily be extrapolated to other emerging democracies or protracted conflicts.

This section analyses two contributing issues at play in such platforms: corporate ownership of personal data and the challenges of content moderation. Following a brief discussion of these issues, the analysis will turn to the future of norm entrepreneurship in cyberspace, advocating for a multi-stakeholder approach centred on human rights.

The data problem

Data has been said to have overcome oil as the most important commodity of the modern age – yet, although it is produced by user activity on digital platforms, these users derive none of the financial gains that are shared by corporations and third-party advertisers. As Nima Elmi of the World Economic Forum reported, in 2020, 'private technology and telecommunication companies control more data on the average person than governments do' (Elmi, 2020). This data is critical to the business model of communications platforms like Facebook, Twitter and YouTube, and its pervasiveness has fundamentally altered modern society through the model's effects on the information ecosystem.

Personal data is defined in the European Union's General Data Protection Regulation (GDPR) as

> any information relating to an identified or identifiable natural person ('data subject'); an identifiable natural person is one who can be identified, directly or

indirectly, in particular by reference to an identifier such as a name, an identification number, location data, an online identifier or to one or more factors specific to the physical, physiological, genetic, mental, economic, cultural or social identity of that natural person. (GDPR Article 4, Definitions)

To maximise profit, platforms employ algorithms: self-learning programs that use ranking criteria to determine what content to prioritise for each individual user based on their behaviours, likes and dislikes, with a goal to maximise user attention and engagement (Ghonim, 2018).

Before international scrutiny turned to the tragedy in Myanmar, Facebook's business model had already come under fire when the Cambridge Analytica scandal unearthed evidence that the platform's use of users' personal data had swayed the results of the 2016 US presidential election. Facebook derives profit from the previously described business model: quickly and cheaply accumulating huge masses of data on individual users, to be analysed and structured for advertisers to personalise content and advertisements that maintain consumer attention (Hand, 2018). This practice has come to fundamentally restructure the way that information is discovered and consumed in digital spaces like Facebook, Twitter and YouTube. Understandably, this has sparked substantial debate that has largely framed the issue in terms of user privacy. However, simply framing the ethics of personal data collection in terms of privacy fails to address other components of the issue: namely, the ability of the business model to promote extremist messaging, and the exploitative nature of the business model.

Tech giants are no longer simply commercial agents in brick-and-mortar-based economies; they are the architects of virtual realities, and the arbiters of engagement in the marketplace of ideas. In a business model that sells user data to third-party marketers and where inflammatory (mis)information is algorithmically centred, for example, consumers are vulnerable to micro-targeting while remaining siloed from fact verification and alternative perspectives. The Myanmar case study provides an informative view of how this functionality can promote extremist speech, especially in a context with low digital literacy and lacking content moderation. Other socio-political contextual factors, such as a period of political and economic transition, set the stage for tensions to mount in Myanmar. But evidence shows that Facebook's sudden and unregulated presence allowed disinformation and calls to action to go viral, facilitating a new level of persecution of the Rohingya. To a certain extent, this phenomenon is aided by individual users' own self-selection towards confirmation bias, avoiding opposing perspectives. As Gerard McCarthy states, research on digital political spheres tends to show that people 'herd into groups or "echo-chambers,"' rather than being engaged in a more diverse and democratic set of opinions (2018, 93). The function of data-fuelled social network algorithms simply amplifies this effect, by continuing to feed content and advertisements that match user preferences, further deepening polarisation, rewarding sensationalism and deepening echo chambers.

If freedom of speech is rooted in a belief that rationally acting humans will be able to discern the best idea, or truth, from a marketplace of ideas – or as the axiom goes, the only cure for bad speech is more, better speech – then speech is only valuable if the medium in which it occurs does not manipulate the outcome. Clearly, there can be vast implications for human rights as a result of a distorted information infrastructure.

The human rights implications are also apparent in considering the issue of data privacy vs. ownership. Multiple movements, organisations and data privacy regulations have developed in response to the violations of user privacy that have become emblematic of Facebook's issues. Mark Zuckerberg, CEO of Facebook, has focused many of the platform's reforms on protecting user privacy in the face of widespread criticism of data breaches and a lack of transparency. Data privacy or cyber security laws like the European Union's GDPR have been introduced in over one hundred countries worldwide, according to UNCTAD statistics. Yet it is questionable whether these regulations truly address the ethical issues inherent in the business model.

Various scholars have argued that a business that derives its profit from a product (i.e. data) produced by users who receive no compensation is, in fact, a form of unpaid labour (see Shoshana Zuboff (2019) and Jakub Kibitlewski's chapter in this volume). As Zuboff suggests, this one-sided extraction is an inherently exploitative model that trades free access to an online space, like Facebook, for real and tangible financial gains shared by the corporation and its third-party advertisers (Zuboff, 2019, 68). Movements like the Own Your Data Foundation and Streamr have introduced new ways of conceptualising personal data, extending beyond privacy concerns and suggesting that a restructuring of the data economy is necessary, such as through data ownership models or the creation of data unions (Malik, 2020).

The content moderation problem

A second regulatory and ethical challenge facing digital communication platforms is content moderation. Upon discovering Facebook's role in propagating the hate speech and disinformation that immediately preceded the ethnic cleansing in Myanmar, local and international observers were quick to point out the platform's complacency in the tragedy.

Most democratic nations have legislation in place protecting freedom of expression. In the United States, for example, Section 230 of the

Communications Decency Act specifically protects freedom of speech and innovation on the internet, freeing service providers from responsibility for the content of their online space (47 U.S.C. § 230). However, events between 2010 and 2020 have produced questions about the ethics of anarchical platforms in practice. An April 2018 open letter to Mark Zuckerberg from members of civil society organisations in Myanmar cited 'an over-reliance on third parties, a lack of a proper mechanism for emergency escalation, a reticence to engage local stakeholders around systemic solutions and a lack of transparency' as issues that had been present and reported in Myanmar prior to the outbreak of violence ('Open Letter to Mark Zuckerberg', 2018). The direct progression from online hate speech to horrific offline violence made it clear to many observers that Facebook must, in reality, hold some responsibility for the effects of its content.

To this end, Facebook is a member of the Global Network Initiative (GNI), a non-governmental organisation whose mission is 'to protect and advance freedom of expression and privacy in the ICT industry by setting a global standard for responsible company decision-making and by being a leading voice for freedom of expression and privacy rights'. The GNI bases its guidelines on existing international law and human rights treaties. In its biennial assessment, Facebook was found to be in compliance with these guidelines, at the same time as identity-based violence flourished on its platform in Myanmar (BSR, 20).

Facebook holds its users to its community standards, which establish the boundaries of what content is allowed on its platform. In order to monitor this content, the Community Operations Team is trained to flag and remove specific slurs and words. In 2018, following the backlash, Facebook committed to increasing the number of moderators in Myanmar, including Myanmar language experts, to better monitor the network (BSR, 21). Facebook has also introduced artificial intelligence technologies to uphold community standards by flagging hate speech, promoting AI as the major solution to future online moderation. However, there is no consensus on whether this is the best option for countering violent speech online. It is not clear that current AI software has the capability to detect context or semantics behind hate speech, or misinformation that is posted as a meme or attached as a link. When it does successfully flag such content, it will not necessarily remove it (Greenemeier, 2018). This solution also assumes that AI and the algorithms of the platform are able to function without an implicit political bias, in addition to explicit decisions to allow popular politicians and groups to remain on the platform.

This dilemma became more pronounced with the suspicion of foreign interference and the use of bots to manipulate elections through social media, and later again when the spread of misinformation about the COVID-19 pandemic posed the risk of widespread ramifications for public health. As already mentioned, the hardening of echo chambers within the platforms of social media giants creates polarised and competing views of reality. The natural progression of this phenomenon is the division of the population into duelling platforms, once the former begins enacting content moderation measures. Immediately following the 2020 US presidential elections, the split off of Trump-supporting conservatives onto newer, free speech-touting platforms like Parler provided evidence that simply enacting moderation measures without industrial legal or normative standards does not effectively solve the structural problems at hand. Dissatisfaction with content moderation can simply spawn copycat platforms that allow dangerous speech to spread without restriction.

Facebook's most recent innovation with regard to content moderation is its Oversight Board, which was created to help the platform protect freedom of expression while determining 'what to take down, what to leave up and why' (Oversight Board, 2020). The board, when fully staffed, will be composed of 40 members from around the world with diverse disciplines and backgrounds, offering independent judgement on select content cases. While too early to tell the outcome of the Oversight Board's presence in the information ecosystem, the development provides a promising start for determining the standards by which the platform will rule its content. Still, the Oversight Board will not affect the ads-based business model, nor the algorithmic ranking system, so speculation remains cautiously optimistic (Douek, 2019).

The evidence shows that the international community does not yet have procedures, norms and institutions developed to actively respond to the new questions of ethics and policy that are provoked by the sudden power of digital networks. Indeed, it's been said that we now have a fifth domain of warfare: land, sea, air, space and cyber (Broeders and van der Berg, 2020, 1). Yet the domain of cyberspace, and data science specifically, holds so many diverse functions and changes so rapidly over time that setting universal, legally binding regulations for its content would simply fail to yield timely and relevant results (Hand, 2018). This chapter argues that a system of dynamic global norm development by multiple stakeholders, grounded in the principles of international law, would positively influence the future direction of these fields.

A human rights-centred, multi-stakeholder approach to cyber norms

Finnemore and Sikkink's foundational discussion defines international norms as 'standards of appropriate behavior for actors with a given identity' (1998, 891), arguing that a norm is championed by 'norm entrepreneurs', before being embraced by a critical mass of relevant actors (895). Norms regarding state behaviour have developed widely over the course of the twentieth century, in attempts to avoid crises that spill over state borders (i.e. the refugee regime), to expand human rights (i.e. women's suffrage) or in the interest of international security (i.e. non-proliferation). Norms differ from international law or regulation in their voluntary and non-binding nature, although norms and international law mutually reinforce and inform each other. For this reason, a dynamic norm regime will likely prove best to address the issues outlined in this chapter. Nye (2014) thoroughly maps out the existing cyber regime complex that regulates certain behaviours and functions of the internet, which provides a starting point for expanding on cyber norms.

Measures to govern cyberspace began to be considered in the United Nations General Assembly as early as 1998, when Russia brought up the risk that ICTs could be used to carry out information wars, fearing a new and destructive digital arms race would occur (Adamson, 2020, 21). In 2013, the United Nations Group of Governmental Experts (GGE) determined that international law applies to cyberspace, although states have been unable to agree on how that regulation should be applied. The protection of human rights is ultimately the responsibility of states, which are the signatories of the human rights covenants enshrined in international law. Yet as the case study demonstrates, much of the infrastructure and regulation for behaviour in the digital space falls to the private sector, demonstrating the increasing influence of private corporations on the rights and democratic principles that have traditionally fallen in the domain of government. It is evident, then, that the most practical way forward is to continue developing a multi-stakeholder approach to norm development. Various associations within the private sector and civil society could already be considered domestic norm entrepreneurs; the Self-Sovereign Identity project, championed by Kaliya Young, provides one reconceptualisation of how personal data should exist in the digital ecosystem (see Tobin and Reed, 2017). The voices of such norm entrepreneurs, well versed in the existing infrastructure of the digital space, clearly have a role to play in determining future standards, or norms, for the industry.

Ultimately, this discussion must be centred on a human rights framework. While states frequently discuss cyberspace in terms of national security and espionage, a lack of norms determining acceptable principles and behaviours online can clearly have far-reaching implications for democracy and human rights. Human rights law exists to govern relations between governments and citizens (Klimburg and Faesen, 2020, 159). Corporations, while legally bound to the local jurisdictions in which they practice, are not party to human rights conventions. Yet as the case of Myanmar has demonstrated, unfettered behaviour of a platform like Facebook, whose profit is generated by the use of personal data and algorithmic manipulation, can have drastic and large-scale ramifications. In a time when a handful of private tech giants create, manage and monitor the bulk of public discourse in the 'marketplace of ideas', new seats at the table are necessary in the process of cyber norm development. The reality of the modern communication network is that the architects, engineers and software developers of the information infrastructure are players in the international system. Non-state actors are already taking steps to determine appropriate standards, such as Microsoft's introduction of the Digital Geneva Convention to Protect Cyberspace and Siemens' Charter of Trust for a Secure Digital World (Eggenschwiler and Kulesza 2020, 250–252). These efforts should be informed by international law and human rights standards to develop a fully robust, effective debate on responsible behaviour online.

Dialogue between the diplomatic and legal elements of the UN GGE model, the corporate, expert participants of the Cybersecurity Tech Accord and representatives of civil society would create a model of norm development that involves each of the relevant stakeholders in determining the world's digital future. Thoughtful dialogue could assist in setting new standards for behaviour by actors online, such as through a reconceptualisation of how personal data is viewed and owned or best practices to identify, archive, and respond to dangerous speech.

Conclusion

The case study of Myanmar and the discussion of the ethical issues of data ownership and content moderation demonstrate that there are many variables to consider and a great deal of further legal and institutional research to be done. This research has demonstrated that discussions of human rights and democratic values must extend to digital and corporate spaces, as the modern challenges outlined before cannot be resolved without a multi-stakeholder approach and a reconceptualisation of the human rights of the digital individual. It is clear that the 'marketplace of ideas' faces unique and troubling distortions as a result of corporate data practices, which could be improved upon with input from those grassroots movements and organisations attempting to develop new approaches to personal data. Determining best practices for content moderation faces additional challenges, given different regimes' practices in censorship and speech (i.e. China's Great Firewall), but the pressing need to address the fractures of the information infrastructure remains. Further research concerned with these subjects would benefit from a closer analysis of international legal frameworks and their application in developing new norms.

References

Adamson, L. (2020). 'International Law and International Cyber Norms: A Continuum?' In Broeders, D. and van den Berg, B. (Eds.), *Governing Cyberspace: Behavior, Power, and Diplomacy*. London: Rowman & Littlefield, 19–43.

Amnesty International. (2017). *"Caged Without a Roof": Apartheid in Myanmar's Rakhine State*. ASA 16/7436/2017. London: Amnesty International.

Banyan. (2012). 'Unforgiving History: Why Buddhists and Muslims in Rakhine State in Myanmar Are at Each Others' Throats'. *The Economist*, 3 November. Available at: https://www.economist.com/news/asia/21565638-why-buddhists-and-muslims-rakhine-state-myanmar-are-each-others%E2%80%99-throats-unforgiving.

Benesch, S., Buerger, C., Glavinic, T. and Manion, S. (2018). 'Dangerous Speech: A Practical Guide'. *Dangerous Speech Project*. Available at: https://dangerousspeech.org/guide/.

Berenger, R. (2013). *Social Media Go to War*. Spokane, WA: Marquette Books.

Bradshaw, S. and Howard, P. (2017). 'Troops, Trolls and Troublemakers: A Global Inventory of Organized Social Media Manipulation'. In Woolley, S. and Howard, P. (Eds.), *Working Paper 2017.12*. Oxford, UK: Project on Computational Propaganda. Available at: comprop.oii.ox.ac.uk; http://comprop.oii.ox.ac.uk/.

Broeders, D. and Van den Berg, B. (2020). *Governing Cyberspace: Behavior, Power, and Diplomacy*. London: Rowman & Littlefield.

BSR. (2018). Human Rights Impact Assessment: Facebook in Myanmar [Online]. Available at: https://about.fb.com/wp-content/uploads/2018/11/bsr-facebook-myanmar-hria_final.pdf.

Carstens, C. (2018). 'Religion'. In Simpson, A., Farrelly, N. and Holliday, I. (Eds.), *Routledge Handbook of Contemporary Myanmar*. New York: Routledge, 126–135.

Cho, V. (2018). 'Ethnicity and Identity'. In Simpson, A., Farrelly, N. and Holliday, I. (Eds.), *Routledge Handbook of Contemporary Myanmar*. New York: Routledge, 43–51.

Douek, E. (2019). 'Facebook's "Oversight Board": Move Fast with Stable Infrastructure and Humility'. *NCJL & Tech*. 21, 1.

Eggenschwiler, J. and Kulesza, J. (2020). 'Non-State Actors as Shapers of Customary Standards of Responsible Behavior in Cyberspace'. In Broeders, D. and Van den Berg, B. (Eds.), *Governing Cyberspace: Behavior, Power, and Diplomacy*. London: Rowman & Littlefield, 245–262.

Elmi, N. (2020). 'Is Big Tech Setting Africa Back?' *Foreign Policy*, 11 November [Online]. Available at: https://foreignpolicy.com/2020/11/11/is-big-tech-setting-africa-back/.

Finnemore, M. and Sikkink, K. (1998). 'International Norm Dynamics and Political Change'. *International Organization* 52(4), 887–917. Available at: http://www.jstor.org/stable/2601361.

Ghonim, W. (2018). 'Transparency: What's Gone Wrong with Social Media and What Can We Do About It?' *Harvard Kennedy School Shorenstein Center on Media, Politics, and Public Policy* [Online]. Available at: https://shorensteincenter.org/transparency-social-media-wael-ghonim/.

Gravers, M. (2015). 'Anti-Muslim Buddhist Nationalism in Burma and Sri Lanka: Religious Violence and Globalized Imaginaries of Endangered Identities'. *Contemporary Buddhism* 16(1) [Online]. DOI: 10.1080/14639947.2015.1008090.

Greenemeier, L. (2018). 'Can AI Really Solve Facebook's Problems?' *Scientific American*, 13 April 13 [Online]. Available at: https://www.scientificamerican.com/article/can-ai-really-solve-facebooks-problems1/.

Hand, D. (2018). 'Aspects of Data Ethics in a Changing World: Where Are We Now?' *Big Data* 6(3) [Online]. DOI: 10.1089/big.2018.0083.

Hlaing, K. (2012). 'Understanding Recent Political Changes in Myanmar'. *Contemporary Southeast Asia* 34(2), 197–216.

Human Rights Watch. (1996). Burma: The Rohingya Muslims: Ending a Cycle of Exodus? [Online]. Available at: https://www.hrw.org/report/1996/09/01/rohingya-muslims-ending-cycle-exodus.

Human Rights Watch. (2013). 'All You Can Do is Pray': Crimes Against Humanity and Ethnic Cleansing of Rohingya Muslims in Burma's Arakan State. [Online]. Available at: https://www.hrw.org/report/2013/04/22/all-you-can-do-pray/crimes-against-humanity-and-ethnic-cleansing-rohingya-muslims.

Ingber, S. (1984). 'The Marketplace of Ideas: A Legitimizing Myth'. *Duke Law Journal* 1984(1) [Online]. Available at: https://scholarship.law.duke.edu/cgi/viewcontent.cgi?article=2867&context=dlj (Accessed November 26, 2020).

Keck, S. (2016). 'Reconstructing Trajectories of Islam in British Burma'. In Crouch, M. (Ed.), *Islam and the State in Myanmar: Muslim-Buddhist Relations and the Politics of Belonging*. Oxford: Oxford University Press, 39–68.

Klimburg, A. and Faesen, L. (2020). 'A Balance of Power in Cyberspace'. In Broeders, D. and van den Berg, B. (Eds.), *Governing Cyberspace: Behavior, Power, and Diplomacy*. London: Rowman & Littlefield, 145–171.

Kyaw, N. N. (2016). 'Islamophobia in Buddhist Myanmar: The 969 Movement and Anti-Muslim Violence'. In Crouch, M. (Ed.), *Islam and the State in Myanmar: Muslim-Buddhist Relations and the Politics of Belonging*. Oxford: Oxford University Press, 183–210.

MacGregor, F. (2017). 'As Tragedy Unfolds in Myanmar, the People's Heroine Stokes the Flames of Hatred'. *Foreign Policy*. 22 September [Online]. Available at: https://foreignpolicy.com/2017/09/22/as-tragedy-unfolds-in-myanmar-the-peoples-heroine-stokes-the-flames-of-hatred-aung-san-suu-kyi-rohingya/.

Malik, S. (2020). 'Privacy Is Dead. Long Live Data Ownership'. *Streamr*. 14 May [Online]. Available at: https://medium.com/streamrblog/privacy-is-dead-long-live-data-ownership-7e5a354e1368.

McCarthy, G. (2018). 'Cyber-Spaces'. In Simpson, A., Farrelly, N. and Holliday, I. (Eds.), *Routledge Handbook of contemporary Myanmar*. New York: Routledge, 92–105.

Mill, J. S. (1989). *On Liberty*. Cambridge, UK: Cambridge University Press.

Mozur, P. (2018). 'A Genocide Incited on Facebook, with Posts from Myanmar's Military'. *The New York Times*. 15 October.

Nye, J. (2014). 'The Regime Complex for Managing Global Cyber Activities'. *Global Commission on Internet Governance Paper Series* 1.

"Open Letter to Mark Zuckerberg." (2018). [Online] Available at: https://assets.documentcloud.org/documents/4432469/Myanmar-Open-Letter-to-Mark-Zuckerberg.pdf.

Oversight Board. (2020). [Online] Available at: https://www.oversightboard.com/ (Accessed 1 December 2020).

Perez, S. (2019). 'Ellen Pao Calls Out Twitter's "Public Town Square" Model as Flawed'. *TechCrunch* [Online]. Available at: https://techcrunch.com/2019/10/04/ellen-pao-calls-out-twitters-public-town-square-model-as-flawed/.

Schissler, M., Walton, M. and Thi, P. (2017). 'Reconciling Contradictions: Buddhist-Muslim Violence, Narrative Making and Memory in Myanmar'. *Journal of Contemporary Asia* 47(3). DOI: 10.1080/00472336.2017.1290818.

Simpson, A., Farrelly, N. and Holliday, I. (Eds.). (2018). *Routledge Handbook of Contemporary Myanmar*. New York: Routledge.

Slaughter, A. (2017). *The Chessboard and the Web: Strategies of Connection in a Networked World*. New Haven and London: Yale University Press.

Snyder, J. and Ballentine, K. (2001). 'Nationalism and the Marketplace of Ideas'. In Brown, M., Cote, O. R., Jr., Lynn-Jones, S. M. and Miller, S. E. (Ed.), *Nationalism and Ethnic Conflict*. Cambridge, MA: MIT Press, 61–96.

Stevenson, A. (2018). 'Facebook Admits It Was Used to Incite Violence in Myanmar'. *The New York Times*. 6 November.

Szep, J. (2013). 'The War on the Rohingya as Buddhist Monks Incite Muslim Killings in Myanmar'. *Reuters*. 8 April.

Tobin, A. and Reed, D. (2017). 'White Paper: The Inevitable Rise of Self-Sovereign Identity'. *Sovrin Foundation*. 28 March [Online]. Available at: https://sovrin.org/wp-content/uploads/2017/06/The-Inevitable-Rise-of-Self-Sovereign-Identity.pdf.

United Nations, Human Rights Council. (2018a). *Report of the Independent International Fact-Finding Mission on Myanmar*. A/HRC/39/64.

United Nations, Human Rights Council. (2018b). *Report of the Special Rapporteur on the Situation of Human Rights in Myanmar*. A/HRC/37/70. 37 Sess. Geneva: HRC.

United Nations, OHCHR. (2017). *Report of OHCHR Mission to Bangladesh: Interviews With Rohingyas Fleeing From Myanmar Since 9 October 2016*.

Van Klinken, G. and Aung, S. (2017). 'The Contentious Politics of Anti-Muslim Scapegoating in Myanmar'. *Journal of Contemporary Asia* 47(3), 353–375.

Zuboff, S. (2019). *The Age of Surveillance Capitalism: The Fight for a Human Future at the New Frontier of Power*. New York: PublicAffairs.

CONCLUSION

Colette Mazzucelli, Andrea Adams, and Anna Grichting

Old paint on a canvas, as it ages, sometimes becomes transparent. When that happens it is possible, in some pictures, to see the original lines: a tree will show through a woman's dress, a child makes way for a dog, a large boat is no longer on an open sea. That is called pentimento because the painter 'repented', changed his mind. Perhaps it would be as well to say that the old conception, replaced by a later choice, is a way of seeing and then seeing again.

Lillian Hellman, *Pentimento* (1973)

This edited volume is published during a time of fundamental uncertainty in our world. Gone are the days when policymakers and researchers could rely on stability to provide explanations of conflict as a consistent, focal reference point in the international system. While the behaviour of states is still influenced by anarchy, the early twenty-first century world is hardly stable. The combination of climate change, forced migration and COVID-19 crisis continues to create a world in flux with the most vulnerable too close to the dangers of life-threatening natural disasters or sea journeys to flee the prospect of physical harm and far removed from the promise of a vaccine.

This unevenness in protection and access, which defines the fragility of life on planet Earth, prompts us to consider the disparities that are the result of new technologies and their applications throughout our world. The main reason we introduce three alternative levels of analysis to those in Waltz's *Man, the State, and War* is to explore the changing nature of agency as a counter to structure, identity as a reference in relation to sovereignty and peace as more than the absence of war. Waltz's images, as well as his assertion as a defensive realist that states can never have enough security, are that conflict may be understood to be caused now and always by human nature, the state and the international system. His third image, the international system, as the privileged level of analysis in a neorealist environment defines the literature in the Western core of international relations.

The questions this volume raises and the ways the various parts speak to alternative images lead us to draw certain preliminary conclusions pertaining to personal data collection risks in a post-vaccine world. Of critical importance is the availability of learning that opens up spaces for collaboration across continents relying on new models, including the Global Network University introduced by NYU president emeritus John Sexton in his volume, *Standing for Reason*. The Global Network University is one model among different emerging models, which, in various ways, aim to transform spaces into places for exchanges of ideas that may contribute to the welfare of humankind.

Lessons learned from the present pandemic are the same as pandemics of the past. Advice to wash our hands, minimise social contact, isolate or quarantine when illness is suspected and protect the most at-risk groups have been proven effective in the toughest of past pandemics. Governments will still battle misinformation about how to protect against the virus. Individuals will still make individual decisions about protecting themselves based on their beliefs about the threat level. Individuals will still have to balance privacy concerns and state interests in community health.

What may be different is how the double-edged sword of technology impacts the legitimacy of nation-states' messages. Scientific breakthroughs using technology have enabled the rapid production of the vaccine while exposing people to unreliable messaging about its validity from unvetted sources. These same breakthroughs have enabled world citizens to access the internet to see behind government propaganda and question whether governments act in their best interests. Local, networked groups may disseminate information that is different from official channels, and world citizens have to determine which version to believe. In Part I of this volume, specifically in the chapters by Kibitlewski as well as Martin-Shields and Al Achkar, it is evident that citizens' moral agency across generations and countries is impacted by the opaque nature of structural responses, notably by firms that operate beyond sovereignty through their profit-driven platforms.

The COVID-19 pandemic gives us reason to pause and to pray, disrupting the pace of globalisation, and providing time to rethink the fundamental nature of security and peacebuilding. In 1959, as the Cold War focused American policy on containment, Waltz's three images came to define thinking about conflict. *Man, the State, and War* asks generations of minds to ponder if the origins of conflict are rooted in human nature, the state or the international system. Sadly, the tragedy of violence in Afghanistan is the latest reminder that this way of thinking limits our capacity to imagine cultural reconciliation by undertaking peacebuilding alternatives that are urgently necessary in our world.

In this world, abuses by totalitarian states require us to rethink the experience of security in terms of the plight of the indigenous, those experiencing sexual violence during conflict, the pillaging of sacred monuments, the hoarding of scarce resources and the absence of climate justice. The forced migration that results from the internal conflict in Assad's Syria and the fall of Afghanistan to the Taliban asks us to see the state in a modified way. Rethinking security and peacebuilding requires a focus on alternative images to those of Waltz. The lines are redrawn to reflect on a twentieth-century pentimento. These reflections must take into consideration not only states, as Kibitlewski asserts in his analysis; profit-driven platforms that operate with impunity in the Western world are central to our ethical concerns.

The organising principle of subsidiarity grounded in the natural law philosophy of Aquinas is most relevant to our task. Waltz's third image of the international system focuses on hierarchy. In contradistinction to Waltz, the starting point for alternative images of security is a less centralised, yet competent, authority. As the distinct parts in this volume indicate, the alternative starting point to assess a broader sense of security, particularly in terms of referencing personal data, is one that highlights the reality of contested identity in a world influenced more and more by forced displacement as a result of internal conflict.

Rethinking security in the twenty-first century, 60 years after the painting of Waltz's original lines, asks us to work from the image closest to the people. For instance, as an alternative to Waltz's first image of human nature, there is a basic human need to counter uncertainties of 'identity dominance', which figure prominently in the collection of people's sensitive personal data about ordinary life in Afghanistan (Guo and Noori, MIT Technology Review, 2021). This need is at the heart of security when state collapse gives way to control by a religious-political movement and military organisation. Internal strife with deep roots in data insecurity is at the heart of identity conflict. The chapters in Part I ask us to consider the ways in which the struggle to control personal data is the alternative first image of security and peacebuilding in a post-vaccine world. In this respect, as Kibitlewski as well as Martin-Shields and Al Achkar indicates, there is movement from reflecting solely in terms of the egoism that the classical realist argues motivates human beings.

In their chapter, Martin-Shields and Achkar reason that that as data from invisible or vulnerable populations becomes less difficult to collect, as digitalisation influences data collection, there must be an evolution in the ways ethics and human subjects' protocols are taught. As data is discovered in fragile spaces and within vulnerable communities, risks are created, which, traditionally, were only seen in face-to-face research, including risks to privacy and safety. Their chapter underlines that digitalisation blurs the lines around what kinds of human subjects' protocols are required to protect the identity of research participants. Looking ahead, these authors recognise that the social sciences need to prepare researchers with a broader range of technical and legal knowledge. Yet, the reality, as Martin-Shields and Achkar explain, is that a focus on eliminating or managing risks hinges on *knowing* all the risks. With the speed at which new technologies and digital research techniques are evolving, the present approach to digital research ethics is impractical at best. In their findings, having references like the Signal Code as ethical guides for understanding the different ways power manifests in digital human subjects' research, and understanding how to make sure that power is managed in a way that protects vulnerable participants, are destined to be critical to future research ethics.

Chapters in Parts II and III of this volume illustrate what Martin-Shields and Achkar recognise in a prescient manner. Research ethics is one societal area that is 'bridging over' in that scholar-practitioners have to cross over to a world where digital systems are both actively and passively part of our lives. In their view, to cross over the space between pre- and post-digital worlds represents these changes, namely, the ways educators re-imagine how we train ourselves to do ethical digital research in vulnerable communities. As their chapter attests, effective management of this particular task may allow ethics and research protocol pedagogy to help derive the most out of using digital tools for research. This essential objective mitigates the probability of carelessly or accidentally putting at risk the people whose lives could be made better through effective scientific research.

The twenty-first century development of what Slaughter terms the Web in her volume increasingly mediates the actions of humans, states and systems. Grichting, in an interdisciplinary manner that resonates with the analyses in this volume, reasons from ego to eco as she considers the significance of ecological concerns in different analyses of conflict as well as possibilities for reconciliation, notably, in her doctoral work in design at Harvard focusing on Berlin, on the divided island of Cyprus and most recently, on the Korean Peninsula. Her background as an architect initially and subsequent responsibilities as an urban planner offers myriad possibilities to reimagine the concept of the boundary in ways that tie into the mesh region introduced in Part II of this edited volume. By positing the boundary as a 'Thirdscape', Grichting (2009) asks her readers to 'depolarised [...] narratives of conflict and envision the boundary as a space for the emergence of new cultures and ecologies, as well as new political and economic dynamics'. Her focus is transformational in this context or, as she explains, healing in community 'from a deep wound to a beautiful scar' (Grichting, LIU Global, 2021).

The tensions inherent in reimagining boundaries of states require bottom-up initiatives that challenge the hierarchy that is posited by international relations theorists, particularly those who reason in the realist school of thought. Working from the bottom up to rethink security and peacebuilding requires a reconfiguration of Waltz's second image, the state, which is the decisive actor in the Westphalian system of international relations. In our world of failed and failing states, the deadly triptych of forced migration, the COVID-19 pandemic and resource scarcity prompt leaders to project 'famines of biblical proportions' (Lederer, 2020) looking ahead. The aforementioned triptych is transnational in scope and depth, which no state can address. This challenge urges the practical consideration of the alternative second image, a 'mesh region', to focus on what anthropologists as well as architects refer to as space and place. Holistically, the transition from a fragile space to one that exhibits resilience and renewal has the potential to facilitate a place for sustainability to take root. The fluidity in the action of placemaking, supported by a mesh of decentralised nodes rather than a structure of centralised hierarchy, nurtures daily lives in the most fragile areas of conflict. As the transformation from no man's land to community occurs, agency is in a constant state of tension with structure, as the most vulnerable to the brutalities of the world's internal conflicts, women and children, struggle for empowerment, fighting to take action materially and spiritually, that resists oppression and, more fundamentally, sustains justice.

In this context, a 'mesh describes a type of network that allows any node to link in any direction with any other nodes in the system. Every part is connected to every other part, and they move in tandem' (Gansky, 2010). The relevance of the mesh is in its capacity, analysing the present, and its potential, anticipating the future, to expand: a larger and larger mesh in any given region maximises a variety of communications that can, despite incessant possibilities for corruption or oppression, provide a structure of resilience (Slaughter, 2017). The focus in the Rossi, Mazzucelli, and Unger chapter is on the agency that makes bottom-up policy-making to address the pandemic in Italy more plausible. The mesh provides a region with the structure of an underlying network that is reciprocal in the interactions nurtured through a return on investment in exponential social network expansion, which can engender trust over time (Fukuyama, 1996).

If the emerging identity of the mesh region is a territorial and virtual space with no basis in sovereignty, developed nation-states must address any unevenness that can drive an undesired reaction. As is the case with Italy, a technology-enabled nurturing mesh might become one that inadvertently subverts the interest of developing countries.

In their chapter, Rossi, Mazzucelli, and Unger further recognise this challenge for Italy, which is at once a developed and a developing state in the European Union. Owing to its late unification, Italy is more of a post–World War II construction, whose elites linked its weak national identity to the European idea, rather than a unified state. As a microcosm of the EU's North–South divide, Italy, in their analysis, must draw the lessons from history being made by COVID-19. As they write, 'An initial lesson is that the scars of pandemic history are primarily within the member states rather than among the EU27. In Italy, this reality necessitates reference to the regions, particularly those hardest struck, notably Lombardy followed by Piedmont and Veneto.' Their reference to the mesh region, introduced with the family as a unit of analysis, asks readers to look below rather than beyond the state.

The distinct and devastating nature of the pandemic's second wave striking Italy during fall 2020 (Paterlini, 2020) raises the most fundamental change to consider given its COVID-19 response in an EU context. Clearly, there is a need to organise new health paths; this is a process in which data collection as well as observation, measurement, description, analysis and evaluation figures prominently (Harari and Vitacca, 2020). The challenge to improve healthcare in local areas within the most vulnerable regions is a call to the scientific community and local populations to share their experiences at the level closest to the citizens most in need.

Further, it may be impossible to prevent the rapid global spread of new and novel infective agents because of affordable air travel and tourism. As Slaughter (2017) suggests, global collaborative networks must be developed to allow rapid responses to new threats using the vast knowledge and resources from all over the globe. In Slaughter's view, a critical aspect of these collaborative networks is to map the network connections so that the 'mesh' is not unknown; rather, the mesh represents a clear path from one destination to another. As inclusionism, the lens introduced in the companion volume to this one, suggests, international relations must dissect and explain the expected cultural boundaries when moving from one spatial and or territorial location to another.

The relevance of the mesh is its capacity, analysing the present, and potential, of anticipating the future, to expand: a larger and larger mesh in a given region maximises the variety of communications that can, despite incessant possibilities for corruption or injustice, provide opportunities for revivification. Our responsibility is to consider all that this expansion implies for the health of the planet and peace in our world. The perpetual encounter in placemaking, regeneratively speaking, is to design the mesh region as the alternative second image of security and peacebuilding in a post-vaccine world.

In his chapter, Pap aims to explain the impact of the COVID-19 pandemic on the Roma, conceptualised at the intersection of a racial, cultural or socio-economic minority, in Europe. The term 'Roma' refers to heterogeneous groups living in various countries under different social, economic, cultural and other conditions. It denotes multifaceted subgroups that overlap, yet are connected by historical roots, linguistic communalities and a shared experience of discrimination in relation to majority groups. Originating from India a millennium ago, Roma have dispersed worldwide and there are no official or reliable statistics on the global population. The status of Roma in this context requires a much more long-term inquiry given the lack of access to available data. The ethical concerns pertaining to data collection in this case are significant given the vulnerable status of the Roma across the Continent. The case study of Hungary for conceptualising the Roma is an essential starting point for this research. Pap's ground breaking analysis introduces an overview of a controversial, arguably benevolent, populist, policing strategy while applying a multicultural framework for the Roma.

The Roma, considered Europe's forgotten people, are a community throughout Europe already disproportionally affected by the virus. As Pap emphasises, many Roma live without running water, have difficulties with physical distancing, are likely to lose their jobs as irregular workers, lack digital skills or online connectivity and face extreme challenges navigating a healthcare system that switched to online and telephone consultations. What connects Pap's case study to the companion volume, *The Ethics of Personal Data Collection in International Relations*, is its position situated in the context of the American 'Black Lives Matter movement' along with current debates on conceptualising and operationalising race and ethnicity; the chapter's focus on ethno-racial disparities regarding the effects of the COVID-19 pandemic as well as various forms of penal populism and nationalism makes Pap's legal and social arguments compelling. His case study clearly demonstrates that the virus exacerbates social inequalities. Yet, it is not the virus itself; the social environment and institutions bear the blame. The implications of Pap's analysis for illiberalism in Hungary as well as for all minorities worldwide make this chapter one that fits well in Parts II and III given the attention focused on the pandemic and the ways in which its prolonged impact affects the Roma across space and time. The alternative third image of the distributed ecosystem highlights the inherent conflict in the discriminatory practices endured by the Roma as a sui generis minority community across Europe and in the world, as the pandemic intensifies the existing shared-fate concerns, notably climate injustice, which threaten the commons.

Pap's chapter provides the basis for us to consider the ideas that Richardson shares in the Afterword, which are relevant to the future of research given the growing needs that institutions of higher learning have to adapt to a changing sensitive data collection environment both in the United States and countries around the world.

As Richardson suggests: 'In this new data ecosystem, academic institutions have proven to be trusted sources of data information, assessment and analysis and should perhaps broaden their mandate and commit to be data stewards to ensure the efficient utilisation of data sources while safeguarding data quality, confidentiality, ethics, and security.'

Pap's chapter is important methodologically in that its content demonstrates the ways in which the Roma have been targeted by populist political rhetoric and securitising law enforcement policies during the COVID-19 pandemic. Examples are cited from outside Hungary since no such relevant cases were reported in country at the time of writing. Models for conceptualisation and policies are pooled in the European space, which is quite distinct in the evolution of integration through law during the post–World War II era. Europe provides the story of regional integration that goes furthest to challenge the anarchy of the international system depicted in Waltz's third image. As more data becomes available, the research that builds on this chapter during the post-vaccine era is likely to require insights pertaining to new ways of understanding social science research protocols in an increasingly digital research environment. The more institutions of higher learning understand about this changing environment, the more likely they are to fulfil their vocation as 'data stewards', in Richardson's words.

The challenges inherent in fortifying the mesh region abound in post-conflict spaces. As Schneider explains, the Dayton Agreement divided BiH into two entities – the Federation of Bosnia–Herzegovina, or FBiH – and *Republika Srpska*, or the RS. Of note is the ethnically mixed nature of the territory within the federation and the devolution of certain powers to local authorities. This chapter highlights the areas of policing and education, which are subject to the highly ethnicised politicking that has been the hallmark of post-war Bosnian democracy. Schneider underlines that the political institutions of BiH are rooted in the entrenchment of ethnic political parties whose longevity relies on ongoing ethnic insecurities, thereby inhibiting the cultivation of an inclusive civic national identity. This societal rift has implications for what has been defined in a companion volume as inclusionism. An international relations lens that addresses state limitations when confronted with the challenges of shared-fate concerns for individual citizens as well as a larger community, inclusionism explains a dynamic that is cosmopolitan in nature given its presence beyond the borders of any one state. When a fragile state apparatus lacks the resources, the political will or the institutions to shed ideological stances in the face of shared-fate global threats, there may not be other options to protect citizens. Given the nexus of climate injustice and the pandemic's impact, the ethical challenges to research in post-conflict spaces call for inclusionism as well to address the methodological concerns emerging in digital research within vulnerable communities.

For Waltz, the environment and health did not figure in reflections on research that explained the nature of war. The international system or third image is an insufficient reference point for research that occurs in the mesh region. Moreover, the pandemic has altered the way that social science research using human subjects can take place. Therefore, as the chapters in Part II suggest, there is a critical need to consider what ethical research in post-conflict spaces might look like in the midst of a prolonged health crisis. Schneider's analysis links Parts II and III to the extent that she identifies long-lasting challenges to researchers in post-conflict spaces as a result of the pandemic. States, including Italy, had to restrict the travel of their own citizens to relatively small radii. The loss of the in-person element potentially compromises the collection of sensitive data.

In the midst of a changed, distorted (Cohen, State of the Planet, 2021) globalisation, rethinking security and peacebuilding urges movement away from a focus solely on Waltz's third image, the international system. Challenges of transnational security define the landscape of a distributed ecosystem, which is the alternative third image in our twenty-first century painting, the eye of reflections on a twentieth-century pentimento.

In Waltz's international system, structure is too focal a point, which thoroughly ignores what is essential to assure the survival of non-human and human species alike, as extremist violence ticks up. As conflict alters in nature and scope, in the variety of its fundamentalist movements and the reach of its geographic space, grappling with the alternative third image of security and peacebuilding in a post-vaccine world is an essential choice, 'a way of seeing and then seeing again' the meaning of an all-embracing arrangement. The overlay to Waltz's original conception addresses, as the structure of his international system cannot, the shared concerns of the commons as the cornerstone of peace.

In fluid contexts of fragility and scarcity, intensified by the prolonged nature of the pandemic around the world, developing states face particular challenges, as the chapters in Part III illustrate in specific ways. In their chapter analysing the Ebola crisis in Sierra Leone, Hlaing and Greenhalgh underline that 'the artificial creation of a state along with a government that lacks complete legitimacy in the eyes of its people suggests that a simple focus on the state as the most important actor is inappropriate in this context'. The authors explain that the brutality of civil war, which ravaged the country, reveals the impact of 'external regional factors, competition for access to natural resources, and poverty and lack of opportunity, particularly for the country's youth population'. Child soldiers were not confined within national borders as the violence marked 'a generation of people who lacked education, proper healthcare, trust in government, and were traumatised by the events'. Hlaing and Greenhalgh purposefully avoid the simplistic explanations that 'only consider the state's actions' about those events depicting recent Sierra Leonean history.

For some, Waltz's images are the original lines painted during the last century. Those among us who 'repented' seize the day, immersing ourselves in locality to grapple with the fear of the global. Our actions are not oriented solely by the structure of the international system; rather our security concerns speak to nurturing agency through multi-faith dialogue in a world that bears witness to religious nationalism as well as religious pluralism, as Salter's analysis in Part III explains in a reference to the Foreword by Secretary General Professor Azza Karam in the companion edited volume. Moreover, the Foreword by President Emeritus Professor John Sexton in this volume speaks to themes elucidated in Salter's chapter, thereby connecting these volumes to an ongoing discussion in the literature.

Salter's case study of the issues in Myanmar supports the notion that lack of governmental protection for human rights violations in an 'algorithmically driven, anarchic cyberspace' results in digital hate speech, disinformation, which can lead to violence. The ethnic cleansing of the Rohingya in Myanmar was fuelled by disinformation campaigns, as the distorted 'marketplace of ideas' allowed extremist views to flourish. Moreover, ethical issues of data ownership must extend to digital and corporate spaces to influence the dialogue about democratic values for the 'digital individual'.

The successive presentation of the case studies in this volume, starting with those in Part I that explain methodological approaches to our subject to those that range from the liberal to the illiberal in Parts II and III, offers the authors of this Conclusion the occasion to revisit Waltz's original images. This is a particularly timely undertaking as the challenges to the post-war liberal international order become more striking in specific national contexts given the enduring impact of the global COVID-19 pandemic.

As this volume demonstrates, evolving research is dependent on the acknowledgement of digital, ecological and health as shared-fate concerns, which are manifest in the distributed ecosystem. The alternative third image is a transformational later choice beyond the short twentieth century's experience of stability during the Cold War, a way of 'seeing and then seeing again' the fluidity of conflict marked increasingly by forced displacement, digital connections and contested identity. Transitioning from the realist's singular focus on ego to a communitarian purpose on behalf of eco, which is Grichting's and Zebich-Knos (2019) focus in research and practice, is the defining challenge of present and future centuries as well as the demanding vocation of local and transnational societies.

References

Cohen, S. 2021. *State of the Planet.* https://news.climate.columbia.edu/author/steve-cohen/.
Fukuyama, F. 1996. *Trust: The Social Virtues and the Creation of Prosperity.* New York: Free Press.
Gansky, L. 2010. *The Mesh: Why the Future of Business is Sharing.* New York: Portfolio Penguin.
Grichting, A. 2009. Thirdscapes: Ecological Planning and Human Reconciliation in Borderlands. *The International Journal of Environmental, Cultural, Economic and Social Sustainability* 5: 239–256.
Grichting, A. and Zebich-Knos, M. (Eds.). 2019. *The Social Ecology of Border Landscapes.* London: Anthem Press.
Grichting, A. 2021. Co-Creating Peace with Nature in the DMZ. New Visions for Borders and Buffer Zones in a Future Ecological Civilization. In: *International Relations World Education Seminar (IRWES) LIU Global Seminar*, 20 October.
Guo, E. and Noori, H. 2021. This is the Real Story of the Afghan Biometric Databases Abandoned to the Taliban. *MIT Technology Review.* https://www.technologyreview

.com/2021/08/30/1033941/afghanistan-biometric-databases-us-military-40-data-points/.

Harari, S. and Vitacca, M. 2020. COVID-19 Spread: The Italian Case. *Respiratory Medicine and Research* 78: 100771.

Hellman, L. 1973. *Pentimento*. Boston and New York: Little Brown & Co.

Lederer, E. 2020. UN Food Agency Chief: World on Brink of "A Hunger Pandemic". *AP News*. https://apnews.com/article/ethiopia-famine-us-news-hunger-virus-outbreak-ddf274a0521fc3047de31f56cb71dd62.

Paterlini, M. 2020. On the Front Lines of Coronavirus: The Italian Response to Covid-19. *BMJ* 368: m106.

Sexton, J. 2019. *Standing for Reason: The University in a Dogmatic Age*. New Haven: Yale University Press.

Slaughter, A.-M. 2017. *The Chessboard and the Web: Strategies of Connection in a Networked World*. New Haven and London: Yale University Press.

Waltz, K. N. 1959. *Man, the State, and War*. New York: Columbia University Press.

AFTERWORD

Annette Richardson

The global COVID-19 pandemic has fostered unprecedented social and economic disruption, forcing most governments to introduce severe measures to contain the virus, such as travel restrictions, bans of public events, closures of non-essential businesses and transition to remote work and education.

To understand and respond better to the COVID-19 pandemic dynamics, countries worldwide are using data and statistics to drive mitigation and eradication-led strategies as well as forecast future pandemics and public health crises.

With an ever-changing data ecosystem, challenges posed by this global pandemic have accelerated the more extensive use of private sector data and intensified the need for improved data governance, principles and tools for data privacy protection.

Rapid deployment and adoption of self-reporting apps and data-analytic technologies to collect new data, use existing data in novel ways (e.g. symptom tracking, contact tracing, mobility and density mapping, quarantine enforcement, health and immunity passes), have raised deep concerns about surveillance tactics, privacy, personal data protection and civil liberties.

The increased speed of technological innovation and goal-directed processes reflect the acceleration of social change (e.g. cultural and institutional norms), and the pace of life affecting the tech industry, where speed acts as an important part of the business model, both among large tech companies and start-ups.

Rapid innovation is important in a crisis, not only so that companies can exploit market advantages in what author of *The Shock Doctrine*, activist Naomi Klein, also describes as 'disaster capitalism': in this context, life-, society- and economy-preserving solutions can be rolled out where needed.

Protecting privacy in the context of any crisis is complex. Risks of abuse, distrust and unaccountability in governments and in technology companies developing these tools and applications may arise and lead to a more fundamental question of whether the technologically enhanced forms of high-tech monitoring and surveillance products for COVID-19-related public health use may become a permanent part of the new normal.

The right to privacy is a globally recognised normative ideal ratified in international treaties and national constitutions. It is of particular importance for protecting global vulnerable and marginalised communities, particularly from small- and middle-income countries at highest risk for contracting and dying from COVID-19.

There are reasons to be concerned that structural inequalities in data access and exposure to privacy invasion disproportionately affect disadvantaged societal groups. The fact that private companies and governments worldwide are tapping the location data of billions of internet and mobile phone users for tracking and monitoring purposes raises a significant equity concern in many of the most-vulnerable communities most significantly affected by the contagion and lethality of COVID-19, including minority and immigrant communities. Risks to these vulnerable communities of both under-inclusion in beneficial public health interventions and over-inclusion in government-administered privacy infringement should be noted.

The use of pre-existing digital products, such as third-party video-conferencing software platforms, also creates new privacy and data protection vulnerabilities.

During the COVID-19 pandemic, both governments and private companies were given the moral license to take extraordinary measures and deployed digital technologies, mostly without proper impact assessment, stakeholder consultation or evaluation, as often described by civil rights advocates, policymakers and the media.

In this volume, we explain the contextual nature of privacy trade-offs during a pandemic and explore how regulatory and technical responses are needed to protect privacy in such circumstances.

Privacy advocates might have reason to be wary given prior instances of governments enacting surveillance programs during times of crisis in ways that, they argue, involve long-term infringement of civil rights.

In this new data ecosystem, academic institutions have proven to be trusted sources of data information, assessment and analysis and should perhaps broaden their mandate and commit to be data stewards to ensure the efficient utilisation of data sources while safeguarding data quality, confidentiality, ethics and security.

With less than a decade to 2030, towards the achievement of the UN Sustainable Development Goals, the global COVID-19 pandemic has been a litmus test of the ability of governments and global stakeholders to harness resources, including data and technology, towards addressing pressing global challenges.

By providing a multidisciplinary conversation on the value of privacy and data protection in the context of a global pandemic and beyond, academic institutions must address the implications rushed or rapid innovations and digital solutions have for the future and explore the issues of expedited privacy assessments to mitigate adverse privacy implications on society, particularly on populations in low- and middle-income countries, which are the most affected.

LIST OF CONTRIBUTORS

Andrea Adams, PhD, JD, MBA, is an assistant professor in the Crime Justice and Security Program in the College of Arts and Sciences at the University of the District of Columbia. Andrea is on the Advisory Board of the RedDot Corporation, the parent of the Safecity.in, a smartphone app. The Safecity app creates awareness of street harassment and provides a place for women and other disadvantaged communities to break their silence and report personal assault experiences. Andrea's work help design the organisation's informed consent, privacy and security provisions of the app, and one aspect of her research agenda focuses on the ethics of smartphone app use. Andrea is a licensed attorney and has 25+ years of business experience in labour and employment law.

Ziad Al Achkar is a PhD candidate and researcher at the Jimmy and Rosalynn Carter School for Peace and Conflict Resolution at George Mason University. His research focuses on the use of digital technologies in support of peacebuilding and humanitarian action, and the evolving relationship with the private tech sector. Before starting his PhD, he worked at the Harvard Humanitarian Initiative where he focused on the use of Information Communication Technologies in conflict analysis and support of humanitarian operations.

Emilie J. Greenhalgh is an international development professional and writer with 10 years of professional experience working for INGOs and the US Government in Cameroon, Morocco, the Democratic Republic of the Congo, Afghanistan, Washington, DC, and most recently, Niger, where she was the deputy resident country director for a $437 million water and infrastructure program. Emilie holds an MA in International Relations and International Economics, with a focus on African studies, from the Johns Hopkins School of International Studies. Emilie is currently an independent consultant based in Indonesia and is finalising her first full-length book.

Anna Grichting is an architect, urbanist and musician at Bordermeetings Switzerland. She graduated with a Doctor of Design in Urbanism from Harvard

University. Anna has taught at the Universities of Qatar, Geneva, Harvard, MIT and Vermont. She is invited to lecture at HEAD Geneva, Politecnico di Milano and NYU. Anna is a senior research fellow at the University of Vermont and the recipient of grants for research, workshops, cultural productions and residencies worldwide. She works on bridging borders and designing Healing Ecologies in Landscapes of Conflict from the Cyprus Green Line and the Korean DMZ to Qatar's borderscapes, www.annagrichting.com.

Thynn Thynn Hlaing is an international development professional and over the past 18 years, she has led various country teams in her own country of Myanmar, as well as Sri Lanka, Cambodia and Liberia. From 2013 to 2018, Thynn Thynn worked as Country Director for Oxfam's program in Sierra Leone, where she managed the successful implementation of the Ebola Emergency Programme, which was staffed by 400 employees. Following completion of the Ebola emergency response, Thynn Thynn was awarded as 'The Best INGO Leader for 2017' in Sierra Leone from the African Watchdog Association. Thynn Thynn is currently the country manager of the Clinton Health Access Initiative's program in Papua New Guinea, where she is leading the country team in assisting the Government of PNG with their development of a national immunisation strategy. A native of Myanmar, Thynn Thynn holds a Master's in Public Administration from the Lee Kuan Yew School of Public Policy at the National University of Singapore and was selected to be one of 16 participants in the Yale World Fellows Program in 2018.

C. Ann Hollifield, PhD, is professor emerita at the University of Georgia in the United States. Her research focuses on media economics, management and news media viability in changing market conditions, work that started while she was a Robert Bosch Foundation Fellow in Germany in 1991–92. In 2006, she founded the first graduate degree program in the United States in media analytics. She is the author/editor of 7 books and nearly 50s other research articles and book chapters. She continues to work internationally as a consultant on news media viability research, and she currently is authoring a textbook on data analytics for media professionals. Prior to her academic career, she spent 15 years as a journalist and senior editor in newspapers and television.

James Felton Keith is an award-winning engineer and economist who was the first black LGBTQ person to run for US Congress or any of America's federal offices. As an author and activist, his Data Unions redefined the labour movement and personal data as the natural resource driving all corporate productivity. As an entrepreneur, he established the first international standard certification for corporate diversity and inclusion and the first insurance policy for a lack of inclusion based on an 'inclusion score'. His bio-political philosophy, Inclusionism, is at the forefront of Human Rights advocacy and International Relations and each week he hosts the WHCR 90.3 FM radio show, Inclusionism, from NYC.

Jakub Wojciech Kibitlewski is a graduate candidate at the John F. Kennedy Institute for North American Studies (Freie Universität Berlin), where he pursues an interdisciplinary degree focused on political science and sociology. Working as an assistant on the 'Trust and Transparency in an Age of Surveillance' research project funded by the German Research Foundation (DFG), Jakub developed an interest in the surveillance-related aspects of digital platform companies, which largely shapes his academic inquiry today. His dissertation-in-progress examines the power dynamics between digital platforms and nation-states in the context of American security policy. As the editor of Gazeta Wyborcza's 'News from Poland', he provides an English-speaking audience with insights into the latest developments in Polish politics. Jakub is a 2019 Ernst-Reuter-Stipend recipient.

Charles Martin-Shields is a senior researcher at the German Development Institute in Bonn, Germany. His research focuses on digitalisation and technological change in developing countries, with a current focus on the roles that digital technology plays in the lives of migrants. Prior to the German Development Institute Dr Martin-Shields was a visiting scholar at the Carter School for Peace and Conflict Resolution at George Mason University and a consultant working with the World Bank on technology and social inclusion. He has worked on digitalisation and governance issues for organisations including UNHCR, the US Institute of Peace and US Department of State, and holds a PhD from the Carter School for Peace and Conflict Resolution.

Colette Mazzucelli, PhD, EdM, MALD, served as First President (Academia), 2020–22, Global Listening Centre, and has taught since 2004 on Graduate Faculty, GSAS & SPS, at NYU New York, https://as.nyu.edu/faculty/colette-mazzucelli.html. She is Lead Editor of the Anthem Press Ethics of Personal Data Collection Series. A BMW Foundation Responsible Leader, Colette is the Founder and Principal of LEAD IMPACT Reconciliation Institute and a member of the Advisory Board for Higher Education of the Irish Tech Society, https://www.irishtechsociety.ie/. At Pioneer Academics, she teaches International Relations (Europe) mentoring students across six continents, https://pioneeracademics.com/. Colette is the author and/or editor of seven volumes, including *France and Germany at Maastricht*, https://www.amazon.com/France-Germany-Maastricht-Negotiations-Contemporary/dp/0815335938. Since 1993, her biography appears in numerous *Marquis Who's Who* publications, including *Marquis Who's*

Who in America and *Marquis Who's Who in the World*, https://wwlifetimeachievement.com/2019/01/07/colette-mazzucelli/.

András L. Pap is a research professor and head of the Department for Constitutional and Administrative Law at the (formerly Hungarian Academy of Sciences) Centre for Social Sciences Institute for Legal Studies, as well as Professor of Law at the Institute of Business Economics at Eötvös Loránd University (ELTE) and at the Law Enforcement Faculty of the Ludovika University of Public Service in Budapest, Hungary. He is also adjunct (recurrent visiting) professor in the Nationalism Studies Program at the Central European University in Vienna, Austria. He was visiting scholar at NYU Law School's Global Law Program and Marie-Curie Fellow at the Slovak Academy of Sciences. In 2018, he founded the International Association of Constitutional Law Research Group on identity, race and ethnicity in constitutional law.

Leslie Prosy is a masters candidate in New York University's International Relations Program, Copy Editor for the *Journal for Political Inquiry* and member of the NYU International Relations and Politics Association. She currently is a research assistant for the CoronaNet Research Project, certified in Monitoring and Evaluation through the International Labor Organization, certified in International Law/Asylum Rights for unaccompanied minors in Germany, received a Bachelors in Psychology concentration Cultural Psychology from the State University of New York, Empire State College. Before attending NYU, she recently concluded a project in Germany mediating for both government agencies, international organisations and refugees during the European migrant crisis.

Annette Richardson is the founder and managing partner at Richardson Partners LLC and a Partner at Ambershore Group. In 2016, Annette launched a consultancy firm to advise global business leaders, social impact investors and philanthropists focused on building sustainability, legacy and advocacy programs to advance, at scale, the Global Goals and foster long-term strategic partnerships. Annette has been one of the most valued collaborating partners in convening business leadership at the United Nations. She served as a senior adviser to the UN Office for Partnerships under the leadership of UN Secretary-General Ban Ki-moon and was instrumental in creating some of the most significant global multi-stakeholder conferences the UN has been engaged in. She is also a former special adviser to the Executive Office of the UN Secretary-General for the Sustainable Energy for All Initiative and a former special adviser to the Under Secretary-General and Executive Director of UN Women. Annette is a frequent speaker on leadership, strategic partnerships and sustainability at business and academic conferences around the world.

Christian Rossi is associate professor of history of international relations at the Department of Political and Social Sciences, Cagliari University, Italy. Since 2018 he is the department's deputy director. His research interests vary from the British foreign politics in the Mediterranean to the European Union History. Among his publications: Partition of Palestine and Political Stability: Ottoman Legacy and International Influences (1922–48), EUI Working Papers, 2010; The United Kingdom and the proposals of Nuclear Free Zones in the Mediterranean between the 1960s and 1970s, in G. Borzoni, C. Rossi, Il Mediterraneo e la sfida che arriva da Est, FrancoAngeli, Milano, 2017.

Laura Salter is a communications assistant for the International Institute for Sustainable Development in addition to volunteering as a social media and marketing coordinator for Human Rights Pulse. Previously, Laura supported Human Rights First's Refugee Representation program in Washington, DC, where she assisted asylum seekers in attaining pro bono legal representation. Laura holds a Master of Arts in International Relations from New York University where she was honoured to serve as Editor-in-Chief of NYU's *Journal of Political Inquiry* and was awarded the school's coveted Masters' Award for Academic Achievement. She also achieved highest honours while completing her Bachelors' degree in International Studies and French at Harding University. Laura speaks English, French and Spanish and currently resides in her hometown of Edmonton, Canada.

Nicole Scartozzi graduated with a Master's in International Relations from New York University. Before attending NYU, she received her BA in Political Science with minors in Philosophy, Business and International Relations. She has worked for a wide variation of conferences and non-governmental organisations throughout her educational career, as she prepares to begin her professional career. She is currently volunteering at her neighbourhood hospital and works as a consultant for a non-profit. Nicole's research interests revolve around refugees, increasing human rights and international development.

Mary Kate Schneider is a lecturer of political science and director of the Global Studies Program at Loyola University Maryland in Baltimore, MD. Her research focuses on post-conflict peace and reconciliation, security, institutions, identity and nationalism, and her regional expertise lies in the Western Balkans (with a recent foray into East Africa). She holds a PhD in Government and Politics from the University of Maryland, an MA from Lehigh University, and BA and BS degrees from Kutztown University of Pennsylvania. Dr Schneider has conducted extensive fieldwork in Bosnia–Herzegovina, where her research on institutional design and peacebuilding among youth was supported by a Fulbright grant.

John Sexton served as president of New York University from 2002 through 2015. He is NYU's Benjamin F. Butler Professor of Law and Dean Emeritus of the Law School. During his presidency, the university's reach and stature grew tremendously, including the emergence of NYU as a global network university, with campuses in Abu Dhabi and Shanghai and 11 international academic centres; a merger with Polytechnic University, now the NYU Tandon School of Engineering; and the largest increase in the number of Arts and Science faculty in the university's history. A fellow of the American Academy of Arts and Sciences, President Emeritus Sexton also serves on the board of the Institute of International Education and is past Chair of the American Council on Education. He received a BA in history, an MA in comparative religion and a PhD in the history of American religion, all from Fordham University, and a JD *magna cum laude* from Harvard Law School.

David C. Unger has taught American Foreign Policy at Johns Hopkins University SAIS Europe in Bologna, Italy, since 2009. He was born in Brooklyn, NY; educated in the New York City public schools; earned a bachelor's degree in history and comparative literature from Cornell University and a doctorate in modern European economic history from the University of Texas at Austin. He did additional graduate studies at the University of Wisconsin (Madison), the University of London (UK) and the City University of New York. He has also been senior foreign affairs writer for the *New York Times* editorial board and a research associate at the University of London SOAS.

INDEX

11 September 2001 48, 169
969 Movement 165

Abdal 81
Act CLXXIX of 2011 on the Rights of Nationalities 86
Africa Governance Initiative 138
Albania 90
Amazon 4, 10–11
Amnesty International 166
analytica xiii, xxvii, 5, 13, 83, 171
Anthropocene xv
Apple 35
Arab Spring 162
Arakanese political party 165
Ashkali 81
Asian 50–51, 54, 80, 82
asylum 77, 87
autochthonous 87
Axial Age xi

Balkans 78
Bangladeshi 51, 80
Banja Luka 107, 112
Belgium 48, 90, 92
Belmont Report 33
Berlin Wall 48
Beyond Platforms Initiative 21
black box xv, xix-xx, xxii, 122
Black Lives Matter movement xxix, xxx, 74, 93, 188
Blackboxing 35
blockchain technology 18
Bosnia-Herzegovina (BiH) xviii, xxiii–xxiv, xxx–xxxi, 102–110, 112, 114, 189
Bosnian War 102
Boyash/Rudari 81
Brazil 80, 82
Brčko District 106, 111

Brexit xiii, 65
Britain 80, 120, 123, 163
Brussels 50–51, 53, 55–56
Budapest Convention xiv
Buddha xi
Buddhist 163–167, 169
Bulgaria 90–92
Burma 164, 167
Business for Social Responsibility (BSR) 168, 173

Calabria 59
Cambridge Analytica xiii, 171
Campania 59
Canada 4, 143
CARE International and International Rescue Committee 80
census 82, 85, 87, 109
Center for Disease Control and Prevention (CDC) 120, 123–124, 138–139, 141, 149
Children's Online Privacy Protection Act 8
China xiv–xv, xxiii–xxv, 49–50, 54, 57, 66, 143, 176
Chinese xi, xxv, 66, 80
Christianity xi
citizens xii, xvii, xxix, xxxi, 6, 37, 52–54, 62, 65–69, 77, 84, 91, 102–103, 105–107, 109, 115, 164, 175, 183, 186, 189
climate change xv, 48, 50, 52, 53, 64, 69, 182
Cold War xxiv, 48–49, 53, 64, 183, 191
Collective trauma 107–108
Communications Decency Act 173
communications technologies vii, xiv
Computational Propaganda Research Project 163, 169
conflict resolution viii, xii, xvi, xix

204 INDEX

Consumer Privacy Bill of Rights Act 8–9
contact tracing xx, 56, 62, 120, 139, 147, 193
coronavirus pandemic xiv, xxix, 11, 48, 65, 67, 68, 69; *see also* COVID-19 Pandemic; global pandemic; novel coronavirus pandemic
Council of Europe 84–86, 92
COVID-19 Pandemic xv, xxiii, xxvi, xxix, xxx–xxxii, 48–54, 68, 74, 77, 79, 89, 93, 110, 114–115, 183, 185, 187–188, 191, 193, 194; *see also* coronavirus pandemic; global pandemic; novel coronavirus pandemic
Croatia 61, 102–105, 108
cryptocurrency 37
curfews 90, 120

Dangerous Speech Project 163
data vii–ix, xiii–xvi, xviii, xxii–xxxiii, 4–20, 26–41, 49, 51–53, 67, 76–77, 80, 82, 90, 101, 106–115, 121, 127, 129–130, 137–140, 144, 149, 151, 161–162, 170–172, 174–176, 182–184, 186–189, 191, 193–195
data collection viii, xi, xiv–xix, xxiv, xxvi, xxix–xxxi, xxxiii, 4, 20, 26–30, 32–38, 51, 77, 90, 101, 108, 113, 115, 129, 137, 139, 144, 149, 151, 162, 171, 182, 184, 186–188
data collection systems 28
data extraction 14, 19
data privacy ix, xv, 6–7, 9, 10, 12, 19, 36, 172, 193
data privacy protection 7, 19, 193
data protection xxvii, xxx, 4, 6–8, 10, 15, 17, 28, 30, 51, 76–77, 170, 193–195
Data Protection Directive 7
Data Protection Working Party 7
Dayton Peace Agreement (DPA) 102, 105
democracy 55, 57, 59, 60, 62, 69, 102–104, 107, 160, 168, 175, 189
democratic xxiv, xxxi, 20–21, 51–52, 57–59, 60, 62, 65, 68, 73, 89, 103, 114, 160, 163–164, 167, 172, 175–176, 191
'Designing Accounting Safeguards to Help Broaden Oversight and Regulations on Data' (DASHBOARD) 15
development xxiv, xxviii, 28, 36, 51, 53–54, 66, 68, 81, 120–121, 124, 127–128, 137, 144, 146–148, 162–163, 174–176, 185, 194

digital footprints 41
Digital Freedom Index xv
Digital Geneva Convention 176
digital identity xv
digital platform providers 4
digital tools 27–28, 31, 33, 41, 185
digitally intermediated research 28
diplomatic xvi, 88, 162, 176
District Ebola Response Centres (DERCs) 129–130, 140–142, 147
domestic intervention xv
drones 28–29

Ebola; *see also Ebola Virus Disease (EVD)* xx, xxxi–xxxii, 120–140, 142–151
Ebola Response Consortium 129
Ebola treatment unit (ETU) 120
Ebola Virus Disease (EVD): *see also Ebola* 120
eco of inclusionism 48
economic policies xv, 64
economist 51, 80
ecosystems xv, xxxi, xxxii
Egyptians 81
Emilia-Romagna 59
England 80–81
Enlightenment xi
epidemic 55, 80, 120–121, 123–124, 126, 128–131, 138, 141, 143–151
ethics pedagogy xxviii, 40,
EU 2020 51
EU Civil Protection Mechanism 66
EU General Data Protection Regulation (GDPR) xxvii, xxxii, 4, 10, 51, 53, 170, 171, 172
EU27 49–50, 69, 186
Eurobarometer survey 83
Eurocentric xviii, xxiii
European Coal and Steel Community (ECSC) 63, 64
European integration xvi, xvii, 47–48, 69
European Parliament 64–65, 76, 89
European Roma community 74
European Roma Rights Centre 90
European Social Survey (ESS) 108
European Union (EU) xvii, xxiii, xxix–xxx, 5–6, 76–77, 82, 109, 170, 172, 186
European Union Agency for Fundamental Rights (FRA) 82

Facebook xiii, xviii, xxvii–xxviii, xxxii, 3–4, 6, 9–10, 12–15, 17–20, 37, 39–40, 164, 168–175

INDEX 205

fake news 68
Family Educational Rights and Privacy Act (FERPA) 8
Federal Trade Commission (FTC) 4, 8
Federal Trade Commission Act (FTCA) 8
federalism 63
female genital mutilation 81
financial crisis of 2007–08 xix, xxii, 48
France 48, 53, 54, 66, 115, 143
Franco-German conflicts 48
fratricide 48

gatekeeper 40
General Data Protection Regulation (GDPR) xxvii, 4, 51, 170
General Framework Agreement for Peace (GFAP) 102
genocide vii, 49, 77, 113, 161, 166
Gens du voyage 81
Germany xviii, xxv, 34, 48, 82, 143
global cybercrime treaty xiv
global financial crisis (GFC) xix, xxii, 48
global international society 48, 50
Global Network Initiative (GNI) 173
Global Network University xii, xv, 182
global pandemic xvii, 50, 69, 193, 195; *see also* COVID-19; novel coronavirus pandemic
globalisation xiv, xvi, xviii, xix, xxi, 48, 53, 69, 183, 189
Google xxv, 4, 10, 14
grassroots 21, 60, 160, 176
Greece xi, 61
Green Deal 69
ground zero 34
Gypsies 81
Gypsy crime 91
Gypsy Criminality 88
Gypsy violence 91
G-Zero World 49

Health Insurance Portability and Accountability Act (HIPPA) 8
Heinsberg study 34
Hispanic 80
human rights viii–ix, xv, xviii, xxvi, xxxi–xxxiii, 5, 20, 53, 77, 80, 84, 90–92, 143, 160–161, 164–166, 168, 170, 172–176, 190, 199
Human Rights Watch 164–165
humanitarianism 28
Hungarian 73, 83, 85–89; *see also* Hungary

Hungarian Central Statistical Office 85
Hungarian National Social Inclusion Strategy 86
Hungary xviii, xxiii, 73–74, 79, 81–82, 85, 90, 187–188; *see also* Hungarian

imaging data 28
inclusionism xvi, xxix, xxxiii, 48, 53, 187, 189
India xi, xxiv, 51, 82, 187
indigenous 87, 89, 148, 164, 183
information and communication technologies (ICTs) 161
information and communications technology revolution 48
information privacy 4–5, 14
informed consent 27–29, 31, 33–34, 38
institutional review boards (IRBs) xvii, xxvii, 25, 31–33, 39–40, 109
international borders xxix, 114
international relations ix, xiii–xiv, xvi, xvii, xviii, xix, xxi, xxiii–xxv, xxvii–xxxiii, 48–50, 77, 121–122, 160, 182, 185, 187–189
International Rescue Committee (IRC) 80, 129
Iran xxiv, 82
Irish Data Protection Commission (DPC) 4, 10
Islam xi, 163, 165, 169
Italian Competition Authority 10
Italian National Health Service (SSN) 65
Italy xviii–xxiv, xxix–xxx, 48–62, 66–67, 90, 115, 186, 189

Jamaica 128
Jewish xi

Kale (Calé, Kaale) 81

labour theory xxvii, 5, 12, 19
Lao-tzu xi
Levant xi
liberal international order (LIO) xiv, 191
liberal internationalism xiv, xv
Liberia 123–124, 126, 131–132, 139, 143–144, 148–149
Libra 37
Liguria 61
Lisbon Treaty 64
Ljubljana 87
Ljubljana Guidelines on Integration of Diverse Societies 87

206 INDEX

Lombardia 59
Lombardy 50, 186
Luxembourg 48

Maastricht Treaty 49
Mahavira xi
Malta 61
Manifesto of Ventotene 63
Marxian theory 13
Mearsheimer xiv, xxiv
medical xxi, 8, 25–26, 38, 55, 66, 77, 125, 128–129, 134, 136–137, 141–149
Mercy Corps 37
Microsoft 162, 176
migration 49, 75, 85, 182–183, 185
Millennium Development Goal (MDG) 127
Ministry of Health and Sanitation (MOHS) 126–127, 130, 138, 142
minority self-governments (MSGs) 85, 86
misinformation xxxii, 68, 168–170, 173, 182
Moldova 90–91
Muslim Uighur xxv
Myanmar xviii, xxiii, xxvii, xxxi–xxxiii, 161, 163–166, 168–173, 175, 176, 191

National Council of Paramount Chiefs 133
National Ebola Response Center (NERC) 120, 124, 129–130, 133, 137–142, 144–145, 147
National Ebola Task Force 126–127
National Health Service 38, 58, 65
national minorities 84, 87, 89
National Research Act 26
NATO 48
neofunctionalism 64
neoliberal xvii, 48–49, 122
neoliberalism xvii, 48–49
neorealism xvii, xix, xxiii, 48–49
Netherlands xxx, 48
New York vii–viii, xii, xviii, xix, xxv, 35, 80, 169
North Macedonia 90
Norway 164
Nova Scotia 128
novel coronavirus pandemic 48, 65, 69; *see also* COVID-19; global pandemic

Obama administration 8
oligarchic 24
Ooredoo 164, 169
Organization for Security and Cooperation in Europe (OSCE) 86, 89
oversight capacity 28
Oxfam xxxii, 124, 129–130, 133–134, 139, 144–145
Oxfam's monitoring, evaluation, accountability, and learning (MEAL) 139

Partito Democratico (PD) 60
peacebuilding 105, 183–185, 187–190
penal nationalism xxx, 74, 77–78, 88
penal populism xxx, 74, 77–79, 88–89, 93, 188
People's Republic of China xxiii
personal protective equipment (PPE) xxi, 55–56, 131, 135–136, 150–151
populism xi, xxx, 74, 77–79, 88–89, 93, 188
populist xviii, xxx, 58, 74, 79, 81, 90, 187–188
post-Cold War era 64
post-vaccine xvi, xviii, xix, xxiii, xxv–xxvi, xxxiii, 182, 187–188, 190
principles of Fair Information Practices 8
privacy ix, xv, xxvii–xxix, 3–10, 12, 14–20, 28, 30–31, 34–37, 40, 75–76, 171–173, 182, 184, 193–195
privacy rights 4, 6, 10, 14, 16, 19, 173

Qatar 164
quantum cryptography 18
quarantine 56, 62, 91–92, 120, 129, 133, 140, 150, 182, 193

realism xiv, xvii, xx,xxvii, xxxiii, 47–48, 53
refugee camps 79, 87
refugees xxii, xxiii, 33, 49, 87, 166
Reuters 77, 165
Rohingya xxxi, 161–166, 169, 171, 191
Roma xxix–xxx, 73–75, 81–93, 187, 188
Romania 82, 90–92
Romanichels 81
Rome 48, 52, 56–62, 83
Russia xiv, xv, 175

São Paulo 80
Sarajevo 102, 105, 107
Sardegna 59
Save the Children 81, 127
Schengen Treaty 66
Schengen zone borders 61
Schuman Plan 51, 63–64
self-sovereignty xvi, xxiii

INDEX 207

sensitive data 38, 77, 107, 109–110, 115, 188, 189
Serbia 90, 102, 104, 105, 109; *see also* Serbs
Serbs 102–103, 106, 109; *see also* Serbia
Sicilia 59
Sierra Leone xviii, xx, xxiii, xxiv, xxvii, xxxii, 120–124, 126–133, 135–136, 138–145, 148–149, 150–151, 190
Signal Code 36, 40–41, 184
Single European Market (SEM) 50
Sinti/Manush 81
Skype xx, 130, 137
Slovakia 82, 90, 92
Smallpox 130
social inclusion 75, 83, 86
social media war xv
Social Mobilisation Action Consortium (SMAC) 129, 130, 145
social network 4, 12–13, 48, 51, 160–161, 169, 172, 186
social protests xvi–xvii
Social Science One 39–41
social sciences 25, 27, 31, 41, 75–76, 83, 110, 184
Soroca 91
Soviet Union xvii, 48–49, 102
Spain 61, 115
Spanish flu 130
surveillance capitalism xxv–xxviii, 5, 13–14, 18
Sweden xxx, 56, 67, 80

Taiwan xv, xxiv
technocolonialism 33
technological change 26, 28, 31
Telenor 164, 169
testing 56
Theory of International Politics xvii, 49
third-party data companies 31
TOR 35
transnational migration 49
Treaty of Rome 48
Tsiganes 81
Turkey 82, 90
Tuskegee syphilis study 26
Twitter xviii, 26, 30, 39, 161, 170–171
typologies 83

U.S. House Judiciary Committee (HJC) 16, 15
Ukraine xiv, xv, 90
UN health and humanitarian mission 142
UN Human Development Index 120
UN Mission for Ebola Emergency Response (UNMEER) 125, 128, 133–135, 141–144, 148
UN Office for the Coordination of Humanitarian Affairs (OCHA) 30, 121, 128–129, 137
Union of European Federalists 63
United Kingdom (UK) xx, 20, 25, 56, 65–66, 68
United Nations (UN) 79, 80, 82, 91, 121, 165, 166, 167, 175
United Nations Group of Governmental Experts (GGE) 175–176
United Nations High Commissioner for Human Rights (OHCHR) 166
United Nations Human Rights Council 165–166
United Nations Human Rights Office of the High Commissioner (UNHCR) 80, 91
United States Federal Trade Commission 4
United States of America (USA) xvii, xxiii–xxiv, xxix, 4–8, 15, 25, 48–49, 56, 58, 80, 82, 102–103, 114, 123–124, 144, 151, 172, 188
US federal law 9

Vareš 106
voting behaviours 31
VPN xv, 35

Waltz xv–xvii, xix–xx, xxii–xiii, xxvii, xxxiii, 48–49, 52, 121, 182–184, 188–191
Waltzian realist international relations theory 121
Washington Consensus xvii, 48
Water, Sanitation, and Hygiene (WASH) 124
weblinks 39
WeRobotics 28–30, 39
West Germany 48
Westphalian system 185
Woodrow Wilson administration 8
World Economic Forum 170
World Health Organization (WHO) 50, 124–125, 127, 135, 138, 141, 144–146
World Trade Organization (WTO) 80

Xinjiang xxv

Yenish 81
YouTube 170–171

Milton Keynes UK
Ingram Content Group UK Ltd.
UKHW012153230624
444366UK00003B/17